COMPUTER
BOOK SERIES
FROM IDG

Borland® C++Builder™ For Dummies®

Cheat Sheet

Frequently Used Buttons

Component Buttons

A	Label
abl	Edit
OK	Button
✓OK	BitButton
	SpeedButton
	Memo
	Table
	DataSource

Action Buttons

	Open Project
	Save All
	Open File
	Save File
	Add File to Project
	Remove File from Project
	Select Unit from List
	Select Form from List
	Toggle between Form and Unit
	Create New Form
▷	Run Program
‖	Pause while Running Program
	Step over a Line while Debugging
	Step into a Function while Debugging

C++ Language Help

Basic Operators

Operator	In Action	Description
+	2 + 2	Add the two numbers
-	2 - 2	Subtract one number from the other
*	2 * 2	Multiply the two numbers
/	2 / 2	Divide the first number by the second
%	11 / 2	Provide the remainder after evenly dividing the two numbers

C++ Language Help

Advanced Operators

Operator	In Action	Description
+	i++	Increment the value of i

... bytes
... bytes

IDG
BOOKS
WORLDWIDE

D1511878

...For Dummies: #1 Computer Book Series for Beginners

Borland® C++Builder™ For Dummies®

Cheat Sheet

C++ String Escape Character Sequences

Character Sequence	Effect
\f	New form or page
\n	New line
\t	Tab character
\b	Backspace
\0	Null character
\"	" character inside a string
\\	\ character

Debugger Keys

Key Combination	Action
F4	Execute program to current line
F5	Toggle breakpoint on current line
F7	Step into function at cursor
F8	Step over function at cursor
F9	Run program
Shift+F7	Trace to next source line
Ctrl+F5	Add watch dialog box
Ctrl+F7	Evaluate/modify dialog box

Editor Keys

Key Combination	Action
Ctrl+Shift+I	Indent blocked text
Ctrl+Shift+U	Cancel indent on blocked text
Ctrl+E	Start incremental editor search
Ctrl+K, N	Convert block to uppercase
Ctrl+K, O	Convert block to lowercase
Ctrl+K, R	Read a block from a file
Ctrl+K, W	Write a block to a file

Delphi IDE Keys

Key Combination	Action
F1	Help
F11	Toggle to Object Inspector
F12	Toggle Form Designer/Code Editor
Ctrl+F6	Toggle unit code/header files
Ctrl+F9	Make project

Surf's Up: Where to Go for Information on C++Builder

Borland Web Site	www.borland.com
Official Borland C++Builder Home Page	www.borland.com/bcppbuilder
Dunstan Thomas (UK) Ltd. Web Site	www.dthomas.co.uk
UnOfficial C++Builder Home Page	www.nh.ultranet.com/~bsturk
Author's Home Page	www.ourworld/compuserve.com/homepages/ jpvokes/cbuilder.htm
"The Bits That [Borland] Forgot"	www.jpmj-group.mcmail.com/bcb.html

...For Dummies: #1 Computer Book Series for Beginners

BORLAND® C++BUILDER™ FOR DUMMIES®

by Jason Vokes

Foreword by Michael Sadler
of Borland (UK) Ltd.

IDG Books Worldwide, Inc.
An International Data Group Company

Foster City, CA ♦ Chicago, IL ♦ Indianapolis, IN ♦ Southlake, TX

Borland® C++Builder™ For Dummies®

Published by
IDG Books Worldwide, Inc.
An International Data Group Company
919 E. Hillsdale Blvd.
Suite 400
Foster City, CA 94404
www.idgbooks.com (IDG Books Worldwide Web site)
www.dummies.com (Dummies Press Web site)

Library of Congress Catalog Card No.: 97-73298

ISBN: 0-7645-0196-8

Printed in the United States of America

10 9 8 7 6 5 4 3 2 1

1O/SY/QY/ZX/IN

Distributed in the United States by IDG Books Worldwide, Inc.

Distributed by Macmillan Canada for Canada; by Transworld Publishers Limited in the United Kingdom; by IDG Norge Books for Norway; by IDG Sweden Books for Sweden; by Woodslane Pty. Ltd. for Australia; by Woodslane Enterprises Ltd. for New Zealand; by Longman Singapore Publishers Ltd. for Singapore, Malaysia, Thailand, and Indonesia; by Simron Pty. Ltd. for South Africa; by Toppan Company Ltd. for Japan; by Distribuidora Cuspide for Argentina; by Livraria Cultura for Brazil; by Ediciencia S.A. for Ecuador; by Addison-Wesley Publishing Company for Korea; by Ediciones ZETA S.C.R. Ltda. for Peru; by WS Computer Publishing Corporation, Inc., for the Philippines; by Unalis Corporation for Taiwan; by Contemporanea de Ediciones for Venezuela; by Computer Book & Magazine Store for Puerto Rico; by Express Computer Distributors for the Caribbean and West Indies. Authorized Sales Agent: Anthony Rudkin Associates for the Middle East and North Africa.

For general information on IDG Books Worldwide's books in the U.S., please call our Consumer Customer Service department at 800-762-2974. For reseller information, including discounts and premium sales, please call our Reseller Customer Service department at 800-434-3422.

For information on where to purchase IDG Books Worldwide's books outside the U.S., please contact our International Sales department at 415-655-3200 or fax 415-655-3295.

For information on foreign language translations, please contact our Foreign & Subsidiary Rights department at 415-655-3021 or fax 415-655-3281.

For sales inquiries and special prices for bulk quantities, please contact our Sales department at 415-655-3200 or write to the address above.

For information on using IDG Books Worldwide's books in the classroom or for ordering examination copies, please contact our Educational Sales department at 800-434-2086 or fax 817-251-8174.

For press review copies, author interviews, or other publicity information, please contact our Public Relations department at 415-655-3000 or fax 415-655-3299.

For authorization to photocopy items for corporate, personal, or educational use, please contact Copyright Clearance Center, 222 Rosewood Drive, Danvers, MA 01923, or fax 508-750-4470.

About the Author

Jason Vokes is an award-winning senior developer and consultant for Dunstan Thomas (UK) Ltd. He has been developing software commercially in C, C++, and Pascal since graduating from Portsmouth University in 1987. Jason admits to being a C++Builder "evangelist" and has been a crusader for Borland's highly successful Rapid Application Development product Delphi ever since its release. He's presented at the Borland Developer's Conference (UK) and speaks regularly to user groups around the UK. In addition to designing and implementing systems, Jason also writes and facilitates Delphi and C++ training courseware.

Jason lives in Portsmouth, Hampshire, UK, and can usually be found either on his PC or playing saxophone for a jazz band at local venues when he's not dreaming up new ways to use program development tools.

Feel free to drop Jason a line at jpvokes@compuserve.com or visit his home page at ourworld.compuserve.com/homepages/jpvokes at your own risk.

ABOUT IDG BOOKS WORLDWIDE

Welcome to the world of IDG Books Worldwide.

IDG Books Worldwide, Inc., is a subsidiary of International Data Group, the world's largest publisher of computer-related information and the leading global provider of information services on information technology. IDG was founded more than 25 years ago and now employs more than 8,500 people worldwide. IDG publishes more than 275 computer publications in over 75 countries (see listing below). More than 60 million people read one or more IDG publications each month.

Launched in 1990, IDG Books Worldwide is today the #1 publisher of best-selling computer books in the United States. We are proud to have received eight awards from the Computer Press Association in recognition of editorial excellence and three from *Computer Currents'* First Annual Readers' Choice Awards. Our best-selling *...For Dummies®* series has more than 30 million copies in print with translations in 30 languages. IDG Books Worldwide, through a joint venture with IDG's Hi-Tech Beijing, became the first U.S. publisher to publish a computer book in the People's Republic of China. In record time, IDG Books Worldwide has become the first choice for millions of readers around the world who want to learn how to better manage their businesses.

Our mission is simple: Every one of our books is designed to bring extra value and skill-building instructions to the reader. Our books are written by experts who understand and care about our readers. The knowledge base of our editorial staff comes from years of experience in publishing, education, and journalism — experience we use to produce books for the '90s. In short, we care about books, so we attract the best people. We devote special attention to details such as audience, interior design, use of icons, and illustrations. And because we use an efficient process of authoring, editing, and desktop publishing our books electronically, we can spend more time ensuring superior content and spend less time on the technicalities of making books.

You can count on our commitment to deliver high-quality books at competitive prices on topics you want to read about. At IDG Books Worldwide, we continue in the IDG tradition of delivering quality for more than 25 years. You'll find no better book on a subject than one from IDG Books Worldwide.

John Kilcullen
CEO
IDG Books Worldwide, Inc.

Steven Berkowitz
President and Publisher
IDG Books Worldwide, Inc.

Eighth Annual Computer Press Awards ≥1992

Ninth Annual Computer Press Awards ≥1993

Tenth Annual Computer Press Awards ≥1994

Eleventh Annual Computer Press Awards ≥1995

Dedication

To my Dad, Ian — thanks for all the support, encouragement, and love. We all love you very much.

Author's Acknowledgments

I've spent many happy hours asking and answering numerous questions on developer forums, but it took just one e-mail message to get me into writing this book. A big thanks to Jill Pisoni for sending that message and for your encouragement in getting me to pursue this project.

Special thanks must go to the Project Editor Nancy DelFavero and all the other IDG Books editors and production people for all of your hard work in making a Dummies book out of my all-too-raw material.

Thank you to Borland for giving so many of us developers what we've wanted from Delphi — C++ RAD!

Selina, thanks for your love, encouragement, support, and friendship and for putting up with my long absences. I'll prove that I'm okay to be around in a room where there's no PC running. Thanks also to Ross and Karen for your encouragement and support. Big hug to Deb and especially Chris. Thanks for the advice and love. Hi, Naomi, Matthew, and Peanut Pete!

Cheers to Kevin Bailey and Mahmood Sheikh whose thorough technical reviewing has been invaluable. Professor Richard Welford — you're a dude for making me do this thing. Damien, what can I say! Allison and Dave, your special help deserves special thanks. Plus, all the people who encouraged and supported me at Dunstan Thomas — I'm proud to work with you guys. Special mention for Colin R. — the RAD man — and John Sands for the right words at the right time.

Finally, Big Mention to the boys in the band (Skunk Funk) for putting up with my bum notes whilst I've had my mind on other things. It's not over 'til the next one!

Publisher's Acknowledgments

We're proud of this book; please send us your comments about it by using the IDG Books Worldwide Registration Card at the back of the book or by e-mailing us at feedback/dummies@idgbooks.com. Some of the people who helped bring this book to market include the following:

Acquisitions, Development, and Editorial

Project Editor: Nancy DelFavero

Senior Acquisitions Editor: Jill Pisoni

Media Development Manager: Joyce Pepple

Copy Editor: Kathy Simpson

Technical Editors: Mahmood Sheikh, Borland International; Kevin Bailey, Dunstan Thomas (UK) Ltd.

Editorial Manager: Mary C. Corder

Editorial Assistant: Darren Meiss

Production

Project Coordinator: Sherry Gomoll

Layout and Graphics: Steve Arany, Lou Boudreau, Angela Bush-Sisson, Mark C. Owens,

Proofreaders: Melissa D. Buddendeck, Kelli Botta, Michelle Croninger, Nancy Price, Rebecca Senninger, Robert Springer, Janet Withers

Indexer: Nancy Anderman Guenther

Special Help

Joell Smith, Associate Technical Editor
Shannon Ross, Project Editor
Susan Diane Smith, Senior Copy Editor
Suzanne Thomas, Associate Editor

General and Administrative

IDG Books Worldwide, Inc.: John Kilcullen, CEO; Steven Berkowitz, President and Publisher

IDG Books Technology Publishing: Brenda McLaughlin, Senior Vice President and Group Publisher

Dummies Technology Press and Dummies Editorial: Diane Graves Steele, Vice President and Associate Publisher; Judith A. Taylor, Product Marketing Manager; Kristin A. Cocks, Editorial Director; Mary Bednarek, Acquisitions and Product Development Director

Dummies Trade Press: Kathleen A. Welton, Vice President and Publisher

IDG Books Production for Dummies Press: Beth Jenkins, Production Director; Cindy L. Phipps, Manager of Project Coordination, Production Proofreading, and Indexing; Kathie S. Schutte, Supervisor of Page Layout; Shelley Lea, Supervisor of Graphics and Design; Debbie J. Gates, Production Systems Specialist; Robert Springer, Supervisor of Proofreading; Debbie Stailey, Special Projects Coordinator; Tony Augsburger, Supervisor of Reprints and Bluelines; Leslie Popplewell, Media Archive Coordinator

Dummies Packaging and Book Design: Patti Sandez, Packaging Specialist; Lance Kayser, Packaging Assistant; Kavish + Kavish, Cover Design

®

The publisher would like to give special thanks to Patrick J. McGovern, without whom this book would not have been possible.

Contents at a Glance

Cartoons at a Glance

By Rich Tennant

page 163

page 319

page 55

page 7

page 245

Fax: 508-546-7747 • E-mail: the5wave@tiac.net

Table of Contents

Foreword

*W*hen Borland introduced Delphi in February 1995, it caused a revolution. It was the first development tool to offer Windows programmers a unique combination of a powerful compiler, strong database functionality, true object-oriented programming, and an extremely productive visual environment. A little over two years on and Delphi has sold more than 600,000 copies worldwide, and is still growing stronger. But customers would often say to me, "Delphi is fantastic, but why can't it be C++ based? I know C++."

Well, now we can offer what our customers have been asking for. At Borland, we are very excited about this great tool for all C++ developers, IS managers, and corporations. We are providing true visual productivity with the power of C++ in one Rapid Application Development environment. Not only does Borland C++Builder provide the speed of visual drag-and-drop development, the productivity of more than 100 reusable components, and the flexibility of scalable database tools, it provides the power and control of industry-standard C++ and the ability to allow developers to make use of their existing C++ projects.

When talking about the outstanding success of Delphi, it would only be proper to acknowledge the impact and importance of the developer community. Without their enthusiastic reaction to the great technologies that Borland delivers, we would not see the multitudes of supporting materials such as this superb companion and, consequently, the success of our products.

With Jason lending his enthusiasm and experience, I'm happy to see a book on C++Builder join the ranks of the excellent . . .*For Dummies* series and watch as C++Builder achieves the popularity it so thoroughly deserves.

Enjoy,

Michael Sadler
Product Marketing Manager
Borland (UK) Ltd.

Introduction

● ●

*Y*ou're about to discover the easiest way ever to write Windows applications using the popular C++ programming language. With Borland C++Builder (and the expert help in this book) you can create easy-to-use, great-looking Windows applications that will make your friends and coworkers envious (and your boss worried that you'll ask for a raise). C++Builder takes the "brain strain" out of programming, which leaves you with more time to experiment with your own ideas.

About This Book

Books that force you to consume large portions of text before you get off of the ground are fine if you want to test your grit and determination. But, I suspect you also have a life. Therefore, *Borland C++Builder For Dummies* is designed to quickly turn you on to what you can do with this tool, and how you can do it.

C++Builder offers you the means to develop applications rapidly with C++ programming, and *Borland C++Builder For Dummies* offers you fast answers when you're developing C++ applications using C++Builder.

What about You?

I would guess that you already use computers on a regular basis and are familiar with Windows and the most-popular Windows applications. You're probably quite self-reliant when it comes to installing software on your machine and would not shy away from setting up program shortcuts and macros that make your life easier. You're probably also at a point where you want to do more than just work with applications and want to begin developing some of your own. You'd like to test the waters of application development, see what makes things tick, and have more *control* over your computing environment.

If you're a "power user" type, I suspect that you've already experimented with configuring your system to suit your individual preferences. Because you're curious and creative, C++Builder is an ideal development environment. You can start gradually by developing simple Windows applications using the speedy drag-and-drop capabilities available with C++Builder. As you gain experience and confidence, you can then increase your use of the C++ language to further tailor and control your applications.

C++ is a very powerful and highly respected commercial development language — the sky's the limit with this language and C++Builder fully supports it (if you use C++Builder, you are developing with C++). That doesn't mean to say that this book will make you an overnight C++Builder expert, but there is nothing stopping you from becoming one once you get started.

Maybe you're someone who has been developing applications for some time and you may even be an experienced commercial programmer. Or, you may be writing programs in non-Windows systems and are looking to switch to a visual Windows development method but still want to make the most of your experience.

Whatever route you have taken to arrive at C++Builder's door, you are probably more interested in getting results than proving something just for the sake of proving it. That's why you chose this book — for the information you need to begin building Windows applications.

What's So Great about C++Builder?

C++ has a reputation for being a very powerful language, but with power comes responsibility (in this case, it means your having to tend to the smallest development details yourself). This requires a great deal of knowledge and experience when you are programming complex Windows applications. The fact is, C++ is a complex language with lots of rules, confusing terms, and the added challenge of the user having to learn object-oriented programming techniques.

Products such as Borland's Delphi and Microsoft's Visual Basic came along to irreversibly change the programming landscape. By using these tools, programmers can create applications much faster than they could before and are freed from the hassle of having to set up project files (the development environment does it for you). Developers just pick out pieces they want to use, modify them accordingly (by just filling in the blanks in many cases), and Presto! — a running application is created.

C++Builder essentially works along the same lines as Delphi and Visual Basic. It's a rapid application development (RAD) tool that provides fast drag-and-drop development capability to the C++ programming environment. (I dare you to try to impress strangers with that information at your next cocktail party.) You get more power with less responsibility (unless you like doing everything yourself).

C++Builder enables you to produce 32-bit Windows 95 or Windows NT .exe files (the program files that your computer can run directly). Because your computer can use C++Builder output directly (the executable files that I just mentioned), your code runs many times faster than it would in an environment that requires you to run a program in order to run your program. I could go on and on about other ways C++Builder makes you a faster and better programmer, but that would be spoiling the story.

How to Use This Book

There's nothing to stop you from reading this book in the bathtub (provided you don't end up fishing it out of the water). You may even find this enjoyable bedtime or poolside reading. (I'm not about to tell you to put this book down and work on your tan — it's your vacation.) But remember that *Borland C++Builder For Dummies* is a "hands on" book for "hands on" activities. So, if you do your reading away from work, be sure to make use of what you've discovered as soon as you get back to your computer.

Because you have ideas of your own from time to time that you want to try out, but aren't sure of the best way to implement them, I've presented the subject matter in sections that are as self-contained as possible. This allows you to dip into the book as needed.

As topics are introduced, you can try out your ideas. The examples I use are independent from one another, so you can hook your own code into them or just try them out as I wrote them.

How This Book Is Organized

You can use this book as a cover-to-cover guided tour of Borland C++Builder, or you can pick up this book as needed during those "Help me!" moments. I also include a number of specific examples that you may want to try out now, and then adapt later for your own work.

This book is separated into five parts for easier digestion:

Part I: Breaking Ground

Part I introduces you to C++Builder — how it looks onscreen and how to start using it. I take you on a guided tour of this powerful product and tell you about its integrated development environment. You're introduced to *forms* — the cornerstone of visually constructing Windows programs, and you can discover how to get forms into shape to build your own applications.

Part II: Components: Your Building Bricks and Mortar

This part introduces some power tools you can add to your developer's kit bag. C++Builder provides you with a whole load of program development components (more than 100) and knowing how to use them really rocket-powers your application building. These components allow you to construct not only fully functioning user interfaces, but also provide the means to access data and create attention-getting reports.

Part III: Wiring Your Building with More Components

Continuing with the step-by-step example format used in Part II, you can find out how to build your own dialog boxes, file management programs, and other Windows interface applications. You also see how to construct report applications that you can connect to databases, and there's even a couple example programs that show you how to add multimedia files to your applications.

Part IV: Advanced C++ Builder Development

Explore the C++ programming language and ways you can use C++ to add the finest details to your applications (underlying C++Builder is an industrial-strength C++ compiler that furnishes you with incredible programming power). You want to be sure that the applications you build are robust enough to stand up on their own out there in the real world. With that in mind, this part shows you how to fix any problems you find in your programs, as well as prevent problems from happening in the first place.

Part V: The Part of Tens

Developing applications is one of those things that will never become a spectator sport. Unlike football, you have to play the game before you can pretend to be an expert on the subject. You need to roll up your sleeves and get your hands dirty (especially if you haven't cleaned the crumbs out of your keyboard for a while). This section gives you some quick tips and ideas (ten in each chapter, give or take a couple) to make your application-building efforts that much better, easier, and stronger.

Icons Found in This Book

Indicates something that saves you time or helps you get the most out of C++Builder.

Some highly techno-nerd information you may want to skip (then again, you may want to read it).

Watch out: This is something to avoid, or at least handle with care!

This item is worth remembering (in fact, it may even bear repeating).

This alerts you to the beginning of specific examples showing new concepts in action. (I created my own examples for you to follow. You may want to substitute the variables to suit your own purposes.)

Put on Your Hard Hat!

Get ready to power up your computer, fire up your tools, and enter the application construction zone with Borland C++Builder.

Part I
Breaking Ground

The 5th Wave   By Rich Tennant

"EXCUSE ME — IS ANYONE HERE NOT TALKING ABOUT RAPID APPLICATION DEVELOPMENT?"

In this part . . .

In this part of the book you can find the real basic stuff, such as system requirements and C++Builder installation tips. I also take you on a guided tour of the Integrated Development Environment, where the C++Builder Component Palette, Object Inspector, Form Designer, and Code Editor all reside happily in one handy workspace. I show you how to fire up a new project and get you started on using the C++Builder tools to get the most from your development time.

Speaking of time-saving features, this part covers C++Builder's Object Repository of reusable, ready-made templates (where you can store your own templates or even whole projects for later use). Chapter 3 supplies essential information about forms — the "bread and butter" of your Windows programming (after all, without forms, you wouldn't have windows).

Chapter 1

The C++Builder Floor Plan

In This Chapter

▶ Determining your PC and memory requirements

▶ Installing C++Builder

▶ Cruising the C++Builder Integrated Development Environment

▶ Selecting your project options

*I*magine the C++ language packaged in a rapid application development (RAD) environment. Then imagine the elements of the environment so seamlessly integrated that you can skip from your visual development tools to your Code Editor without a lot of clumsy stopping and starting. I'm happy to report that's exactly what you have with C++Builder, and in this chapter I take you on a quick cruise through the C++Builder environment, with which you can become intimately familiar in future chapters of this book.

If you read the Introduction, you already know that C++Builder is designed to make you a faster and more proficient Windows programmer. You can create the elements of a user interface (the boxes, buttons, menus, and bars that make Windows so intuitive), or even create a working database program, in a matter of minutes. You really do have all the tools you need to create a commercial-strength application.

So, now that I have you salivating with anticipation, you're probably wondering how to get started. A later section of this chapter covers that, but first let me briefly mention the three versions of C++Builder.

Sampling the C++Builder Flavors

Borland offers three different versions of C++Builder — including the "get up and go" basic version to the "all singing and dancing" professional versions. Which one of the following versions you plump for depends on your requirements, not to mention your budget.

- ✔ **C++Builder Standard** — Provides everything you need to develop database applications. This version takes up about 75MB space on your hard disk.

- ✔ **C++Builder Professional** — Gets you "under the hood" of C++Builder with team development and some other beefy tools, plus library source code you can learn from. This version provides some features you probably won't require immediately, but you will be glad you invested in it once you become more familiar with C++Builder. It takes up about 100MB space on your hard disk.

- ✔ **C++Builder Client/Server Suite** — We're talking giant database capability here. This version is geared to professional developers who need to link to large corporate databases held on client/server architecture. Allow at least 130MB of hard disk space for this version.

What Are the PC Requirements?

To begin with, you need a PC with sufficient processing power and ample memory. It's a simple equation: The more muscular your PC is, the more productive you can be. C++Builder is a fairly powerful product and as such makes significant demands on your machine.

To use C++Builder, you need at least a 486-based microprocessor and preferably one based on a Pentium processor. You also need at least 16MB RAM, although Borland recommends at least 24MB. Because C++Builder develops programs that run on 32-bit PC operating systems, you must be running either Windows 95 or Windows NT. The amount of hard disk space you need depends on which version of C++Builder you're using.

Installing C++Builder

If you haven't installed C++Builder on your PC yet, you can remedy that right now. Slip the Borland C++Builder CD into your CD-ROM drive. You won't have to type a thing — the installation program kicks right in for you. Once the installation process begins, you're led through the installation routine by a series of prompts, each of which ends with clicking on the Next button.

As you run through the routine, you are asked to make selections regarding your program preferences. You can't go too far wrong if you select the default settings provided for you (but you do have to enter your own personal information in order to register the product).

After running through a handful of screens, you're presented with the Install button. Click on it and C++Builder is copied over to your machine.

 After the installation routine is completed, you're left with a new program group on your desktop. Double-click on the Borland C++Builder icon (shown at left) to run the C++Builder program (it looks like a skyscraper under construction).

 You can choose from three installation types — Full, Compact, or Custom. If you're going to be using C++Builder regularly, then you should opt for the Full installation. This option copies over all of C++Builder to your hard disk, including the full online help files.

 If you're really hard up for disk space you can go ahead and install the Custom version, but be prepared to have to keep the C++Builder CD in your CD-ROM drive whilst you work with C++Builder. You can also expect the processing to be somewhat sluggish.

What Do You See? The Integrated Development Environment

When you launch C++Builder, you notice straightaway that instead of seeing a single window as you would with many applications, C++Builder presents you with a group of windows scattered around its main window (see Figure 1-1).

What you're seeing are elements of the C++Builder Integrated Development Environment (IDE). Each part of the IDE's visual designers and code editors works seamlessly with the other — something you can really grow to appreciate. I cover each element of the IDE later in this section.

 If you are running your screen at a resolution of 480 x 640, the multiple windows in the C++Builder interface can create a bit of a squeeze. Ideally, you want to use a screen resolution of at least 800 x 600, or maybe higher. This gives you room to arrange everything on your desktop and still have ample work space. But remember that when designing your forms, your end user may not be working with the same screen resolution that you are. You have to design forms to the end user's setting. The simplest way to do this is by making sure that your forms are never larger than 640 pixels in width and 480 pixels in height. (See Chapter 3 for information on sizing forms.)

Object Inspector

Toolbar   Main menu bar   Component Palette

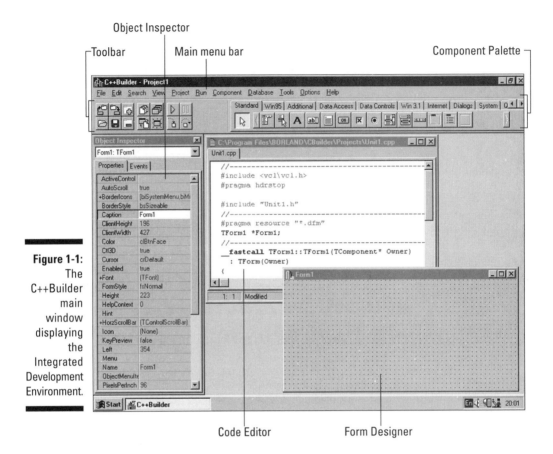

Figure 1-1:
The
C++Builder
main
window
displaying
the
Integrated
Development
Environment.

Code Editor   Form Designer

The main menu and toolbar

Refer to Figure 1-1, which obligingly points out where the main menu resides. Many of the options that you can access from the main menu are also available through the configurable panel of speed buttons on the toolbar (also shown in Figure 1-2). In general, toolbars provide a fast way of performing program operations by simply clicking your mouse.

You can configure the toolbar (the area in the upper-left corner of the main window) by right-clicking on the toolbar to activate its speed menu, and then choosing the Properties option from the menu. You then get the Toolbar Editor, shown in Figure 1-3.

As you can see from Figure 1-3, managing the Toolbar Editor is highly intuitive. To add buttons, just click into them and drag them onto the toolbar. To remove them, just click onto them and drag them anywhere off of the toolbar.

Open project

Save all files

Add file to project

Select unit from project list

Select form from project list

Run program

Figure 1-2:
Many of the
C++Builder
main menu
options
can be
accessed
through the
toolbar.

Pause while running program

Step over line while debugging

Step into function while debugging

Create new form

Toggle between selected form/unit

Remove file from project

Save selected file

Open file

Figure 1-3:
The Toolbar
Editor
makes it
easy to
reconfigure
the speed
buttons.

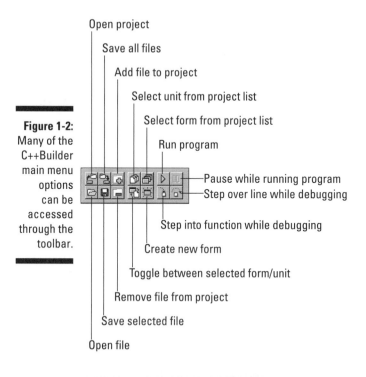

Speed menus are widely available within the C++Builder IDE. Wherever you are, it's worthwhile to right-click to see what options are available.

The Component Palette

Expect to become "best buddies" with the Component Palette. It provides some of the real programming speed of C++Builder. The Component Palette is somewhat like a catalog of ready-made reusable parts that you can order up as you need to build your applications (there's no need to make them from scratch by cutting loads of code). What's really cool is that you never have to replace any parts that you use. You have an endless supply of each component or control on the palette and each component is reusable for other applications.

The Component Palette is divided into tabbed pages, which neatly group components according to their functions. (In Figure 1-1, the QReport and OCX tabs on the far right are partially hidden by buttons.)

Adding a component to a Form Designer (I cover that later in this chapter) takes just a few steps: First, click on the desired tab, then click on a the button for the desired component, and then click into the form to drop in a copy of the component. Presto — the component appears! (In the case of nonvisual components, which the user doesn't see at run time, C++Builder substitutes the component on the form with an icon that looks just like the Component Palette button.)

To select a component after you've dropped it into a form, just click on it. When you select a component, sizing handles surround the component to indicate that it's selected.

The coverage of the Component Palette in this book is not meant to be exhaustive (actually, it would be exhausting to cover the Component Palette in its entirety — the C++Builder environment supports dozens of components and countless component characteristics, such as properties and events). This book does cover enough of what's available that you can build robust applications; then you can explore further as you gain development expertise.

The Form Designer

When you launch C++Builder, the work space area automatically supplies you with a form window (refer to Figure 1-1 and the window titled "Form1"). This form is known as the C++Builder Form Designer (or Form Editor if you prefer).

Each *form* represents an individual window (such as a dialog box) in your application. Within the Form Designer you can add, delete, or reconfigure components as you create your application.

Just to give you a preview of how you can use forms in C++Builder, check out Figure 1-4. The figure shows a form with three ready-made components — a label, an edit box, and a button — dropped into the form.

The Object Inspector

The word *inspector* can fill people's hearts with dread. Fortunately, I am not referring to the Tax Man! This inspector allows you to view the characteristics, or *properties,* of components that you place in a form and change the values of those characteristics. The Object Inspector also lists the events associated with an object and the means to change the event you want to handle. When you select a component, the Object Inspector automatically changes its contents to reflect the properties and events of that component. The Object Inspector could, as such, be called an "object editor," because it allows you to modify the properties of objects.

Properties

When you begin a project, the Object Inspector displays the properties of the main form (see Figure 1-5 for an example). The properties shown in the Properties tab page of the Object Inspector change according to the type of component selected in the Form Designer. The properties available for a particular component are shown in the Object Inspector as you move from component to component.

If at any time you can't see the Object Inspector, you can summon its appearance by pressing F11.

Events

The Events tab page of the Object Inspector displays the events for each component (see Figure 1-6). When you select the Events tab, you find that nearly every component has several events associated with it. These events are fired, or triggered, by either user actions or the Windows operating system itself. For example, the OnMouseDown event of a TLabel component is triggered when the user clicks on that label component (I cover "mouse events" in Chapter 3).

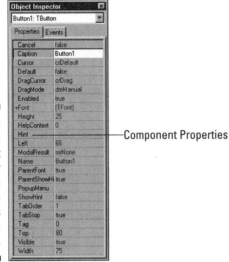

Figure 1-5:
C++Builder's
Object
Inspector
displaying
the
properties
of a
component.

———Component Properties

If you want something to happen when an event is triggered for a component, you have to enter some code for that particular component in the component's *event handler*. Using an event handler is like hooking your own functionality to empty clothing hangers (that is, if your program were a wardrobe closet). Just as you can leave your closet empty or fill it with designer outfits, you can use as many events or leave as many events blank as you want to. But, your application won't do much of anything if you choose not to use any events at all!

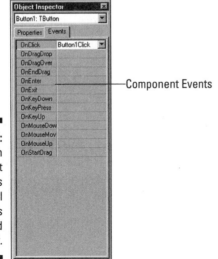

———Component Events

Figure 1-6:
Each
component
usually has
several
events
associated
with it.

If events already exist in a form, you can hook in an existing event handler rather than create another one (if an existing one can perform the task you need). Event handlers are often shared between menu items and speed buttons, for example.

To add functionality to an event handler, first click on the Events tab of the Object Inspector. Then double-click in the blank field in the right-hand column next to the name of the event to be handled. C++Builder provides a name for this event automatically (refer to Figure 1-6). Once you do this, you invoke the Code Editor (covered in the next section).

The Code Editor

Lurking behind the Form Editor is the Code Editor window. The Code Editor pops up when you name an event handler (see the previous section of this chapter). The Code Editor window contains the actual C++ code that drives your application. Figure 1-7 shows you how the event handler code is displayed after you double-click on the empty field next to the event handler name in the Object Inspector. The line place your code here in Figure 1-7 is where you get in on the action by entering your event handler code.

To generate a default event handler, double-click on the component in the form. The Code Editor displays the default event handler that the compo-nent most commonly needs to handle at runtime (for example, a button's default event is OnClick).

Certain components don't need to handle user events. For those compo-nents, double-clicking on them in the form won't generate an event handler. Double-clicking certain other components, such as the Image component or either of the Menu components, opens a dialog box in which you can perform design-time property edits.

Figure 1-7:
The Code
Editor is
where you
enter code
when you
create your
programs.

```
C:\Program Files\BORLAND\CBuilder\Projects\Unit1.cpp

Unit1.cpp

//---------------------------------------------------
#pragma resource "*.dfm"
TForm1 *Form1;
//---------------------------------------------------
__fastcall TForm1::TForm1(TComponent* Owner)
    : TForm(Owner)
{
}
//---------------------------------------------------
void __fastcall TForm1::Button1Click(TObject *Sender)
{
    //  place your code here !!

}
//---------------------------------------------------

18: 3   Modified   Insert
```

The Project Manager

A real C++Builder project is seldom composed of just one file. A project is often an accumulation of many forms, and you'd be surprised by how quickly they can pile up. In order to manage these forms as they accumulate you need the Project Manager. It can tell you at a glance the contents of a current project.

 Choose View⇨Project Manager to get the Project Manager dialog box shown in Figure 1-8. If you have a file that you want to include in your project, click on the Project Add button to show the Add to Project dialog box. Then select the .cpp file that you want to add, and click on OK to close the dialog box. You can see the name of the file added to the list in the Project Manager dialog box.

 For the flip side, click on a file name in the File list, and then click on the Project Remove button. The file is deleted from the list.

Add file to current project

Remove file from current project

Display selected file in Code Editor

Display form in currently selected file

Display project option dialog box

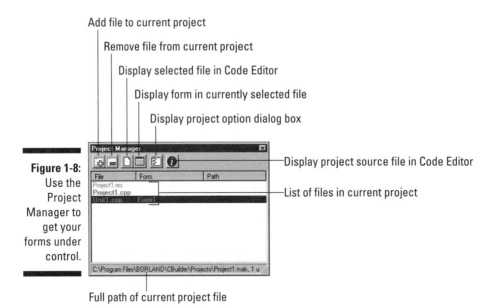

Figure 1-8: Use the Project Manager to get your forms under control.

Display project source file in Code Editor

List of files in current project

Full path of current project file

Projecting Yourself with the Project Options Dialog Box

Nearly all your work in C++Builder is done within a *project*. For instance, your program file is made up of individual code files that you group within a project.

The end result of a project is a program's .exe (executable or "run") file. When a user runs the program, this single file performs the tasks that you build into the program.

You can access the details of a current project's configuration settings by choosing Options⇨Project from the main menu. This command opens the Project Options dialog box. The Project Options dialog box holds the settings for every project and can be accessed anytime during development. You may want to explore the six tabbed pages of the dialog box to see what options are available to you and what those options do. Just click on any of the page tabs (see Figure 1-9). In general, the default settings are fine to start with.

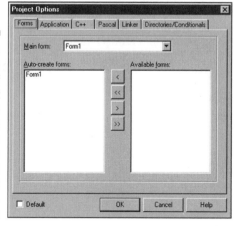

Figure 1-9:
Access the
details of
current
project's
configuration
settings
with the
Project
Options
dialog box.

The Forms page

By default, forms in your project are included in the Auto-Create Forms list box. Auto-creation means that C++Builder takes care of creating a form within an application automatically, relieving you from the chore of having to create a form with code.

The Application page

The Application page contains three application settings. The text that you enter in the Title text box becomes the title of the application; it is displayed along with the Icon selection in the Windows taskbar when the application is minimized. The Help file setting lets you choose which help file to associate with your application.

The C++ page

The C++ page is where you set the options you're using for the compiler in a particular project (see Figure 1-10). Most of the time you want to select the debugging options. They enable you to step through a program's code line by line to view the contents of variables and generally poke around the internals of your program to fix any problems whilst the program is actually running.

Be prepared for a shock when you see the size of a program with debug settings on. Even a project that does absolutely nothing can be hundreds of kilobytes.

Refrain from using the Release option until you have killed all the bugs that you're aware of in your program and sufficiently tested your code before turning your project loose on the outside world.

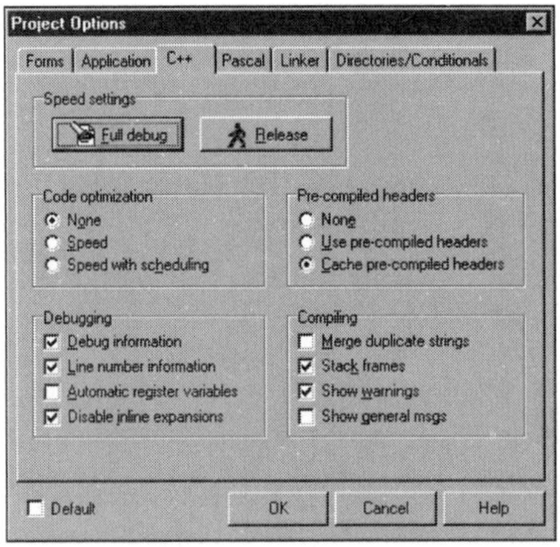

Figure 1-10:
The C++
page gives
you access
to debug
and
compile
settings.

Selecting the Pre-compiled headers option saves you a great deal of time, although it does use up some extra disk space. The C++ compiler has many things on its mind as it runs through checking, compiling, and linking a program. One of the tasks the compiler must perform is including references to other code units that you borrow to include in your program. This process of code collection means that there's more code to be compiled than you may expect when you build your application. Pre-compiled headers save time because they're built only once and then stored, ready to be slotted into another program.

When in doubt, just click on the Full Debug or Release buttons and you end up with an adequate set of compiler options.

The Pascal page

C++Builder has an older sibling called Delphi. Delphi is also a RAD tool, but it uses Pascal as its underlying language. You may have even used Delphi. Borland cleverly built these products so well that you can seamlessly include Delphi forms and code in C++Builder applications. You can use in your own programs parts of those cool Delphi forms that your friends have written (as long as you ask the friends first, of course!).

The Linker page

Linking is the stage that follows compiling as your code goes through the processing "mill." The Linker pulls all the compiled files into one machine-readable executable (.exe) file. Unless you're a bit of a programming guru, not many of the settings on the Linker tab (shown in Figure 1-11) are going to change your life. (The Include Debug Information check box is set or not set according to the Full Debug or Release buttons in the C++ page.)

Most of the time, you may want to set the Application Target option to Generate exe. At some point, however, you may want to build a library of code that different programs can use (at the same time, even!). In that case, you can build what is called a *Dynamic Link Library* (DLL) by clicking on the Generate DLL RadioButton.

The Directories/Conditional page

You really don't need to touch the settings under the Directories/Conditionals tab. At this early stage in your C++Builder programming career you have much more basic stuff to handle than the settings on this page, so just take it easy and let C++Builder take care of them for now.

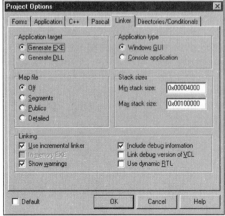

That's it for the introductory tour around the various parts of the
C++Builder environment that team up to create an awesome C++ RAD tool.
The following chapters show you how to use this tool to build professional-
looking Windows programs in a flash.

Chapter 2

Laying Down the Foundation of a C++Builder Program

· ·

In This Chapter

▶ Creating a new application

▶ Using templates in the Object Repository to speed your development

▶ Examining how and where your work is saved

▶ Getting acquainted with file formats

▶ Cleaning out unneeded files

· ·

*M*aybe you've been skipping around this book to see what kind of juicy applications you can whip up with C++Builder, or maybe you plan on taking this book page by page to absorb every morsel of information I supply. Whichever way you're using this book, if you keep on reading this chapter, you can find out how to create a working Windows 95 program in less time than it takes to set the dining room table (unless you're one of those people who customarily dines over the kitchen sink, in which case you can build an application faster that you can microwave leftovers).

Before C++ and object-oriented programming came along, there was the C++ predecessor C — the popular structured programming language that was one of the first languages that let developers implement Windows applications. In the days of C, there were no object classes from which you could derive other classes to speed your programming. (I'm showing my age, but if you remember this, so are you.)

Borland C++, while powerful, has no extensive drag-and-drop user interface to make development really simple — loads of code-writing grunt work is still required to create even a basic program. (Some folks may argue that C++Builder has more of a pluck-and-place interface — nevertheless, C++Builder does much of the code-creation work for you.)

A Form Plus a Component Plus Properties Equals a Program

You probably want to get going on creating a program of your own using C++Builder. You can use the following steps to build a simple example program designed to display an on-screen message:

1. **Select File⇨New Application from the main menu to get a blank form in a new application.**

2. **Click on the Standard tab of the Component Palette and then click on the Label component button.**

3. **Move the mouse pointer to the blank Form Designer and click somewhere in the center of the form to drop in a new Label component.**

4. **Using the Object Inspector, change the contents of the Caption property from** Label1 **by clicking on the property value and entering** Hello Universe!.

   The programming part's done. Next, you compile, link, and run the program. That process sounds far more complicated than it really is, and you can do it in any one of the three ways listed in Step 5.

5. **Choose Run⇨Run, or press the F9 key, or click on the Run speed button in the C++Builder Speed Bar to run the program.**

   Allow C++Builder a few seconds to do what's necessary to produce the .exe (executable) file and run your application. The program should look like the one in Figure 2-1.

Throughout the rest of the chapters of this book I tell you to run a program by simply pressing F9. But if you like the menu or button methods, you may want to keep in mind the other options listed in Step 5.

Figure 2-1:
Your first
program —
and no
code
required!

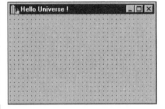

Your first C++Builder program is a success. How many lines of code did you have to write to get this basic program going? None. Yes, that's right, *none*!

Adding Ready-Made Objects from the Object Repository

C++Builder provides far more than just a blank form for you to build your applications on. A number of template objects are stashed in the C++Builder Object Repository.

The Object Repository stores predefined forms, dialog boxes, and even other applications that you can incorporate in your own programs. You can also store your own applications in the repository. Any new application can copy, inherit, or reference an existing structure from the repository — and that includes forms, dialog boxes, reports, menus, or whole C++Builder projects. This helps to ensure consistency across applications.

To view the templates that are available in the Object Repository, choose File⇨New to get the Object Repository dialog box (which Borland titled "New Items") shown in Figure 2-2. There are five pages of templates (objects, that is) in the New Items dialog box that you can add to your applications:

- **New:** For creating a new form, application, code unit, component, or data module
- **Forms:** For creating standard forms from prebuilt form templates
- **Dialogs:** For choosing from a number of basic dialog box type components
- **Data Modules:** For choosing from a number of data modules
- **Projects:** For accessing complete projects

Don't worry too much at the moment about what's available on the New page of the New Items dialog box; it's the other pages that give you access to the Object Repository. (Figure 2-2 happens to show the Dialogs tab page within the Object Repository window.)

Figure 2-2: The Dialogs page of the Object Repository contains time-saving dialog box templates.

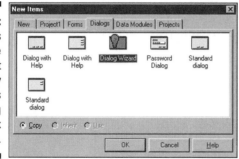

Click on the Forms tab to get the Forms page that provides not only templates for forms, but also some generic reports (see Chapter 11 for more on reports). You can include any of these dialog boxes or forms in an application you're currently building by simply double-clicking on the template that you want to use. Because only one application project can be open at a time, the template is automatically added to the current project.

At the bottom of each page in the Object Repository are three radio buttons — Copy, Inherit, and Use — that are used to select form, dialog box, and data module options. These three options (refer to Figure 2-2) each have a different effect on how the form that you add to an application is implemented.

✔ If you select the *Copy option,* all the code for the object that you copy is added to your project, and you can modify the copy to suit your purposes without affecting the original object or any other applications that may also use the object that was copied.

✔ If you select the *Inherit option,* you retain a link between the form that you added to your application and the original repository form (or any other type of original object). Then any modifications made to the original form will automatically be made to your application form. The reverse is not true, however. Any modifications you make to an inherited form won't affect the original object.

Remember that if you inherit from the template for your application and the template is changed, you need to recompile each application that uses an inherited version of the template in order to update the application. When you use the Inherit option, you can't remove any of the original objects (text boxes, buttons, and so on); it would be like selling the family silver. The form must retain the components that it inherits from the parent. You can only add to the decor of the form by increasing the number of components placed in it.

✔ If you select the *Use option*, you are opening the actual template object. Any changes that you make inside your application are made to the object in the repository and will be reflected in *all* other projects that use that template. This option creates a permanent change to the original object and should only be used when you want those changes to be reflected in any other form that inherits from it. Proceed with extreme caution if you are including template forms in your applications with the Use option; otherwise you can really muck up your other applications.

Grabbing a form from the Object Repository

Getting your hands on objects held in the Object Repository is a simple task. For example, you can use the following steps to add an About Box form from the Object Repository to a sample application.

1. **Select File⇨New from the main menu to get the New Items dialog box.**

2. **Click on the Forms tab of the New Items dialog box, then click on the About Box icon in the dialog box, and then click on the Inherit button.**

3. **Click on OK and you get an About Box form ready to tailor to suit your application.**

Adding a form to the Object Repository

You can expand the contents of Object Repository by adding any of your own forms, applications, dialog boxes, or even entire projects. Then you can reuse an object whenever you need it without having to re-create anything, which saves you valuable time.

To add a form to the Object Repository, use the following steps:

1. **Right-click on the form that you want to add to the repository.**

   This gives you the form's speed menu.

2. **Choose the Add to Repository option to display the Add to Repository dialog box (shown in Figure 2-3).**

Figure 2-3:
Adding your own forms to the Object Repository can be done in a few steps.

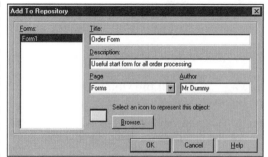

3. **Enter details about the form that you are adding into the Add to Repository dialog box.**

   You are provided with text boxes to enter the Title that you want the form to have, a brief Description, and the name of the object's Author.

4. **Select which page of the repository you want the form to be added to from the Page drop-down list.**

5. **Click on OK and you're done.**

If you want to add an entire project to the repository, choose Project⇨Add To Repository from the C++Builder main menu.

You can also create your own repository pages to help organize your additions to the repository. Choose Options⇨Repository from the main menu and you see the Object Repository dialog box shown in Figure 2-4.

The Object Repository dialog box is used for managing repository pages and the New Items dialog box is used for accessing the repository objects. Is this confusing enough?

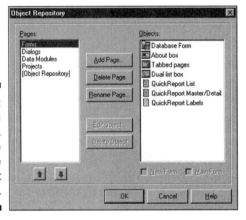

Figure 2-4:
You can add, delete, or rename pages in the Object Repository.

To add your own page to the Object Repository, follow these steps:

1. **Click on the Add Page button on the Object Repository dialog box to show the Add page dialog box.**

2. **Type in the name of the new page that you want to create and then click OK.**

You can also use the Object Repository dialog box to reorder the repository pages by using the up- and down-arrow buttons, or use it to edit the details held on individual repository items by selecting from the Objects list and then clicking on either the Edit Object or Delete Object button.

The Object Repository is actually held in a subfolder of the Cbuilder installation folder called Objrepos. The source code for all the forms and dialog boxes is copied to this folder. Any projects that are included in the repository are included as subfolders of Objrepos. It all adds up to this: You don't have to copy forms and projects manually from folder to folder.

The Object Repository is an amazingly powerful tool in the fight against "zero-code-reuse" syndrome. When you write a form that may be useful in another application, you don't have to re-create it — just stash it in the Object Repository and then go get it when you need it!

C++Builder File Formats

When you write an application with C++Builder, your insight into solving the problem at hand is what counts the most, so you need to preserve the files that represent all your hard work. When you back up your work (I know that you're conscientious enough, or just plain lazy enough, not to want to have to redo everything if a file is lost), you want to know which files are the ones you need to keep permanently and which can be discarded when you're done with a project.

This section is divided into two parts: The first part covers source files that you want to guard with your life; the second part covers files essential to a particular project but that you can discard later if disk space is at a premium.

Project source files

A distinction exists between the files that you create yourself (even with the help of C++Builder) and those that C++Builder uses in its role as the facilitator for your programming ideas. The files that you, the programmer, create are called *source files*. Source files contain the details of your form layouts and event-handling code. They're the most critically important files to a project because they're the ones you labored over. Store your source files to disk and be extremely careful not to lose these files because you can use them to re-create an application without having to do all that work from scratch.

The default file names that C++Builder gives to your source files are listed here (you can change these default names as you want during the course of building an application). Any file that has one of the following file extensions (indicating it's a source file) is vital to your C++Builder project.

- ✔ **Project1.mak.** This is the project options file, more commonly called a makefile. One .mak file is required for each project. The is a text file that you can examine by choosing View⇨Project Makefile. This file contains instructions to C++Builder on how to construct the .exe (executable) program file for a project.

- ✔ **Project1.cpp.** This is the main source code unit for a C++Builder project. It shares the same first part of the file name as the project makefile except that the extension is different. (The .cpp extension stands for C Plus Plus, in case you're wondering.) This file contains the code that starts the application; from here, the application launches into action. If you want to view this file for the project, choose View⇨Project Source from the main menu. You don't want to make many changes in this file to start with (later, maybe).

- ✔ **unit1.cpp.** When you're working in the Code Editor window (see Chapter 1 for information on the Code Editor), the window opens with this type of .cpp file by default. This file contains the code that drives your forms, as well as all the event handlers for the components that you place in those forms. You should be extremely careful to protect these files (unless you find recreating code particularly thrilling).

- ✔ **unit1.h.** Form files come in pairs. For every .cpp file, C++Builder automatically creates a corresponding .h (header) file. The header file contains the declaration of the form; it tells C++Builder what components have been placed in the form and what events have been handled. If you were to drop a few buttons and labels into a form (using steps described in later chapters of this book), there's a way to see what changes have been made to this file. Go to the Code Editor and right-click the unit1.cpp file to bring up the speed menu; then choose the Open Source/Header File option to open this file or press Ctrl+F6. C++Builder keeps the names and types of all components contained within a form.

All .cpp files need a corresponding header file in order to work. When it comes time to back up or move a form from one folder to another, the .h file must go with it.

- ✔ **unit1.dfm.** The .h and .cpp files hold a form's declarations and definitions, but another important source file also holds information about forms. The .dfm file holds the details of the form's properties (size, color, text, and so forth), as well as details on each of the components placed in the form. The file also stores all property values that you have changed from their starting values.

  The .dfm extension indicates that this file holds the data for the form in a binary format (computer-readable zeros and ones). You can't read this file as is, but you can convert it to view its contents. Just click on the form, then right-click on it to bring up the speed menu, and choose the View as Text option to see all of the form's vital statistics. Figure 2-5 shows the inner workings of the example form back in Figure 2-1 displayed in all their coded glory.

```
object Form1: TForm1
  Left = 336
  Top = 186
  Width = 215
  Height = 171
  Caption = 'We Are Not Alone !'
  Font.Charset = DEFAULT_CHARSET
  Font.Color = clWindowText
  Font.Height = -11
  Font.Name = 'MS Sans Serif'
  Font.Style = []
  PixelsPerInch = 96
  TextHeight = 13
  object Label1: TLabel
    Left = 29
    Top = 48
    Width = 150
    Height = 24
    Caption = 'Hello Universe !'
    Font.Charset = ANSI_CHARSET
    Font.Color = clBlack
    Font.Height = -19
    Font.Name = 'MS Sans Serif'
    Font.Style = [fsBold]
    ParentFont = False
  end
end
```

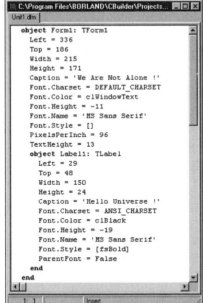

Figure 2-5: The inside story on Figure 2-1 as seen through the Unit1.dfm file.

Files that are good housekeeping candidates

Nobody likes housework — except maybe the truly weird. But after a while, the mess gets to you and you eventually have to clean it up or find a new place to live.

What does this have to do with C++Builder? You need to know which files you should hang on to and which you should throw out once they've done their job. The files described in this section are important for doing the job of enabling C++Builder to construct the .exe (executable) file for your project and build it as quickly as it can, but they're not critically important to a project, and in some cases use up hard disk space unnecessarily.

- **unit1.obj.** Producing a computer-readable program file requires a two-stage process. The first stage involves compiling source files into binary .obj (object) files, the second is linking together the compiled files into the program's .exe file. (Every source file in your application has an .obj file, no matter how small the source file is.)

  The object files are recompiled every time you choose Project⇨Build All from the main menu. If you choose Project⇨Make instead, only those object files that are older than their corresponding source files are rebuilt (for example, if you changed some source code using the Code Editor since the source file was last compiled). That's why a "make" takes much less time to complete than a "build."

✔ **Project1.exe or Project1.dll.** These files are what the whole process of compiling and linking is all about. The .exe (executable) and .dll files consist of machine-readable code that is produced by compiling and linking your work. A project produces only one or the other of these file types — the .exe file is a program file that you can run and the .dll file (Dynamic Link Library) is a code library that can be called from either a program or from other .dll libraries.

✔ **Project1.dsk.** This file contains desktop setup information — such as which windows are open in C++Builder for a project, the size of the open windows, where windows are located on-screen, as well as any debugging that you may have set up. If you opt to store the desktop settings for your project, when you boot up your machine the next time you use it and then open the project, you can carry on straight from where you left off earlier; everything will be just where you left it.

You can save desktop settings by choosing Options➪Environment from the main menu to get the Environment Options dialog box. Then click on the Desktop check box in the AutoSave options group on the Preference page. This file is a nice one to have and could be a bit inconvenient to lose, but it's hardly the raison d'être of the project.

✔ **Project1.il?.** (The ? stands for any letter after il, for example, ilc, ilf, ild, and so on.) When you see the .il? extension, it indicates a file used for *incremental linking*. C++Builder uses very fast compiler technology, but it can be made even faster the second time that you compile a project by its storing a load of preprocessed data in the program code. This makes compiling lightning-fast, but it does temporarily cost you some hard disk space (but it's well worth it).

So that's what .il? stands for!

Threading together all the different source files that constitute an application can be a big task for C++Builder, and after it performs this task the first time, it doesn't want to have to repeat it. So for the first compile of an application, a sort of "halfway house" of information is created in the form of *incremental linking* files. These files really save on compiling time later on during project development.

Incremental linking (.il?) files can grow to be quite large, and once you've saved more than

a handful of C++Builder projects, you can end up with many megabytes of incremental linker files on your hard disk. The .il? files are invaluable for the project you're currently working on, but once you move on to another project you should delete them to free up your disk space.

When you do remove these files, you have to wait a bit longer the first time you recompile the new project, but after that the C++Builder compile times get cooking again.

✔ **~??, ~ma, ~cp, or backup files.** Every time you save a file in C++Builder, the current version is renamed and its file extension changes. For example, .cpp files become ~cp files, .dfm files become ~df files, and so on with other file extensions. This is actually a safety feature. This file renaming allows you to go back the last version of a file using the Windows Explorer if you happen to mess up the current copy of a source file.

By knowing which files are created as your project progresses, you can pick out the ones to discard that eat up space on your hard disk, but you can also save yourself a lot of disk-shuffling when backing up your project. Make sure to back up C++Builder project source files — those with the file extensions .mak, .cpp, .h, and .dfm. The others you can keep or delete, depending on how much time and memory you have to spare.

Chapter 3

Forming a Working Relationship with Forms

In This Chapter

▶ Using properties to change a form's appearance and behavior

▶ Working with subproperties

▶ Triggering mouse and keyboard events for a form

▶ Programming a system event for a form

*I*f you read through the previous two chapters of this book, you already toured the C++Builder development environment and sat in on the creation of a C++Builder program. Stepping into the spotlight next is the *Form* object. Form components are a big deal in C++Builder because most everything that you develop is based on a form or contained within a form.

The term *form* refers to any application window that you create during your program development. With C++Builder's visual programming environment, you use the actual program forms to create your applications. You accomplish this in the Form Designer, which is basically an application form in design mode. Figure 3-1 shows a simple form in design mode with several components already in place.

Developing with Form Properties

Like any object in the real world, a Form object has characteristics that allow you to distinguish it from other types of objects. These characteristics are called the *properties* of the form. A property holds information about an object such as its size, color, name, and other distinguishing features. You can change these properties using the Object Inspector, which parks itself on the left side of the C++Builder workspace window.

Figure 3-1:
A simple
form in
design
mode with
a few
components
dropped
into place.

I start out this section with an example of a *character-entry property,* which determines the characteristics of a form when you enter text into the Object Inspector. You can use the steps in the following example to change the *Caption property* of a form.

1. **Choose File➪New Application from the main menu to get a blank form in a new program.**

2. **Select the form by clicking on it, and then click on the Object Inspector (if you don't have the Object Inspector showing, press F11).**

3. **In the Object Inspector, click on the empty field in the right-hand column next to the line that reads** Caption.

   The contents of this column is named Form1 by default to designate the first form of a C++Builder project. This column contains the values for each property.

4. **Remove the current contents of the** Caption **property by deleting it and then enter a caption of your own.**

   I typed "Hello Universe!" into the Caption property of the form shown back in Figure 3-1.

You have now successfully changed the contents of the Caption property using the Object Inspector (see Figure 3-2).

The Hint property

The *Hint property* is a simple text property used to hold a short "help" message for users; you can type whatever text you like that describes the form into the property's value field using the Object Inspector. As long as the form's *ShowHint property* has been set to true (also using the Object Inspector), the text that you enter into this property appears near to the mouse pointer whenever the user slowly passes the mouse pointer over the form.

Caption property name

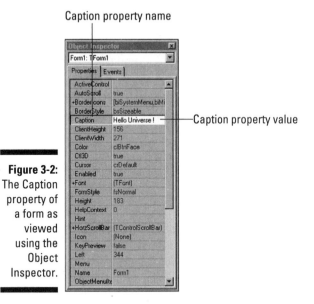

Caption property value

Figure 3-2:
The Caption
property of
a form as
viewed
using the
Object
Inspector.

Height and Width properties

When you resize a form by clicking on a form's edges and dragging with your mouse, certain numeric-type properties change value in the Object Inspector. Try resizing a selected form and watch as the values in the *Height* and *Width* properties on the Object Inspector change accordingly. You can also resize a form by entering numbers directly into the properties on the Object Inspector; some properties, such as *Left* and *Top*, even allow you to enter negative values.

The *ClientHeight* and *ClientWidth* property values refer to the amount of space that you actually have to work with on a form. The working space on a form is called the *client area* and is essentially the size of the form minus its title bar, status bar, and scroll bars.

The Visible property

Some properties offer you a choice of values, but you can choose only one value at a time. Other properties, such as the *Visible property,* offer only true or false values (for example, when the `Visible` property is set to `true` using the Object Inspector, the user can see the form when the program runs; when the property is set to `false`, the user can't see the form).

To select a value when the property has multiple values, you can either

✓ Click on the drop-down list button for the property in the right-hand column of the Object Inspector (see Figure 3-3) and then make your choice from the list.

✓ Double-click on the field in the right-hand column next to the property name in the Object Inspector to cycle through the available alternative values.

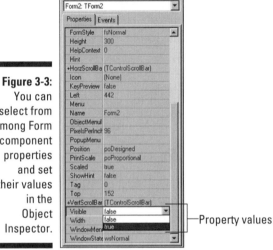

Figure 3-3:
You can select from among Form component properties and set their values in the Object Inspector.

Property values

Set type properties

One way to distinguish *Set type properties* is by the plus sign (+) next to the property name on the Object Inspector. (Other properties also have a plus sign in front of them, such as `enum` types, properties that can be selected through windows dialog boxes, or properties that are actually other objects.) Clicking on the plus sign expands the property within the Object Inspector to display a list of options that you can select (by setting the option to true) from as many or as few of these settings as you require.

You can find multiple items in a set of subitems, and you can select as many subitems as you want from a set. You expand the list of available options by double-clicking on the Set-type property name.

Whenever you select an option from a sublist and set its value to true, the option appears in brackets and highlighted in the field next to the property itself. For example, with the BorderIcons Set-type property, if biSystemmenu and biMinimize are set to true in the Object Inspector, those options appear in the BorderIcons value field as shown in Figure 3-4.

Property selection sublist

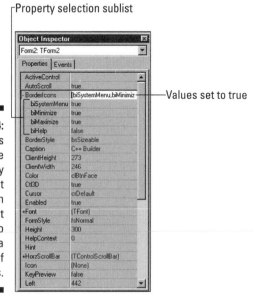

Values set to true

Figure 3-4: BorderIcons is a Set type property that expands in the Object Inspector to show a sublist of settings.

The properties of a component can actually be other objects. For example, a Form component has a TFont property, and TFont itself is an object with its own subproperties. When you look at objects within components, you come across other property categories. The *Font property,* for example, is made up of other properties, such as Color, Height, and Name (see Figure 3-5).

Another way that you can set the values for properties that have more than one type of subproperty is by using a property editor. If a property is complex, when you click in the value field next to the property on the Object Inspector an ellipsis button appears. Clicking on the ellipsis button displays a property editor dialog box, which functions as a friendly user interface for what would otherwise be a complicated procedure. The property editor for the Font property is shown in Figure 3-6.

Figure 3-5:
The Font
property is
actually a
combination
of
subproperty
types.

Font subproperties

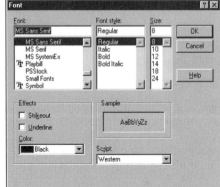

Figure 3-6:
The Font
property
editor.

The Borderlcons property

Once you have a feel for how you can manipulate properties, you can begin
to customize your forms. The *Borderlcons property* is a Set type property
that allows you to specify which icons appear in the title bar of a form. (The
title bar is the dark horizontal strip at the top of each window that contains
the name of the program and sometimes the name of the file you're currently working in.)

The following table lists the value choices within the BorderIcons property and the effect those values have when set to `true` using the Object Inspector.

BorderIcons Subproperty	What Happens When It's Set to True
biSystemMenu	The currently selected form offers a control menu, which you can access by right-clicking anywhere on the title bar.
biMinimize	The title bar of the currently selected form contains a minimize button, which when clicked on reduces the form to an icon in the Windows 95 taskbar.
biMaximize	The title bar of the currently selected form includes a maximize button, which when clicked on resizes the form to fill the application window.
biHelp	Places a "?" button on the form. When the user clicks on the button, the mouse pointer changes to a question mark and then the user can view context-sensitive help and definitions by clicking on form components.

Figure 3-7 shows what the title bar of a form looks like with the `biMaximize` and `biMinimize` options set to `false` in the Object Inspector. A close button (showing an X) is visible, but the maximize and minimize buttons are missing (refer to Figure 3-1 for a comparison).

Figure 3-7:
A title bar
with no
minimize or
maximize
buttons.

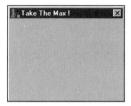

If you turn off all the options within the BorderIcons property, you have to provide the user a way of closing the form either through a button or popup menu. If you don't, your users are going to get stuck with a form they can't get rid of!

If you end up with a window that you can't close, choose Run⇨Program Reset from the C++Builder main menu to get rid of the guest that won't leave!

The BorderStyle property

The six *BorderStyle property* settings (bsDialog, bsNone, bsSingle, bsSizeable, bsSizeToolWin, and bsToolWin) in the Object Inspector are divided between those that allow a form to be resized and those that don't.

When a form has the following BorderStyle property settings, the mouse pointer doesn't change when you move the mouse over the edges of the form (which means, of course, that you can't resize it).

✔ The bsNone setting results in the user not being able to move or resize a form. If you set BorderStyle to bsNone you need to provide the user some way of closing the form because no title bar is shown.

✔ The bsDialog and bsSingle settings provide a standard dialog box border. Either of these BorderStyle settings results in a slightly thinner border than you get with the resizable border settings. That's because the nonresizing borders aren't meant to be selected or dragged.

✔ The bsToolWindow setting is used for utility or tool-type forms, such as property editors, in which you just want provide some options and perform some actions. The border of this form is thinner than forms you may have seen so far and the title bar is a bit skinnier than usual (see Figure 3-8).

Figure 3-8:
With the
bsTool
Window
option
in the
BorderStyle
property,
the form
has subtle
differences.

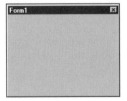

Although the differences between the border style property settings may be too subtle to distinguish at design time (or in the pages of this book), once you compile and run these programs you can see how they differ.

Most of the time, you won't have a problem with allowing the user to resize forms, such as a dialog box window. In that case, you can use one of the following settings in the Object Inspector:

✔ The bsSizeable setting — a default value that provides a resizable border

✔ The bsSizeToolWin setting — a cross between bsSizeable and bsToolWindow

 How these options translate to actual measurements depends on the type of font that you select for your form text — which means they vary. But, I can give you some basic guidelines: The bsTool setting is not used in applications, but rather for programming utilities that are added into C++Builder components; the bsNone setting is used for *splash screens* (the initial bitmap or other graphic that appears to tell the user that Windows is loading your application); the bsSizeable setting works for most normal application forms; and the BsDialog setting is used for anything that returns a *modal result* (such as a dialog box in an application in which an option is selected before anything else is done).

The Color property

Color can dramatically change the appearance of a form. You can use the Object Inspector to set the *Color* property in any one of several ways:

✔ Enter the text definition of a color (**clBlue**, **clGreen** are examples) directly into the property if you're already familiar with the color names and what they produce. (Techno-whizzes may prefer to enter the color in a numerical format.)

✔ Select from the extensive color assortment in the Color property's drop-down list.

✔ Double-click on the Color property field in the Object Inspector to display the Color dialog box (shown in Figure 3-9). Then you can go nuts mixing your own custom colors.

You won't see the right-hand part of the Color dialog box when you open it until you click on the Define Custom Colors button (grayed out in Figure 3-9). When you experiment with the color mixer, you soon discover that you can concoct some amazingly vibrant (and some truly horrible) colors for your forms.

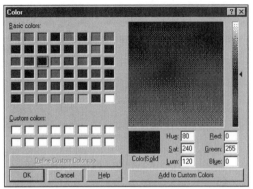

Figure 3-9:
Choose
from basic
colors, or
mix some of
your own,
to add color
to your
form.

The *FormStyle* property gives you four options to choose from. The default setting is fsNormal, which you can leave as the setting for most forms used in your applications. If you want to keep a form under your user's nose the whole time that the form is active, set the FormStyle property to fsStayOnTop, and that is exactly what the form does — it always appears on top of every other form on the screen and other forms can't cover it no matter what the user tries to do.

The FormStyle property and MDI forms

Two related options — fsMDIForm and fsMDIChild — within the FormStyle property allow you to create applications using a main form that acts as a container for other application forms. You may have already used applications in which one form "contains" several other forms, a technique commonly used in word-processing and spreadsheet programs. This type of form treatment, called a *Multiple Document Interface* (MDI), is easy to create. In fact, you can use the following steps to create a MDI application right now.

1. **Choose File⇨New Application from the main menu to provide a blank form in a new program.**

2. **Using the Object Inspector, set the** Caption **property of the new form to** MDI Parent Form **and the** FormStyle **property to** fsMDIForm.

3. **Add a second form to the project by choosing File⇨New Form; another form appears.**

4. **Change the** Caption **property of the new form to** MDI Child Form **and the** FormStyle **property to** fsMDIChild **using the Object Inspector.**

    That's all you need to do to create a simple MDI application.

5. **Press F9 to compile, link, and run the application.**

When you run the example MDI application, you see that the *child form* becomes a permanent part of the *parent form* and moves in tandem with the parent form. The child form can still be moved, or closed or opened, but only within the boundaries of the parent form. Scroll bars appear to allow users to view the whole child window if the parent form is resized so that part of the child form is no longer visible. Figure 3-10 shows two child windows, with the one on the left minimized.

Figure 3-10:
MDI applications feature child forms that operate only within the confines of a parent form.

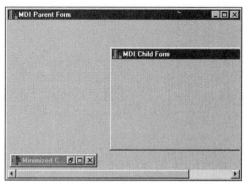

The Icon property

By default, the *Icon* property of a form is the Borland C++Builder logo (a sky-scraper image) but you can pick out another icon to display. To load a new icon into a form, click on the ellipsis button within the Icon property on the Object Inspector. A dialog box titled "Picture Editor" (shown in Figure 3-11) appears. Click on the Load button to browse the icon files that you have on disk and select an icon file (icons have an .ico extension).

You can choose from some sample .ico files in C++Builder's cbuilder\images \icons folder.

Try experimenting with the Image Editor to create icons of your own. You can open the Image Editor by choosing Tools➪Image Editor from the main menu.

The Position property

A form's *Position property* determines where a form is first displayed on the computer screen when the user activates the form. If you select the default setting (poDesigned) for the Position property, wherever you leave the form on screen at design time is where the form appears when the program is run.

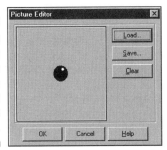

One of my favorite settings for this property is `poScreenCenter`. When you use this setting, the form remains at the same size that you designed but the form appears in the exact center of the screen's desktop (the user can always relocate the form by clicking into its title bar and dragging).

The `poDefault` setting gives control back to Windows in terms of where the form is placed and sized. If you run more than one copy, or *instance,* of your form at the same time, every new copy appears down and to the right of the preceding one. When you use the `poDefaultPosOnly` setting, the positioning of the form is left up to Windows; Windows does, however, use your design size. When you use the `poDefaultSizeOnly` setting, the form is sized for you but placed where you left it at design time.

The WindowState property

WindowState is another property that determines how your form makes its entrance "onstage." This property has three settings: `wsNormal`, `wsMaximized`, and `wsMinimized`. The `wsNormal` setting you want to use most of the time because the form is displayed the way you designed it. Setting WindowState to `wsMaximized` fills the entire screen with the form, no matter how you positioned the form at design time. The `wsMinimized` setting reduces the form to a small caption and icon bar when the form is loaded. No matter how the form is initially loaded onto the screen, you can still move and resize the form as desired.

Making Events Happen

Way back when, programmers could decide the exact order in which end users performed tasks and just how many tasks users could perform at a time. With the advent of Windows, end users have been liberated somewhat from the tyranny of programmers. Now users can open multiple programs simultaneously, merrily jumping from program to program, copying data from one to the other as they go. Users can even load a program at dawn and leave it unused until dusk if they want to.

When you are developing in Windows, you don't know what's going to be thrown at you until it occurs. Therefore, you have to respond to occurrences that are triggered by either the system or the user. These occurrences are known as *events* and the actual function that is called when an event is triggered is an *event handler* (example applications created in future chapters of this book make extensive use of event handlers).

A wide variety of events can happen to and around a form. As is true of nearly all objects within C++Builder, forms have "hooks" on which you can "hang" your code. As a program executes, it cruises by these hooks, even if the hooks are empty. When the program encounters a hook that has some of your code attached to it, the program knows that at that point it must perform the set of instructions that you wrote. (Your instructions are coded in C++.) This list of instructions is executed only if the program happens to pass that way while running (that's up to the end user). But, if and when the program does encounter a hook, the program needs to know how to react to your instructions.

In C++Builder, the code that handles events in your applications (and the "hooks" that they hang on) can be seen by clicking on the Events tab of the Object Inspector (see Figure 3-12), and then double-clicking on any of the fields in the right-hand column of the Events page. C++Builder then moves over to the Code Editor, where a basic functional skeleton of code awaits you.

Figure 3-12:
You gain access to a form's events (and the Code Editor) through the Events page of the Object Inspector.

Clicking with mouse events

The OnClick event occurs whenever the user clicks on a blank area of a form using the main mouse button (in most cases, that means the left and not the right button). The following steps demonstrate how the OnClick event operates:

1. **Choose File⇨New Application from the main menu to create a new form in a new application.**

2. **Click on the Event tab on the Object Inspector, and then double-click on the blank field to the right of the word OnClick in the Object Inspector.**

   The Code Editor is invoked.

   C++Builder then creates a framework function called Form1Click and places the cursor exactly where you can start typing your list of instructions. Now, you're ready to write your first line of C++ code for this example.

3. **Enter the following line into the Code Editor (as shown in Figure 3-13):**

   ```
   ShowMessage("I've been clicked !") ;
   ```

Figure 3-13: The Code Editor is where you enter a form's event handlers.

```
C:\Program Files\BORLAND\CBuilder\Projects\Unit1.cpp

Unit1.cpp

//---------------------------------------------------------
  __fastcall TForm1::TForm1(TComponent* Owner)
    : TForm(Owner)
{
}
//---------------------------------------------------------
void __fastcall TForm1::FormClick(TObject *Sender)
{
    ShowMessage("I've been clicked !") ;
}
//---------------------------------------------------------

17: 39  Modified    Insert
```

4. **To see what this line of code does, press the F9 key or choose Run⇨Run to run the program.**

   C++Builder automatically compiles and links your program before running it.

5. **Click on the background of the form.**

   The program and its OnClick event then delivers the I've been clicked! message shown in Figure 3-14.

Figure 3-14: A mouse event made this message appear.

You can see that C++Builder provides a framework to which you just add the instructions for what you want to happen.

The `OnDblClick` event handler is triggered when the user double-clicks on a blank area of a form. For example, follow the preceding steps for the OnClick event, but this time double-click on the blank `OnDblClick` event handler in Step 3. Place the same message in the event handler function. (You need to prevent the OnClick event handler from being called by clicking on the OnClick event handler name in the Object Inspector and then using the Del key to remove the reference to the function from the Object Inspector event name.)

You're in trouble if you include both an `OnClick` and `OnDblClick` event in a form: The double-click event never gets called because the first of the two mouse clicks always sends the program to the `OnClick` event first.

Like many event handlers, the names of `OnMouseDown`, `OnMouseUp`, and `OnMouseMove` provide clues as to when they're triggered. The `OnMouseDown` event is fired when the mouse button is depressed. The `OnMouseUp` event is fired when the mouse button is released. The `OnMouseMove` event is called whenever the user drags the mouse pointer over a form. You, as a developer, have more control over these functions than you do with the OnClick event handler functions, because the program can determine which mouse button was clicked on and whether any keys (such as the Shift key) are being pressed by the user at the same time. You can accomplish this by using an argument that's passed into the event handler function (see Chapter 15 for more on arguments).

To experiment with mouse events some more, follow these example program steps:

1. **Choose File⇨New Application to get a new form.**

2. **Press F11 to move over to the Object Inspector.**

3. **Click on the Events tab of the Object Inspector, and then double-click on the empty field next to the `OnMouseDown` event handler name.**

   You're now in the Code Editor, where you enter the following line shown in bold:

```
//-------------------------------------------
void __fastcall TForm1::FormMouseDown(TObject *Sender,
        TMouseButton Button,
  TShiftState Shift, int X, int Y)
{
  Caption = "I'm Feeling Down !" ;
}
```

4. **To make this example a bit more interesting, click on the Events tab of the Object Inspector and then double-click on the blank name field for the** `OnMouseUp` **event handler.**

   This puts you in the Code Editor, where you're ready to type the following line of code:

   ```
   Caption = "";
   ```

   C++Builder is *case sensitive,* so be certain to use uppercase and lowercase letters exactly as required by the code or your code may not work correctly (or at all).

5. **Click on the Events tab of the Object Inspector and then double-click on the blank** `OnMouseMove` **event handler name. Once you're in the Code Editor, enter the following line of code:**

   ```
   MessageBeep(0);
   ```

6. **Press F9 to run your program.**

   As you move the mouse over the form, you hear a series of beeps. Keep your eye on the title bar of the form as you press and release the mouse buttons. The message that you placed in the `OnMouseDown` event handler in Step 4 appears in a dialog box when either the right or left mouse button is clicked on; the `OnClick` event works only when the left mouse button is clicked on.

I list the entire `FormMouseDown` event handler function in Step 4 of this section so you can see that C++Builder is trying to tell you something — the TMouseButton button is being clicked on. The `OnMouseDown` event handler can manage up to three mouse buttons, but PC mice normally have only two buttons. One of the arguments (`TShiftState Shift`) tells you about any keys that the user is holding down. The coordinates indicating the mouse's positions on the form (X pixels across and Y pixels down) are also provided.

Entering key events

In Windows applications, a *key event* is triggered every time a user presses or releases a key. The `OnKeyPress`, `OnKeyDown`, and `OnKeyUp` key events are similar to their equivalent mouse events, which you can see in the following example program steps.

1. **Choose File⇨New Application to create a blank form in a new program.**

2. **Press F11 to display the Object Inspector.**

3. **Click on the Events tab on the Object Inspector and then double-click on the empty** OnKeyPress **event handler name.**

   You end up in the Code Editor, where you enter the following code:

```
if ((Key >= '0') && (Key <= '9'))
  MessageBeep(0) ;
```

   The two previous lines translate to the following instructions: If the keyboard key pressed is greater than or equal to 0 *and* the keyboard key pressed is less than or equal to 9, make a beeping noise.

4. **Press F9 to run the program.**

   Try pressing some keys on the keyboard. You hear a beep only when you press a number key.

Having no events associated with some keys is useful for preventing certain key combinations from having any effect on a program.

Form events, courtesy of Windows

Not all events are instigated by users; some are triggered by the Windows operating system itself. Those events are known as *system events,* which are listed in the following table:

Event	*Occurs*	*Use It to*
OnActivate	When the form becomes active	Bring the form up to date
OnClose	Before the form is closed or destroyed when the application closes	Close or free the application or resources that have been used during the running of the form
OnCloseQuery	When an attempt is made to close a form	Check that data is saved and files are closed; or to prevent the close
OnCreate	When the form is constructed	Place initialization code
OnDeactivate	When the form stops being active	Store any temporary variables (generally, the reverse of OnActivate)
OnDestroy	At the last opportunity to hook in code before the form is removed from the computer's memory	Free any memory used in the form

(continued)

(continued)

Event	Occurs	Use It to
OnPaint	When the form needs to be repainted; when another application window is moved over the form	Draw graphics and repaint text to the form's background area
OnResize	When the form's size changes	Move or resize any components in the form

To see how the OnResize system event works for example, follow along with these steps to make a program that always keeps its component in the center of the form.

1. **Choose File⇨New Application to create a new form in a new program.**

2. **In the Standard page of the Component Palette, click on the Label component button, and then click anywhere in the center of the form.**

   C++Builder places a new Label component onto the form.

3. **Using the Object Inspector, click on the Caption property of the Label component and delete the text** Label1.

   Replace it with the text **My Label.**

4. **Click on the background of the form to load its details into the Object Inspector.**

5. **Click on the Events tab of the Object Inspector, and then double-click on the blank field next to the** OnResize **event handler name.**

6. **You're next in the Code Editor, ready to enter the following code:**

   ```
   Label1->Left = (ClientWidth/2) - (Label1->Width/2) ;
   Label1->Top = (ClientHeight/2) - (Label1->Height/2) ;
   ```

7. **Press F9 to run the application.**

   You should see a form like the one shown in Figure 3-15.

Figure 3-15:
The Label
component
automatically
locates
itself in the
center of
the form,
thanks to
OnResize
event code.

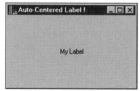

If you resize the form by clicking on its bottom right-hand corner and then dragging, you see that the label that you placed on the form in Step 2 always automatically locates itself in the center of the form, thanks to the OnResize event handler.

Part II

Components:
Your Building
Bricks and Mortar

THE GREAT THING ABOUT OBJECT-ORIENTED PROGRAMMING IS, IT'S MADE SOFTWARE DEVELOPMENT AS EASY AS PUTTING ONE FOOT IN FRONT OF THE OTHER.

In this part . . .

You can see first-hand what makes visual programming so downright cool — ready-to-use program components that you can add to a project with just a few mouse clicks. Tap into the C++Builder Component Palette and you'll find edit boxes, list boxes, buttons, main menus, and many other components that simplify your program development.

You can build applications right from the start by following the step-by-step examples provided throughout these chapters. Just drop components onto a form and then tailor the componentsto your individual needs by setting their properties and defining events. Your programs will do exactly what *you* want them to (in this case, power trips are definitely allowed).

Chapter 4

The Object of Building: C++Builder Component Basics

In This Chapter

▶ Exploring the C++Builder Component Palette

▶ Adding components to your program

▶ Manipulating and aligning components

▶ Building applications using some basic components

Stop for a second and take a look around you. What do you see? A desk, a chair, a computer screen plastered with sticky notes, yesterday morning's cup of coffee? We're surrounded by countless *objects,* and our perception of the world is influenced by our understanding of these objects and how they work.

Objects are described in terms of their distinct characteristics — size, color, composition, and so forth. Descriptions such as "John's big red van" or "Mary's fiberglass surfboard" are basic ways to identify objects. In this chapter, you see how developing programs in C++Builder is an extension of how we understand the real world and the objects in it.

Using *objects* to achieve a particular end result is exactly what you're doing in C++Builder. Just like real-world objects, C++Builder objects have certain characteristics. For example, a Windows button can have a text caption (which means it's identified with a label of sorts) and can support certain operations that distinguish it from the other bits and stuff on your computer screen.

In object-oriented programming, an *object* consists of data and a *routine* to process data, and each object is just one of many objects that make up a program that has real-world applications.

So What Do Objects Have to Do with Components?

The applications you construct with C++Builder are designed to solve real-life problems. To problem-solve effectively, you need a way of creating "models" of the objects in the world. The more realistically you can represent the real world within your applications, the more relevant your applications are to the task at hand and the more readily the applications can adapt to changes that you need to make to them as real-world situations change. C++Builder provides a way of representing real-life objects through the use of *components*.

Components allow you to determine both the characteristics of objects (by using the *properties* that are available) and the operating capabilities of objects (by using function *methods* and *events*). For example, you can change a Form object's color characteristic by changing the value held in its Color property. Or, by entering your own instructions into the Form's OnMouseMove event, for example, you can change how the form behaves when an end user moves a mouse across it. (I talk about properties throughout the rest of the chapters of this book.)

I just threw a few terms at you that you may already know from your programming background, but here's a refresher anyway. A *property* is a single characteristic of an object or component and holds data specific to that characteristic only. A *method* is any function that defines an action that an object can perform. An *event* is an application occurrence for which you can define code that will be run every time that application occurrence arises. Events can be triggered by either Windows itself, or as a result of the user interacting with the program.

Exploring the Component Palette

The Component Palette (the top window in C++Builder, which is shown in Figure 4-1), is like one of those spring-loaded display racks you find in a retail store. When you remove an item (the top component), the next one takes its place. The difference is, when you take a component from the palette, you don't have to replace it. You can just go on forever taking the items that you require without replenishing the stock.

Figure 4-1:
The
C++Builder
Component
Palette
showing the
Standard
page set of
components.

Before I go into detail about each of the parts in the never-ending supply of components, I briefly touch on the various kinds of components that you have available and how to use them.

The Component Palette is divided into several groups according to their functions. You can access each group of components by clicking on each of the tabs directly above the Component Palette bar (see Figure 4-1). Here's a rundown of the purpose of each tab:

✔ **Standard:** This tab contains the parts that make up the bread-and-butter Windows applications. Nearly all Windows applications make some use of the components this tab provides, including components for displaying and editing text, as well as buttons, scroll bars, and menus.

✔ **Win95:** These components allow you to access the Windows 95-type user-interface controls. The most prominent are the TreeView component (you know it from Windows Explorer), Page Control (for creating tabs of your own), Track bar (for creating sliding-bar values), Status bar, and the Rich Text editing component.

✔ **Additional:** The Additional tab, far from being an afterthought as its name suggests, contains some of the coolest gear in the Component Palette — such as the bitmap and speed buttons, grid components, and a shape component.

✔ **Data Access and Data Controls:** You gain access to data from your applications by using the components that reside in the two data tabs. The Data Access tab allows you to hook into data tables and queries. The Data Control tab enables you to automatically link the user interface to these tables.

✔ **Win 3.1:** Many of the controls on the Win 3.1 tab have equivalents in the Win95 tab, but they can be useful for giving a 3.1 feel to your applications. The tab includes an outliner as well as page controls and a notepad component.

✔ **Internet:** This tab gives C++Builder its Internet savvy and is referred to as the Internet Toolkit.

✔ **Dialogs:** Ready-made dialog box components can really speed application development by providing boxes for opening and saving files, for selecting fonts, colors, and printers, and much more. Dialog boxes can really boost productivity and enhance program standardization.

✔ **System:** Individual controls for selecting files, folders, or drives reside on this tab. You can also get your applications talking to one another by using DDE (Dynamic Data Exchange) and OLE (Object Linking and Embedding). Do you need a wake-up call or do you want to schedule tasks? That's no problem if you use the Timer component that lives here.

✔ **QReport:** C++Builder offers its own built-in form-based reports. The QReport (or Quick Report) tab provides components that take the headache out of generating user reports. By dropping these components into a simple form and then setting properties in the usual way, you can rapidly get even complicated reports up to speed and looking good. The tab also includes a preview facility.

✔ **ActiveX:** This tab contains an ActiveX spell checker, as well as several impressive graphing components (in Figure 4-1, the ActiveX tab is there, but it's covered by directional arrow buttons).

This book is not designed to give you an exhaustive tour of the entire C++Builder Component Palette. Coverage that extensive would take several books of this size. In the following chapters, I show you how to build applications using many but not all of the components on the palette. Nevertheless, you still get a good taste of how you can use this tool to create your own fully functioning programs.

You can view a list of all components, regardless of which pages they reside on, by selecting View➪Component List from the main menu.

Using Components

You may have already discovered in previous chapters of this book that introducing components into your program requires just a few simple steps. If you can use Windows, you can start to program in C++Builder.

Selecting and deselecting components

To select a component from the Component Palette, simply

1. **Click on the desired palette page tab (such as Standard, Win95, and the rest).**

2. **Click on the speed button that displays the component's icon.**

   You can select only one speed button at a time and the button for the selected component remains depressed until it is deselected.

At this point, you can click into the form you're working on and the component is dropped in (this process is repeated many times in the following chapters).

 To *deselect* a component, either select another component or click on the mouse-pointer button (shown in the margin) to the left of the Component Palette tabs. This action puts the original component in "neutral gear."

 If you're not sure which button under the Component Palette tabs controls your component, pass your mouse pointer over each icon for a moment until an on-screen message appears identifying the button.

If you have components placed in a form, you can *select* them by simply clicking on them. The selected components display small squares in each corner, or sometimes halfway up each side. Figure 4-2 shows some selected components.

Group select/deselect indicator

Figure 4-2:
Gray boxes
appear at
the corners
of selected
components.

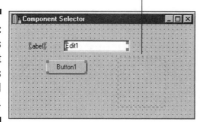

 You can always select a group of components by clicking just outside of the group and then dragging with your mouse until each component is selected. When you release the mouse button, any components that were already selected are deselected. Figure 4-2 shows the rectangle that appears when you group select or deselect.

Placing components

After you select a component in the palette, you can place it on a form by moving the mouse pointer to the desired location on the form, and then clicking the left mouse button. A copy of the component appears at the spot where you click.

You can also select components directly from the Component List dialog box, which you can display by choosing View⇨Component List. This dialog box shows all the components in the Component Palette in alphabetical order, rather than sorted by component-group tabs.

Locking components in place

When you first construct a form, you often need to place several components of the same type in the form at a time. There's a way you can avoid having to reselect the component each time.

Assume, for example, that you want to place seven EditBox components in a form. Hold down the Shift key and click an Edit box component in the Component Palette. The Edit box button is highlighted, indicating that it's selected. Now move to the form and click on the mouse seven times in different locations. You get a copy of the component for every click without having to ferry back to the Component Palette to pick up another one each time.

When you're done, don't forget to change the mouse pointer to its normal state by clicking on the mouse pointer button on the palette.

Choosing visual or nonvisual components

You can place two types of components onto forms: those that you can see at runtime and those that you can't see. *Visual components* such as edit boxes, labels, and gauges, are visible to the user. Other components, such as timers and tables, disappear at runtime; you get to see those elements only at design time and the user works with them only indirectly. They're known as *nonvisual components.*

Place nonvisual components in an orderly fashion in an unused area of the form (so that you don't have to move them out of your way every five minutes). You can actually set the form during design time to be larger than you need for the final program and then set the Height and Width properties as part of the OnCreate method for the form.

Figure 4-3 shows a form with three nonvisual components placed off the Panel to the right side of the form. Now you know what nonvisual components "look like" at design time — they resemble their respective icons from the Component Palette button bar.

Figure 4-3:
A form
showing
three visual
components
on the left
and three
nonvisual
ones on the
right.

Resizing components

You want to make the most of the space that is available in a form and part of that task is moving and sizing the components that you place in the form.

To move a component, select it by clicking on it and then dragging it around the form anywhere you like. Another way to move a selected component is to hold down the Ctrl key and then press the arrow keys to move the component up, down, left, or right.

You also have a choice in the way that you resize a component. Select the component or components that you want to resize and then use one of these two methods:

✔ Place the mouse pointer on any one of the handles (those black squares) on the component's border; the pointer changes to indicate the direction you can drag to resize. Then hold down the mouse button and drag to adjust the component as you need. Figure 4-4 displays sizing handles on a Button component.

✔ You can also resize components by using the arrow keys. Hold down the Shift key and press the arrow keys to adjust the bottom and right sides of the component as required.

Figure 4-4:
Click and
drag the
squares
surrounding
a compo-
nent to
size the
component
as needed.

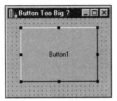

Moving and resizing collective components

You can move or resize any number of components in one fell swoop by group selecting them and then using the Shift and Ctrl keys in conjunction with the arrow keys.

You can resize only visible components. Nonvisible ones spring back to their original size when you let go of the mouse button.

When you need to create several components of matching size, use the Size dialog box, shown in Figure 4-5. With the components that you want to resize selected, just right-click anywhere on the form to bring up the speed menu and then choose the Size option to display the Size dialog box.

Figure 4-5:
Use the
Size dialog
box for
sizing
several
components
at once.

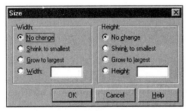

Copying or moving components between forms

You can copy or move any number of components between forms. This procedure uses the Windows Clipboard in the same way that you may have used it with other tools. Try this:

1. **Create two new blank forms by selecting <u>F</u>ile⇨<u>N</u>ew Application from the C++Builder main menu twice.**

2. **Place a few components in one of these forms.**

   Use the steps in the sections "Selecting and deselecting components" and "Placing components" earlier in this chapter. You can use components of any type.

3. **Select as many of these components as you like by holding down the Shift key and clicking on the ones that you want to choose.**

4. **After you select some components, choose <u>E</u>dit⇨<u>C</u>opy from the main menu.**

5. **Click on the form that is still blank.**

6. **Choose <u>E</u>dit⇨<u>P</u>aste from the main menu.**

   An exact match of the components is placed in the second form.

Check out the <u>E</u>dit⇨Se<u>l</u>ect All command, which picks up all the components at the same time without your having to click all over the place. Then you can deselect individual components as needed, which may be a method that's faster for you.

If you have several components of the same type to replace or change in a form, choose <u>S</u>earch⇨<u>R</u>eplace while viewing the form as text.

Table 4-1 offers some helpful tips for working with components.

Table 4-1	Component User's Quick Reference
Operation	*How To*
Select	Click on the desired component; *or* click and drag around a group of components; *or* hold down the Shift key and click one by one to multiple-select.
Place	Move the mouse to a location in a form and click.
Deselect	Click the Neutral button (the arrow button on the Component Palette) to deselect the Component Palette. Click on the form itself to deselect a component in a form.
Moving	Select a component and then drag; *or* select a component, hold down the Ctrl key, and use the arrow keys.
Sizing	Select a component and then click onto one of the sizing handles and drag; *or* select the components, hold down the Shift key, and use the arrow keys.

(continued)

Table 4-1 (continued)

Operation	How To
Copy	Select components by clicking on them, and then choose Edit⇨Copy; or press Ctrl+C.
Cut	Select components by clicking on them, and then choose Edit⇨Cut; or press Ctrl+X.
Paste	Place components in the Clipboard and then press Ctrl+V on a form.

Aligning: View alignment from the main menu

Your applications should look as smart as possible. Part of achieving that professional look is lining up your components neatly in the form.

You can spend a long time setting the Left and Top properties of components or using the Ctrl and arrow keys to make sure that all the components line up, or you can choose some quicker methods.

In Figure 4-6, four buttons that are in serious need of alignment have been dumped into an empty form. You can align these components by choosing View⇨Alignment Palette for the Align palette (see Figure 4-7). By clicking on a button in the palette, you can right-align, left-align, center vertically or horizontally, or evenly space and align groups of selected components on a form.

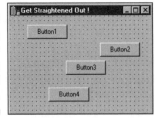

Figure 4-6:
Four buttons in need of alignment.

Another tool in the battle against crooked controls is the Alignment dialog box, shown in Figure 4-8. You can gain access to this alignment selector by clicking on the controls that you want to straighten out, and then right-clicking anywhere on the form to bring up the speed menu and choosing the Alignment option from this menu.

Figure 4-7:
The Align
Palette
offers
options for
aligning
selected
components.

Figure 4-8:
The
Alignment
dialog box
offers
methods of
aligning
your
controls.

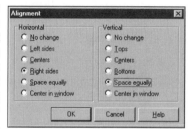

Working with Standard Components

This section introduces you to some components you're sure to rely on heavily. Because at least one component on the Standard page of the Component Palette appears in virtually every application you create, these components are a good place to start for basic application development.

The Label component

The Label component is an unassuming little fellow that is represented by the "A" button. You can use the Label component to identify other components in a form or to display text that you don't want the user to change.

Use the *Alignment property* (it's shown in the Object Inspector Properties page when the Label is selected) to state how you want your text to be placed inside the Label component — either left-justified, right-justified, or centered, but you'll probably get the most professional-looking results out of the Center option.

If a Label sizes itself around the text when you enter the text into the Caption property in the Object Inspector, that means the *AutoSize property* is set to true. To make the label stick to one size, set AutoSize to false in the Object Inspector. This setting enables you to set a fixed size for the label. You may want to use this setting when you plan on changing the caption while running the program or when you're using several Labels.

You can use the Label as a link to another component on the form by using the *FocusControl property* and by following these example steps:

1. **Place a Label on a form by clicking on the Label component button and clicking anywhere into the form.**

2. **With the Label selected, click on the down-arrow button inside the** FocusControl **property value field in the Object Inspector.**

   You then see a list of the other controls on the form that are not Labels.

3. **Select one of those controls from the list.**

4. **Enter text into the Caption property of the Label and prefix any one letter with an ampersand (&).**

   That character becomes a shortcut "hot key" to menu items when used with the Alt key.

Now, when you run your program and press Alt plus the underlined character, the cursor moves to the component that you specified in the FocusControl drop-down list.

Use the *Color property* to set the background color of the label. If you need to, you can even remove the background by setting the *Transparent property* to true. This leaves you with just the text floating over whatever background you choose to place (see Figure 4-9).

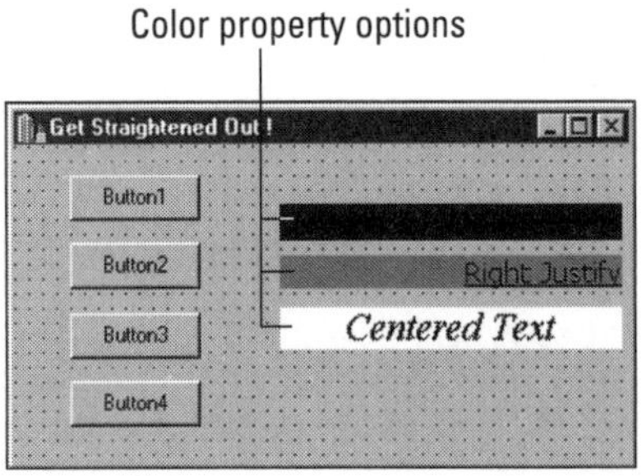

Color property options

Figure 4-9:
Use the
Color
property to
set the
background
color of a
label.

Get Straightened Out !

Button1

Button2   Right Justify

Button3   *Centered Text*

Button4

If you need labels that take up more than one line, set the WordWrap property to true. You can adjust the caption and even see how your label is going to look at design time. The centered text example in Figure 4-10 shows this arrangement.

Figure 4-10:
The
two-line
"Centered
Text" was
achieved
with the
WordWrap
property.

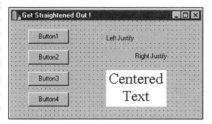

The EditBox component

Your program users need some sort of method to enter text-based data (or what nontechies like to call "words"). The EditBox component provides a way they can do this.

To place EditBoxes onto your forms

1. **Select the EditBox component button from the Standard page of the Component Palette.**

2. **Click in the form wherever you want the EditBox to appear.**

   As with the Label component described in the previous section, once you have selected the Edit component on the form (by clicking on it) its properties are shown in the Properties tab on the Object Inspector.

EditBox properties

The EditBox component has a single-line edit control, the contents of which are stored in the *Text property*. The property is initially set to the name of the component when you first place it in the form. The Text property can accept many more characters than you would expect a user to enter in one line, and in many cases you may want to use the *MaxLength property* from the Object Inspector to restrict the number of characters that users can enter.

Use the *AutoSelect property* with caution when it is set to true, because all the text entered in an EditBox component is highlighted to be overwritten as the user moves to the EditBox. If you press a key by mistake when all the text is highlighted, you lose the current text. To be honest, all is not lost if you do make this error, because you can use a combination of Alt and Backspace (or Ctrl+Z) to retrieve the overwritten text.

The user can enter information into the Edit component in a couple of ways:

✔ The *CharCase property* can be used to indicate that you want all input converted to either lowercase or uppercase characters; the default setting of `ecNormal` allows for mixed-case entry.

✔ If the user needs to enter confidential information, you can hide the user's typed entry behind the single character of your choice by setting the *PasswordChar property.* Figure 4-11 shows this setting in action.

Figure 4-11:
The
Password-
Char
property
at work,
disguising
the user's
password
entry.

Using the Edit control to validate user entry

The Edit component events allow you to impose data-entry validation rules on a user entering text in the Edit control (these events can be accessed from the Events page on the Object Inspector after you've selected an EditBox). Combinations of the OnChange event, which is triggered every time the user makes a change in the EditBox, and the OnKeyPress event can be invaluable in preventing the user from entering rogue or garbage data.

The following steps show you how you could set up an EditBox that accepts only numeric keys to allow entry of a number no larger than 9,999.

1. **Choose File➪New Application from the main menu.**

2. **Drop an EditBox component into the form by clicking on the EditBox button and then clicking into the form.**

3. **In the Events page of the Object Inspector, double-click on the blank** OnKeyPress **event name field and enter the following code:**

```
if ((Key < '0') || (Key > '9'))
  {
  MessageBeep(0) ;
  Key = '\0' ;
  }
```

This code means that if the integer entered is less than 0 or greater than 9, the computer beeps and sets the integer to a blank character. This setting ensures that the user can enter only positive numeric values in the EditBox.

4. **Set the MaxLength property to 4.**

This action sets the maximum value of the number that the user enters at 9999.

5. **Compile, link, and run this program by pressing F9, or by clicking on the C++Builder Run button (the one with the green arrow on it), or by choosing** Run⇨Run.

Play with this application a little to see how it controls what you enter.

The OnEnter and OnExit events are triggered as the user enters and leaves a field. These events can be used to validate the text as a whole rather than by one character at a time.

Be aware that if you change the Text property within the OnChange event, the event handler triggers itself again. You may create a cyclical call that results in your having to reset your machine!

The Panel component

The Panel component can be used as a background component in order to group components within forms. Panels are also useful for understanding some of the more-complex components that have a great deal of behavior in common with Panels.

You can place a Panel onto your form by selecting the Panel button from the Component Palette and then clicking into your form wherever you require a panel. With the Panel selected, you can access the properties and events for the Panel component by using the Object Inspector.

The Caption property of a Panel is always initially loaded with the name of the Panel. Even though a Caption may not be required for many panel applications, Panel components always have a Caption property so don't forget to clear out the Caption property if you are not going to use it.

One of the most significant properties of Panels is the *Align property,* which allows you to insert panels into a form that tailor themselves to fit the available space and remain where you set them even when the user resizes the form. Figure 4-12 shows an example of this property.

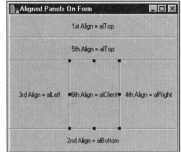

Figure 4-12:
Panel
alignment
options.

To produce the example form in Figure 4-12, follow these steps:

1. Select File⇨New Form from the main menu.

2. Click on the Panel button on the Standard page of the Component Palette.

3. Using Steps 1 and 2, drop six Panels in the free space of the form.

4. Set the Align properties for each Panel as indicated back in Figure 4-8.

I also indicate the order in which I placed each Panel on the form.

After you have placed the Panels in the form, resize the form by clicking into the bottom-right corner of the form and dragging; then pull the form around the C++Builder workspace to see how the panels react. When the form is resized, the Panels align themselves automatically.

By using the Align property, you can lock Panel components into place on a form. In addition, if you select a Panel and then place another Panel within it, you can experiment with aligning panels within other panels.

Don't confuse the *Alignment property* with the *Align* property. Alignment provides the same function for the Panel component as it does for the Label component — it tells C++Builder how you want the *text* of a Caption property aligned within the panel: left, centered, or right.

In the example that follows, a pair of properties — *BevelInner* and *BevelOuter* — are used on a panel. Why surround one component with two bevel borders? By using a combination of these two properties, each of which has three options — alLower, alNone, and alRaised — you can create up to nine "3-D" panel effects, which are shown in Figure 4-13.

The two letters in the middle of each panel in Figure 4-13 indicate the settings of each of the properties: alNone/alNone is in the top-left corner, alLower/alRaised is in the center, and alRaised/alRaised is in the bottom-right corner.

Figure 4-13:
An assortment of "3-D" panel effects, courtesy of the Bevel properties.

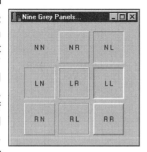

The Memo component

The Memo component has similarities to the Edit component with one major advantage — the Memo component can hold multiple lines of text.

You can select the Memo component using the Memo button on the Standard page. Once you have placed a Memo component onto a form, you can gain access to its properties and events in the Object Inspector.

The Memo component also shares one functionality with the Panel component — the Align property. This property allows you to set aside an area of the form for note entry. Once again, don't confuse Align with the Alignment property, which is set to `alLeft` by default.

The *Lines property* enables multiple lines of text to be held within a Memo component. This property can hold a list of strings (a *string* being a sequence of characters).

If you want to preload some lines of text for your user

1. **Click on the** `Lines` **property field in the Object Inspector.**

2. **Click on the ellipsis button in the** `TStrings` **field to display the String list editor shown in Figure 4-14.**

   A couple lines of text that I entered for this example appear in the Lines property.

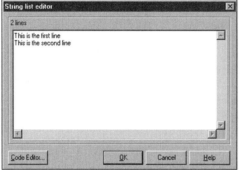

Figure 4-14:
Use the String list editor to enter text in a Memo component.

Several properties add versatility to the Memo component:

- ✔ By using the *ScrollBars property,* you can turn the vertical and horizontal scroll bars on and off. This property has four settings: `ssNone`, `ssHorizontal`, `ssVertical`, and `ssBoth`. These settings provide either vertical or horizontal scroll bars, both vertical or horizontal scroll bars, or no scroll bars at all alongside the Memo.

- ✔ The properties *WantReturns* and *WantTabs* determine whether the Enter and Tab commands that a user enters in a Memo are held as part of the text or are sent out to the form. If you set WantReturns to false, the Enter key does not drop the text to the next line in the Memo, but instead sends it out to the form. The same applies to the WantTabs property; if it's set to false, a Tab entry sends the focus to the next control, rather than placing a tab in the text of the Memo.

- ✔ If the *WordWrap property* is set to true, the user doesn't have to be concerned with overrunning a line. The user can keep typing away and the component takes care of moving to the next line as the user reaches the right side of the Memo.

The following example program puts the Memo component to work creating a dedicated code file editor.

1. **Choose File⇨New Application from the main menu.**

2. **Click on the Memo button on the Standard page and then click on the form to drop in a component.**

3. **Set the Align property of the Memo component to** `alClient` **from the Object Inspector.**

   The component then fills up the whole form.

4. **Click on the background of the form and then click on the Events tab on the Object Inspector.**

5. **Double-click on the blank field next to the** `OnCreate` **event handler to get into the Code Editor.**

6. **Enter the following lines in the Code Editor.**

   ```
   Memo1->Lines->LoadFromFile("unit1.cpp") ;
   Memo1->Lines->SaveToFile("unit1.bak") ;
   ```

7. **Double-click on the blank field next to the** `OnCloseQuery` **event handler, and then enter the following line of code in the Code Editor:**

   ```
   Memo1->Lines->SaveToFile("unit1.cpp") ;
   ```

8. **Run the program by pressing F9.**

   You should see the same code that you just entered displayed in the Memo component in the program. The program reads in the contents of the `unil.cpp` file as it starts using the `LoadFromFile` method. It then makes a backup version of the file called `unit1.bak`. When you close the program, it automatically saves any changes that have been made using the `SaveToFile` method.

If you save your work in a directory other than the C++Builder default directory, you may receive an error message telling you the program can't find the unit1.cpp file.

The ListBox component

The ListBox component can prevent users from making text-entry mistakes by limiting choices to those that are already valid. A ListBox can contain up to 32,000 items that users can choose from (of course, if you include anywhere near that many, both you and your end users may need to develop a real life).

To start, take a look at the ListBox component:

1. **Click on the ListBox button and then click on the form to drop the ListBox into position.**

2. **Click on the ListBox to display its properties and events in the Object Inspector.**

The *Items property* bears a resemblance to the Lines property of the Memo component described in the previous section of this chapter. You can enter a list of data into the ListBox component at design time by using the following steps:

1. **Click on the ellipsis button on the Items property in the Object Inspector to open the String List editor.**

2. **Enter the lines of text that you want the ListBox to hold.**

3. **Click on OK on the String List editor to save your changes.**

If you set the `IntegralHeight` property to true, only items that can be shown vertically in their entirety in the ListBox are shown at all.

If you are writing a program that picks tracks to play from a CD, for example, you can allow the user to select more than one item at a time by using a combination of the *ExtendedSelect* and *MultiSelect* properties. The following table summarizes how these properties affect the behavior of the ListBox component.

MultiSelect Setting	ExtendedSelect Setting	Effect
true	true	Holding down the Ctrl key while clicking allows user to select noncontiguous items in a list; holding down the Shift key while clicking allows user to select a range of items.
true	false	User can select multiple options without using the Ctrl or Shift key but can no longer select a range of options.
false	N/A	Only individual items can be selected.

You can create a ListBox that contains more than one Column, as shown in Figure 4-15, by increasing the *Column property* number (by default, the Column property is set to 0). You may not use this option very often, but it's there if you happen to need it.

Figure 4-15:
You have
the option
of including
more than
one column
in a ListBox.

When your program is in use, the OnClick event is triggered every time you select an item from the ListBox list by pressing the arrow keys or by clicking on the ListBox. In this event, you determine what you want the program to do when the user makes selections.

The steps that follow provide an example program using the OnClick event:

1. **Choose File⇨New Application from the main menu.**

2. **Click on the ListBox component button and then click into the position on the form where you want to drop in a ListBox.**

3. **Click on the ellipsis button in the Items property field to show the String List editor and then enter ten lines of text.**

4. **Click on OK.**

5. **Click on the Label button on the Standard page of the Component Palette and then click on the form.**

6. **Click on the ListBox component on the form, then click on the Events tab on the Object Inspector, and then double-click on the empty field next to the** OnClick **event handler.**

   You're then in the Code Editor, where you enter the following line:

   ```
   Label1->Caption = ListBox1->Items->Strings[ListBox1-
           >ItemIndex] ;
   ```

7. **Run the program by pressing F9.**

   As you click items in the ListBox, the Label's caption changes with your choices (see Figure 4-16).

Figure 4-16:
The ListBox
OnClick
event
enables you
to create
label
captions
that change
with the
user's list
selection.

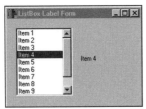

The ComboBox component

The ComboBox component combines the features of an EditBox and a
ListBox. ComboBoxes can offer your users a selection box that doesn't take
up as much room on your form as a full ListBox does. Three types of
ComboBox components are available: Simple, DropDown, and DropDownList:

✔ The Simple type of ComboBox isn't capable of showing drop-down
menus (see Figure 4-17). It functions much like an Edit control attached
to the top of a ListBox. The user can choose from the list or enter text
in the edit box.

Figure 4-17:
Simple
ComboBoxes
scroll rather
than drop
down.

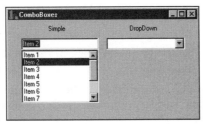

✔ The DropDown components offer a far more compact alternative to the
Simple type of ComboBox. The user can't see the list of choices until
clicking on the down-arrow button on the right side of the EditBox. The
user still has the option of entering text in the edit box.

✔ Typing new entries is not a user option for the DropDownList ComboBox;
users can select from the list but can't enter text of their own.

The ComboBox shares many properties with the Edit and ListBox components. One of them is the *DropDownCount property,* which allows you to
determine how many choices are displayed when the drop-down list

appears. If the Items property contains fewer items than the DropDownCount property does, the ComboBox is clever enough to use up only the room that is needed to show the available items. When you've crammed more than DropDownCount items into a ComboBox, the ScrollBar component automatically arrives on the scene, offering assistance with navigating to the choices that aren't visible.

The *OnDropDown event* is triggered when the user opens the ComboBox. The OnDropDown event gives you the opportunity to update the values in the Items property or to make other components visible in your form when the user clicks on the down-arrow button on the ComboBox.

To add a ComboBox to a form, click on the ComboBox component button and click into the form where you want it to appear. If you then select the ComboBox on the form, you have access to its properties and events through the Object Inspector.

The following example program shows you how to add items to the ComboBox Items list while the program is running.

1. **Choose File⇨New Application from the main menu.**

2. **Click on the EditBox component button, and then click on the form.**

3. **Click on the ComboBox button, and then click on the form.**

   The Style property of the ComboBox is set to csDropDown by default.

4. **Click on the Events tab on the Object Inspector and then double-click on the empty field next to the onDropDown event handler and enter the following in the Code Editor:**

```
ComboBox1->Items->Add(Edit1->Text) ;
```

5. **Press F9 to compile, link, and run your application.**

6. **With the application running, enter any word of your choice in the EditBox and then click on the down-arrow button in the ComboBox.**

   The new word is added to the ComboBox list of items.

You now have complete control over the selections that a user sees at runtime. As a bit of an extension to this example, you could perform the following steps to enable the user to clear out the ComboBox list while the program is running.

1. **Close the program by clicking on the program window's Close button.**

2. **Select the ComboBox and click on the Events tab on the Object Inspector.**

3. **Double-click on the empty** `OnDblClick` **event handler field to get into the Code Editor, where you enter the following line:**

```
ComboBox1->Items->Clear();
```

4. **Press F9 to run the program again.**

The GroupBox component

The GroupBox component is designed to cluster together related components. Suppose that you are building a client database, and part of the database form holds addresses. You may want to show the user that each edit box in a data form is part of the same cluster of information. In this case, you'd place a GroupBox in a form and then set up some EditBoxes as shown in Figure 4-18 (refer to the section "The EditBox component" earlier in this chapter).

 To access the GroupBox component, click on the GroupBox button on the Standard page and then click wherever you want it on the form. With the GroupBox selected on the form, you will have access to its properties and events in the Object Inspector.

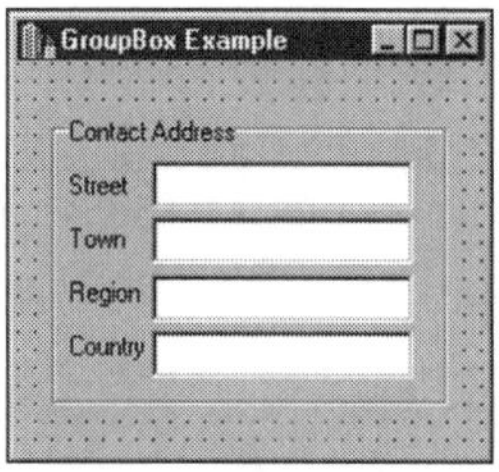

Figure 4-18:
The
GroupBox
component
in action.

GroupBox Example

Contact Address
Street
Town
Region
Country

And One Additional Component: The ScrollBar

ScrollBars are used most often in partnership with other controls, but it's difficult to imagine how many Windows programs could work without a scroll bar. (The ScrollBar component resides on the Additional page of the Component Palette.)

Click on the ScrollBar component button on the Additional page and then click on a form anywhere you want to place the ScrollBar. With the ScrollBar selected on the form, you have access to its properties and events.

✔ The *Kind property* allows you to set scroll bars to run vertically (ScrollBar components run horizontally by default).

✔ The *Max* and *Min properties* hold the value of the scroll button's position relative to the scroll bar's two end positions; all positions in between each end are automatically graded relative to the Max and Min values.

✔ The *Position property* holds the current value for the scroll bar that controls how other components are scrolled.

✔ The *LargeChange property* sets the distance that the scroll bar moves when the user clicks on either side of the scrollbar button.

✔ The *SmallChange property* adjusts the distance the Position property moves when the user clicks on one of the end-arrow buttons.

 The following steps can be used to create an example program using a ScrollBar Component:

1. **Create a new application by choosing File⇨New Application from the main menu.**

2. **Click on the ScrollBar button on the Additional page and then click on the form.**

3. **With the ScrollBar component selected, set the following values for the ScrollBar properties:**

Property	Value
LargeChange	32
Max	255
SmallChange	16

4. **Press Ctrl+C to place a copy of the ScrollBar in the Clipboard, and then press Ctrl+V twice.**

This step places two more copies of the ScrollBar on the form.

5. **Arrange the scroll bars in the form as shown in Figure 4-19.**

6. **Click on the Panel component button on the Standard page and then click alongside the ScrollBars on the form.**

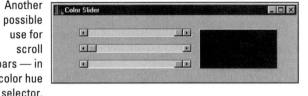

7. **Remove the name from the Panel's Caption property.**

   You won't need it for this example.

8. **Select all three ScrollBar components by pressing Ctrl and clicking on each one.**

9. **In the Events tab on the Object Inspector, double-click on the empty field next to the OnChange event handler.**

10. **You'll then be in the Code Editor, where you enter the following lines:**

```
Panel1->Color = RGB( ScrollBar1->Position,
       ScrollBar2->Position,
       ScrollBar3->Position ) ;
```

   This single event handler is cleverly triggered for a change in position of any of the scroll bar buttons. For example, in Figure 4-19 each bar represents the amount of red, green, and blue that goes into making up the color that the solid panel on the right displays.

11. **Run your application by pressing F9 or by clicking the Run speed button, or by selecting Run⇨Run from the main menu.**

Experiment with your new color selector application by sliding the scroll bars back and forth. Don't forget to examine the LargeChange and SmallChange properties in the Object Inspector to see the degree to which they change.

You can also place a Label component next to each scroll bar and enter the relative position of each scroll bar button in the Label's Caption property. Do this by entering the following code after the Panel color assignment entered in Step 10 in the OnChange event handler:

```
Label1->Caption = IntToStr(ScrollBar1->Position) ;
Label2->Caption = IntToStr(ScrollBar2->Position) ;
Label3->Caption = IntToStr(ScrollBar3->Position) ;
```

The result is what you see in Figure 4-20 — the improved version of the previous example. This one keeps track of the numerical value of each setting as you move through the color spectrum, and it illustrates the power of integrating components.

Figure 4-20:
ScrollBars
working
with other
components
for
precision
control.

Label components   ScrollBar components

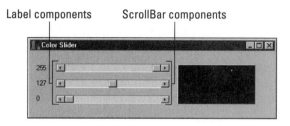

Chapter 5

Button It Up! Adding Buttons and Boxes to Forms

● ●

In This Chapter

▶ Selecting button properties

▶ Adding graphics to a button

▶ Using check boxes

▶ Using radio buttons and radio groups

● ●

*Y*ou don't have to go very far in a Windows application before you're required to click on a button of one kind or another. Buttons are part of what a graphical user interface environment (GUI, to you acronym fans) is all about.

Buttons can be used to lead users through complicated situations by allowing them to react in the most primitive of ways: by punching something! Buttons are used for many Windows application tasks including opening and closing dialog boxes and changing program settings, such as fonts or colors.

No doubt, you have already been using buttons extensively and now you can start controlling how they work in your own applications.

Adding a Button to a Form

The "plain vanilla" standard Windows button resides on the Standard page of the Component Palette. To get this button into place on a form, just follow these steps:

 1. **Click on the Button component button on the Standard page of the Component Palette.**

2. **Move the mouse pointer to the location on the form where you want to place the Button and then click.**

   A Button component appears on your form.

Specifying Button Properties

As with all other C++Builder components you can find on the Component Palette, Button components have characteristics (such as color and size) that you set using the Object Inspector. To load the properties of a Button component into the Object Inspector, simply select the component on the form by clicking on it.

Setting Button text

The *Caption property* is an essential part of a button application. This property displays the button text that the user sees and indicates to the user the likely outcome of clicking on a button.

By placing an ampersand (&) before any letter in the text of the Caption property of a Button component, you can use that letter as a menu *hot key*. This means that instead of clicking on the Button with the mouse, you can press the Button's hot key in combination with the Alt key and that essentially "clicks" the button. Here's an example of how you can do this:

1. **Select File⇨New Application from the main menu.**

2. **Press and hold down the Shift key and then click on the Button component button on the Standard tab of the Component Palette.**

   This "locks" the mouse pointer to the selected component for placing it more than once on the form.

3. **Place the mouse pointer within your new form and click it three times, each time in a different location on the form.**

   Move the pointer down slightly after each click so that the three new Button components don't overlap each other.

4. **To deselect the Button component button, click on the Pointer button on the far-left side of the Component Palette button bar.**

5. **Click on one of the Buttons and, using the Object Inspector, enter the text string** &abc **into the Button's** Caption **property.**

6. **Repeat Step 5 for the other two Buttons using the text strings** a&bc **and** ab&c.

7. **Select all of the Buttons by holding down the Shift key and clicking on each.**

8. **Click on the Events tab on the Object Inspector and then double-click on the empty field next to the** OnClick **event handler.**

   This transports you to the Code Editor, where you type in the following line:

   ```
   ShowMessage("Hi there!") ;
   ```

   Each of the Buttons will display the text "Hi there!" when clicked by the program user.

9. **Compile, link, and run the program by pressing F9.**

   Each of the letters (a, b, and c) that was preceded by an ampersand is underlined, as shown in Figure 5-1.

Figure 5-1:
Three
buttons
equipped
with "hot
keys" in
their
captions.

Once you have created the Buttons in this example, press the Alt key and then a, b, and c in turn to see the Buttons selected (pushed in). Don't forget that you can still click on the Buttons with the mouse, if you so choose.

As you place components into a form, you can quickly align them (including Buttons) by selecting all of the components and then using the Alignment Palette dialog box found under View⇨Alignment.

How properties affect a Button's behavior

Properties can affect the way that a Button component reacts. For example, if you set the *Cancel property* of a Button to true using the Object Inspector, when the user presses the Esc key or clicks on the Button, the OnClick event (which is automatically created for you when you set the Cancel property to true) for that Button is triggered.

Hello? Buttons to program

Here's a Button component property that comes in handy if you are creating a dialog box in which your user is supposed to perform a specific task and then, once that task is completed, close the dialog box. It's called the *ModalResult property* and you find it using the Object Inspector. This property enables a value to be returned by the buttons in a dialog box to the main form of your program.

The default value for the ModalResult property of a Button is mrNone (which pretty much does nothing). If you change this value to something else using the drop-down list in the Object Inspector, when the user clicks on the Button the ModalResult property of the Button is returned to the main form.

For example, if you provide a dialog box for the user to make an immediate decision, place two buttons onto the dialog box — one with the ModalResult set to mrYes and the other to mrNo. When the user presses either of these buttons on the dialog box, the dialog box is closed and the mrYes or mrNo result is returned accordingly.

If the *Default property* of the Button is set to true using the Object Inspector, when the user presses the Enter key it triggers the Button's OnCiick event (see the next section of this chapter, "Specifying a Button event").

By setting the Default property to true for one of the Buttons on a form, the user is free to move around all the buttons in the form by pressing the Tab key. A dotted line around the Caption text indicates which button is going to be selected when the user presses Enter. (Refer to the top button in Figure 5-1.) The Button with this dotted outline is called the *focus button*.

Specifying a Button event

Button components must be able to react to relevant actions (or *events* in programming-speak) going on within your program. You can define what happens as these Button events occur via the Events tab on the Object Inspector. The most critically important event for a button is the *OnClick event*. This event tells the button what to do when the user clicks the mouse or presses a key combination that "selects" the button.

You can also play some tricks with Button events. You can try this example for fun:

1. Choose File⇨New Application to open a new form.

2. **Click on the Button component button on the Standard page, and then click anywhere on the new form.**

3. **With the Button component still selected on the form, click on the Events tab on the Object Inspector, and then double-click on the empty field next to the** `OnMouseDown` **event handler.**

   You're then in the Code Editor, where you enter the following line:

   ```
   Button1->Caption = "I feel Down" ;
   ```

4. **Double-click on the** `OnMouseUp` **event handler name in the Events page of the Object Inspector.**

   Enter the following line in the Code Editor:

   ```
   Button1->Caption = "I'm Up" ;
   ```

5. **Press F9 to run this example program.**

   You can see that the caption of the Button component changes as you press and release the mouse button.

The previous example hints at two things: First, you can perform a task whilst a button is down and then stop the task once the button is released. Second, you can change the action of a button at run time. Is this dangerous and confusing? That depends on how you change the action of the Button.

Why place more buttons onto a form than you really need when you can save space in a form (and save yourself some work) by having one button do two things? (As long as the button isn't doing the two things at the same time, though!) This comes in handy for a program in which the user toggles (switches back and forth) between modes of operation — for example, from read-only to edit. The buttons in Figure 5-2 allow the user to set a program into edit mode by clicking the Edit button and then save any changes by clicking on the Save button.

Figure 5-2:
You can set this up so the user can toggle between the two buttons.

You can save some space on the form in Figure 5-2 by alternating the Caption property of a single Button between Edit and Save. In this example, the code in the OnClick event would look like this:

```
if (Button1->Caption == "&Edit" )
  {
  Button1->Caption = "&Save" ;
  // Do other code here

  }
else
   {
  Button1->Caption = "&Edit" ;
  // Do other code here

  }
```

This single-button approach produces a win-win situation — you don't have to worry about which button the user may press next and the user is left in no doubt of the appropriate action to take, because only one action is offered at a time.

Getting the Picture: Adding a Graphic to a Button

I'm going to demonstrate how to improve on the appearance of the rather bland Edit and Save buttons back in Figure 5-2. Wouldn't they look more interesting with a graphic or two?

Don't worry; you don't have to draw any pictures for the buttons yourself. You've got 162 graphics to choose among in the C++Builder cbuilder\images\ buttons folder (you'll find bitmap images there to suit most of your needs). The graphics that I placed in the buttons to create Figure 5-3 are Edit.bmp and FileSave.bmp, the ones best suited to this purpose.

Figure 5-3:
Edit and
Save: Two
buttons
made a
bitmap
better.

BitButton is a component that acts as a standard button but allows you to embed bitmap pictures as well as text in a button. You can find the BitButton component on the Additional page of the Component Palette.

You can put pictures into your BitButtons by using the somewhat strangely named *Glyph property* on the Object Inspector. Try using the steps in the following example:

1. **Click on the BitButton component button on the Additional page of Component Palette.**

2. **Click into a form in the location that you want to place the BitButton component.**

3. **With the new BitButton still selected on the form, select the Glyph property on the Object Inspector.**

   An ellipsis (. . .) button appears.

4. **Click on the ellipsis button on the Glyph property to get the Picture Editor, shown in Figure 5-4.**

Figure 5-4:
The Picture Editor enables you to select a bitmap image for a button.

If you are not in the directory called cbuilder\images\buttons, then go to that directory using the Browse button.

5. **To select a bitmap graphic, click on the Load button in the Picture Editor box to bring up a Load Picture dialog box.**

6. **Locate the file that you want to use in the BitButton using the Load Picture dialog box and then click on the Open button.**

   This returns you to the Picture Editor, except that now your picture is visible in the center of the framed area of the Picture Editor.

7. **Click on OK to close the Picture Editor.**

   The graphic that you have selected is now displayed on the button.

Me and my shadow Glyph

You may wonder why back in Figure 5-4 the graphic in the center of the Picture Editor box appears to be two images in one — the left half an icon with recognizable images and the right half a mere shadow of the other side.

This happens because the graphics that are shown on a button change according to the state of the button. The *NumGlyphs property* states how many images are within a Glyph (the default is two). One of the images is the complete one, which is shown to the user when the button is clickable. The second one is normally much dimmer (often grayed) and is shown to the user when the button has been disabled (the Enable property has been set to false). When the button is dimmed, it can't be clicked. And you thought you were seeing things!

By selecting one of the four *Layout property* options available to you in the drop-down list in the Object Inspector, you can determine exactly how the Caption and the Glyph should be placed in relation to each other on the button. The four layout choices are: `blGlyphRight`, `blGlyphLeft`, `blGlyphTop`, and `blGlyphBottom`. The result of all four choices is shown in Figure 5-5.

Figure 5-5:
The four Glyph layout choices in action.

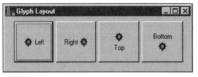

You can also modify the default of four pixels of space between button text and button image by using the *Spacing property* in the Object Inspector. If you set this value to –1, the picture and the text are evenly spaced out for you on the button.

A useful property included in the BitButton is the *Kind property* — again, you gain access to this property using the Object Inspector. The Kind property offers 11 different settings, the results of which are shown in Figure 5-6. Setting this property not only chooses your Caption and Glyph properties (in other words, you have text and a picture already made for you), but also sets the ModalResult of the button (see "How properties affect a Button's behavior" earlier in this chapter for details on the ModalResult property). Talk about a helping hand!

Figure 5-6:
The Kind property gives you 11 different glyph and caption combinations to choose from.

Working with SpeedButtons

SpeedButton components provide users with an alternative way of executing a task that can otherwise be accessed as a selection on a menu bar. The SpeedButton component provides a special type of button that usually displays a graphic. Because SpeedButtons also often appear in groups, they have special properties, such as *GroupIndex* and *AllowAllUp,* that allow you to manage clusters of SpeedButtons.

Many Windows applications make extensive use of speed buttons, usually by organizing SpeedButtons on a Panel component (refer to Chapter 4 for details on Panel components).

You're probably no stranger to speed buttons. A cluster of speed buttons is shown in Figure 5-7. Do they look familiar? They're the project and file speed buttons from the C++Builder main window.

Figure 5-7:
A group of C++Builder SpeedButtons ready to go.

You can group SpeedButton components by using the *GroupIndex property* in the Object Inspector. SpeedButtons with a GroupIndex property set to the same value remain in a depressed position when the user clicks on any of them, while the other buttons in the group pop up in turn.

Using the Object Inspector, set the *SpeedButton Down property* for a group of SpeedButtons that you want to appear depressed (or selected) when the form is first shown in the program. You can also take control of SpeedButtons by setting the Down property from within your code by using this line:

```
SpeedButton1->Down = True ;
```

Note: This setting does not trigger the button's OnClick event. If it did, the program would perform the action that has been associated with the OnClick event. By setting the Down property in code, you're just changing the button's appearance.

You can set the *AllowAllUp property* if you want the user to be able to deselect all the buttons at once. If one of your program options must be in use at all times, don't use this property.

If a SpeedButton has no text caption, use the *Hint property* in the Object Inspector to enter some text to give the user a clue as to the button's function. Then, when the user passes the mouse pointer over a button, a label pops up identifying the button's purpose.

Give the SpeedButton component a test drive. Just follow the steps in this example:

1. **Select File⇨New Application for a new form.**

2. **Hold down the Shift key while you click on the SpeedButton component button in the Component Palette on the Additional page.**

   This locks the component selection on the SpeedButton component.

3. **Click four times in line anywhere on the new form.**

   Four SpeedButton components are placed.

4. **Click on the Pointer button on the Component Palette to "unlock" the component selection.**

5. **Use the Object Inspector to change the Caption properties for each SpeedButton.**

   Enter the < and > characters as shown in Figure 5-8 for the Caption properties. The resulting buttons resemble those you'd see on a VCR or CD player.

Figure 5-8:
Directional
arrows
were added
to this
SpeedButton
component
by using the
Caption
property.

6. **Use the Object Inspector to enter a value of 1 into the** GroupIndex
property for each SpeedButton on the form.

Now each of the SpeedButtons on the form belongs to Group 1. Setting
the GroupIndex property for each of the SpeedButtons to the same
value gives them the look and behavior of a set of push buttons.

7. **Click on the SpeedButton at the far left in the row of four
SpeedButtons and using the Object Inspector, set the** Down **property
for the SpeedButton to** true.

If you follow the steps in this example, you end up with a set of buttons
similar to those in Figure 5-9. You can see that the far-left button has
the *focus,* that is, it looks selected.

8. **Press F9 to run the program.**

When you click on an unselected button, the button in the depressed
position automatically pops up.

Figure 5-9:
By using
SpeedButton
properties,
you can
give a
button
focus.

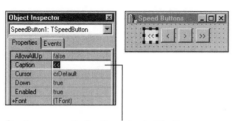

Caption property for the selected button

Checking Out Check Boxes

At times, you may want your users to check off a list of items, or you may want to offer a list of settings that can be clicked to either on or off, true or false, or done or incomplete.

 CheckBox components, selected via the CheckBox button on the Standard page of the Component Palette, give you this ability. (Even though check boxes are not truly buttons, they have so much in common with button components that this chapter is the best place to cover them.)

You can place a check box on either side of a caption in a dialog box. In Figure 5-10, I put one check box to the right of the top caption and the rest of the check boxes to the left of the captions. (Use the *Alignment property* on the Object Inspector to make this kind of choice.)

If you use the Object Inspector to set the *AllowGrayed property* to true, the CheckBox component has three states: checked, unchecked, or grayed out. You can access these options via the *State property* on the Object Inspector. As you can see from Figure 5-10, a check box can be both checked and grayed out. Does this mean that I am not sure whether I have walked the dog? No, in this case it means I'm halfway around the park with the mutt. The task is neither completely done nor undone. If I didn't care how far I got with the dog, I would omit this halfway notation and set the state to the default value of false.

Figure 5-10:
What a to-do! A check box created by the author with checked and unchecked boxes, and one box that's checked and grayed-out.

At the end of the day, I can check through the list I created in this example by using the Checked property to see which jobs are completed. You could do this in your own code by using the following:

```
if (CheckBox1->Checked == true)
  ShowMessage("Check Box1 is Checked !!") ;
```

Tuning in to Radio Buttons

Radio buttons take their name from the old-fashioned car radio buttons that would pop out as others in the set of buttons are pushed in. Like speed buttons, radio buttons normally come in groups. RadioButton components are used when you are looking to provide a set of choices to the user in which only one choice can be selected at a time. (Such as, how do like your coffee — black or au lait?)

You can select a RadioButton component by clicking on the RadioButton button on the Standard page of the Component Palette. Once the RadioButton is selected, click on a form to drop in the component. C++Builder automatically groups radio buttons for you in a form or panel (and you don't have to limit yourself to just one set of buttons if you want more).

As with the CheckBox component described in the previous section of this chapter, use the Alignment property (on the Object Inspector) to choose which side of the RadioButton you want the Caption property text placed — either left or right. Examine the *Checked property* on the Object Inspector to see whether the RadioButton component is selected.

Follow these steps to include RadioButtons in an example program:

1. **Select File⇨New Application for a new form.**

2. **Hold down the Shift key while you click on the RadioButton component button on the Standard page of the Component Palette.**

3. **Click five times to form a column of five RadioButton components on your new form.**

4. **Use the Object Inspector to change the** Caption **property of each RadioButton to correspond to the five lines of text shown in Figure 5-11.**

5. **Click on the BitButton button on the Additional page.**

This selects the BitButton component.

Figure 5-11:
Enter
captions for
radio
buttons in
this box.

6. **Click on the bottom center of your form to place a new button.**

7. **Using the Object Inspector, select** bkOK **from the drop-down list in the Kind property for the BitButton component.**

8. **Press F9 to run the program.**

The next steps in this example program create a *radio group,* so that your buttons can work as a team. The RadioGroup component offers a way of adding radio buttons while providing an integrated heading for the group at the same time.

 Select the RadioGroup component using the RadioGroup button on the Standard tab of the Component Palette. Once selected, click onto a form to drop in the RadioGroup component.

You can add RadioButtons to a RadioGroup by doing the following:

1. **Click on the** Items **property on the Object Inspector.**

2. **Click on the ellipsis button on the** Items **property to display the String list editor (refer to Figure 5-11).**

   Each line of text that you add to the String list editor becomes a caption for a radio button in the RadioGroup component shown in Figure 5-12.

Figure 5-12:
An
integrated
group
of radio
buttons
courtesy of
the Items
property.

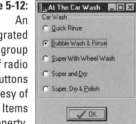

If you wanted to split a Radio Button group into several columns, use the *Columns property* in the Object Inspector.

You can either set or read a selected radio button by using the *ItemIndex property*. If ItemIndex is set to –1, the user hasn't touched the button. The ItemIndex value for the first button in a RadioGroup component starts, in good old computer style, at 0 for the first selection. If you wanted to determine if the first radio button was set in a RadioGroup component, you could use the following code:

```
if (RadioGroup1->ItemIndex == 0)
   ShowMessage("Radio Button 1 has been set !") ;
```

Chapter 6

Developing with the Additional Components

● ●

In This Chapter

▶ Limiting user input with EditMasks

▶ Displaying a graphic on a form with the Image component

▶ Using Shapes to real effect

▶ Scrolling with ScrollBox components

▶ Getting a line on Grid components

● ●

*T*he components that reside on the Additional page of the Component Palette may seem to be a mixed bag of items (which indeed they are). In this chapter, you can find example programs built with StringGrids and DrawGrids, plus Shape, Bevel, MaskEdit, Image, and ScrollBox components.

So what do the Additional controls have in common? They're all standard components that Borland enhanced for added capabilities (for instance, the MaskEdit component, which is coming up, is basically an Edit component with an input filter attached to it).

Unveiling the MaskEdit Component

The term *mask,* in computer-speak, is a digital "overlay" of sorts that prevents a user from entering invalid data into a data field. Or, put another way, a mask is a mechanism for validating data input.

The MaskEdit component allows you to construct patterns of code that restrict the type of characters that a user can enter into a MaskEdit text box.

To see how the MaskEdit component works, you want to first place a component in a form:

1. **Choose <u>F</u>ile➪New Applica<u>t</u>ion from the C++Builder main menu to get a new form in a new application.**

2. **Click on the MaskEdit button on the Additional page of the Component Palette.**

3. **Click on the form where you want the MaskEdit control to appear.**

Entering EditMask property values

Understanding the MaskEdit component has a lot to do with understanding its *EditMask property* from the Object Inspector. Assume that a program requires a user to enter an account code that consists of exactly four letters, followed by four numbers. After placing a MaskEdit component on a form, you could do the following:

1. **Double-click on the empty name field next to the** `EditMask` **property in the Object Inspector, or click on the ellipsis button in the empty field.**

   This action invokes the Input Mask Editor dialog box (the property editor) shown in Figure 6-1.

2. **Enter the following value in the <u>I</u>nput Mask field of the dialog box:**

   ```
   LLLL0000
   ```

   The four Ls placed in the `EditMask` property restrict users to entering only text characters in the first four positions and the four 0s (zeroes) restrict a user to entering only numbers for the last four characters. This means the user could successfully enter ABCD1234 but not 12ABCD34 (in fact, the user wouldn't be permitted to get past entering the first character).

Table 6-1 summarizes the basic character code you can enter in the EditMask property of a MaskEdit component. This code determines which characters a user can enter into an edit box and in what position those characters will appear.

Option to save formatting characters

Mask characters loaded into EditMask property

Ready-made sample masks

Figure 6-1:
The Input
Mask Editor
dialog
box — the
property
editor
for the
EditMask
property.

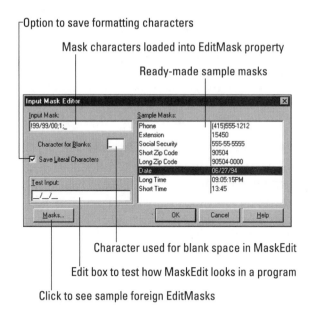

Character used for blank space in MaskEdit

Edit box to test how MaskEdit looks in a program

Click to see sample foreign EditMasks

Table 6-1	Character Code Used for EditMask Property
Mask Character	**Description**
A	Permits letter or number characters (for example, A–Z, a–z, 0–9 character ranges are permitted)
L	Permits letter characters only (for example, A–Z, a–z character ranges are valid)
0	Permits numeric characters only
#	Permits numeric characters (including numbers with a plus or minus sign)
_ (underscore)	Inserts a character space in the MaskEdit text
>	Converts all characters to uppercase until a < character is found
<	Converts all characters to lowercase until a > character is found
!	When entered as the first character in a mask, removes leading spaces (that is, character spaces) from strings loaded into the MaskEdit's Text property (for example, the four space characters at the beginning of the " acbd1234" string would be removed)

Examining the property editor

You don't have to string a bunch of mask characters together yourself inside the EditMask property before you can get a useful MaskEdit component. C++Builder provides some ready-made masks for you. But in order to use them, you need to cruise around the Input Mask Editor a bit more. In case you didn't use the steps from the previous section, do the following:

1. **Choose File⇨New Form from the main menu.**

2. **Click on the MaskEdit button on the Additional page, and then click on the Component Palette.**

3. **With the MaskEdit component still selected on the form, click on the `EditMask` property in the Object Inspector, and then click on the ellipsis button for the property.**

   These steps produce the Input Mask Editor dialog box.

In the example shown back in Figure 6-1, I highlighted the Date mask by clicking on it. The Date mask's string of coded characters is then loaded into the Input Mask edit box in the top-left corner of the window. The Mask entry is divided into three sections, or *fields,* separated by semicolons:

✔ The first field shows the mask characters.

✔ The second field (in this example, the number 1) indicates that you want to retain the formatting characters. For example, if you place a zero in the second field in this example, the slash (/) characters are not stored in the Text property for the MaskEdit.

✔ The underscore character in the third field represents characters not yet entered into the MaskEdit component by the user at run time (an indication to users that they need to enter something here).

The following is a sample mask string that provides a MaskEdit component formatted for displaying a date:

```
!99/99/00;1;_
```

If you managed to resist the temptation to try out the Masks... button in the bottom-left corner of the Input Mask Editor (refer to Figure 6-1), go ahead and click on it now. You will see an example of the international appeal of C++Builder — the Open Mask File dialog box, shown in Figure 6-2. Mask files are available for 13 countries. When you choose one of these files, you see the appropriate time zone, postal rates, currency, and more information specific to that country.

Figure 6-2:
The Open
Mask File
dialog box
is where
you can find
masks for
different
countries.

Previewing how a mask looks in use

You can find out how a mask is going to look and react at design time by using the Masked Text Editor. After you choose the date mask, and with the MaskEdit component selected, click on the Text property in the Object Inspector. You'll see that an ellipsis button has been added, which when clicked opens the Masked Text Editor (see Figure 6-3). If you don't have a mask entered into the EditMask property of this MaskEdit component, you won't see much going on in there. If the date mask is chosen, it enables you to test how the MaskEdit is going to look and act for real.

In Figure 6-3, I selected a date mask from the Input Mask Editor (refer to Figure 6-1) and entered the short format date for the 31st of January 1997 into the Input Text edit box. The contents of the MaskEdit component's EditMask property are also shown in this dialog box so you know what your Input Text entry is being checked against.

See how the mask looks before you put it on!

Type any six digits in the Text property of the MaskEdit component using the Object Inspector and then click on the ellipsis button. Did C++Builder display an `Invalid input value` message? If so, you entered text that was not in the format that the MaskEdit requires according to its EditMask. If you choose a date mask, as shown in Figure 6-1, the MaskEdit accepts entries in a date format only. The standard U.S. date format, for example, is MM-DD-YY, so 31st January 1997 must be entered as 01/31/97.

You can check how the edit line is going to look and react at design time by using the Masked Text Editor (see Figure 6-3). Don't forget to also use the Masked Text Editor first to check out any masks that you create yourself.

Figure 6-3:
Use the
Masked
Text Editor
to see how
the mask
looks at
design time.

Putting the MaskEdit to work in a program

The following steps put the MaskEdit to use to create an example age-checking program:

1. **Choose File➪New Application for a new form.**

2. **Click on the Label button on the Standard page of the Component Palette and then click on the form to drop a Label component into the form.**

3. **Click on the Button component button on the Standard page and drop a Button component into the form.**

4. **Click on the Panel button on the Standard page and then drop a Panel component into the form.**

5. **Click on the MaskEdit button on the Additional page and then drop a MaskEdit component into the form.**

6. **Click on the Label component and press F11 to bring up the Object Inspector.**

7. **Click on the Caption property in the Object Inspector and type** Please Enter Date of Birth.

8. **Click on and drag the Label component to position it alongside the MaskEdit component.**

9. **Select the MaskEdit component, then select the EditMask property in the Object Inspector, and then click on the ellipsis button to get the Input Mask Editor.**

10. **Choose the Date type mask from the list and click on OK to close the Input Mask Editor.**

11. **Click on the Panel component and then select the alBottom option from the Align property's drop-down list on the Object Inspector.**

The Panel moves down to the bottom of the form.

12. Size the panel by clicking and dragging out its top edge so that it can show a single line of text in its Caption property.

The components can be laid out in a fashion similar to Figure 6-4.

13. Click on the background of the form.

The form's details are loaded into the Object Inspector.

14. Click on the Events tab of the Object Inspector and then double-click on the blank OnCreate event name for the form.

You're then in the Code Editor, where you enter the following line of code in the event handler:

```
MaskEdit1->Text = DateToStr(Now()) ;
```

This code loads today's date into the date field as the program begins.

15. Click on the Button component button and then enter the text How Old Am I? **into its Caption property.**

16. Click on the Events property in the Object Inspector of the button and then double-click on the empty name field of the OnClick event handler to get into the Code Editor, where you enter the following:

```
unsigned short nYear, nMonth, nDay ;
if (Now() < StrToDate(MaskEdit1->Text))
  {
  ShowMessage("Hey, you're not born yet ?");
  }
  else
  {
DecodeDate(Now() - StrToDate(MaskEdit1->Text), nYear,
      nMonth, nDay) ;
Panel1->Caption = "You are " + IntToStr(nYear%100) + "
      years" ;
```

This code is designed to figure out the difference between today's date and the date that you entered, and places the number of years between them in the Caption of the Panel. (This nifty application comes in handy if the end user happens to be an insurance agent or financial planner.)

17. Run the application by pressing F9 and enter some dates into the MaskEdit that was just built.

Don't forget to click on the "How Old Am I?" button to perform the calculation that you placed in the OnClick event handler, the result of which is placed in the caption of the Panel.

Figure 6-4 shows the age-calculator application created using these steps.

Figure 6-4:
An age
calculator
built
with the
MaskEdit
and other
components.

 You may find that when you run the example program and enter a invalid date, you see something like `Project Project1.exe raised exception class EConvertError with message "...` with more details following the message. This is not actually an error. C++Builder is checking your program and notifying you of an exception (see Chapter 17 for more on exceptions). Try running the program from outside C++Builder or you can turn off the Exception Handling Mechanism by choosing Options⇨ Environment and then deselecting the Break on Exception setting. Then you won't be bothered with this message.

Working Out with the Shape Component

The Shape component on its own won't shake the earth from its axis (fortunately), but when fused with other components (plus a modicum of imagination and a smidgen of coding) it can end up being the life of the party.

 You can get a Shape component going by clicking on the Shape button and then clicking on a form at the location where you want the Shape component to be placed. With the component selected, you can check out its properties in the Object Inspector.

The Shape property

The Shape property determines how a component is going to be configured in a form. You select the shape that you want by clicking on the Shape component placed on the form and then choosing from the Shape property drop-down list on the Object Inspector. You have a choice of the six shapes that are shown in the All Shapes All Sizes . . . box in Figure 6-5.

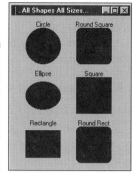

Figure 6-5:
The shapes
of things to
come:
Shape
property
assortment.

Height and Width properties

You can also adjust the size of a component. Just select the component and modify the Height property and Width property in the Object Inspector, or click on and drag the edges of the Shape component to resize it as needed.

Pen and Brush properties

You determine the way that a shape is drawn by using the Pen and Brush properties in the Object Inspector. By setting the Pen property, you can control the way that the outline of the shape is defined. The Brush property fills the area contained by the shape.

The Pen property contains three subproperties:

- *Width* determines the thickness of the shape's outline.
- *Color* sets the tint of the outline.
- *Style* provides a range of fixed settings including psClear for no outline around the Shape and psSolid for an unbroken outline. These can selected using the drop-down list that appears in the Style property on Object Inspector.

The Brush property has only two subproperties: Color and Style. You can access these by double-clicking on Brush in the Object Inspector. By using the Style property, you can fill in or clear the contents of the shape, and you can choose whether you want the shape to be filled with diagonal, horizontal, or vertical lines.

Creating a sample program

To create a Shape program of your own, you can use the following steps, which will give you the sample program shown in Figure 6-6.

1. **Choose File⇨New Application to get a blank form in a new program.**

2. **Click on the Panel button on the Standard page and then click on the form to place the Panel component.**

3. **Set the Width property of the Panel to 40 and the Height property to 90 by dragging out the edges of the form.**

4. **Remove the Caption property text in the Object Inspector and select** clBlack **from the Color subproperty drop-down list of the Brush property.**

5. **Place three Shape components in a vertical column on the panel by clicking on the Shape button and then clicking on the Panel component.**

   Click on and drag each shape so that they each take up a third of the panel.

6. **Set the Shape properties of the three components to** stCircle **using the Object Inspector.**

   You now have three circles stacked one on top of the other.

7. **Also in the Object Inspector, set the Color subproperties in both the Brush and Pen properties to** clRed **and the Name to** Red **for the top circle; set the middle circle to** clYellow **and** Amber**; and the bottom circle to** clGreen **and** Green**.**

8. **Click on the Button component button on the Standard page and click on the form to place a component.**

   Repeat this step twice to drop in three buttons.

9. **Arrange the Buttons on the form one above the other, next to the three Shape components by clicking on and dragging them.**

10. **Select the top Button component and enter** Ready **into the Caption property using the Object Inspector; do the same for the middle and bottom buttons except enter** Steady **on one and** Go **on the other.**

11. **Double-click on the top button to get into the Code Editor and enter the following code:**

```
Red->Visible = True ;
Amber->Visible = False ;
Green->Visible = False ;
```

12. Double-click on the middle button and enter the following code:

```
if (Green->Visible!= True)
  Red->Visible = True ;
Amber->Visible = True ;
Green->Visible = False ;
```

13. Double-click on the bottom button and enter the following code:

```
Red->Visible = False ;
Amber->Visible = False ;
Green->Visible = True ;
```

The end result should look like Figure 6-6.

14. Press the F9 key to run the program.

To try out your new program, click on the buttons to run the OnClick event handlers you've just written.

Figure 6-6:
Follow the steps for the Shape events exercise and you can be your own traffic cop.

Getting the Picture with the Image Component

Whenever you want to display a graphic image on a form, you can do so by using the Image component.

To give the Image component a trial run, just follow these steps:

1. Select the Image component by clicking on the Image button on the Additional page and then click on the form wherever you want the Image control to appear.

2. **With the Image component selected, click on the** `Picture` **property on the Object Inspector.**

3. **Click on the ellipsis button of the Picture property to invoke the Picture Editor dialog box.**

4. **Click on the Load button to invoke the Load picture dialog box.**

5. **Find and select the picture file that you want to use in the Image component and then click on the Open button.**

   The Load picture dialog box closes and the picture is shown in the Picture Editor.

6. **Click on OK to close the Picture Editor and load the Image into your picture.**

   You don't have to compile and run your application to view the image in the form.

If you set the *Stretch property* of an Image component to true using the Object Inspector, the image is proportioned to the size that you set for the Image component in the form. If the image is too large for the Image component and the Stretch property is set to false, the image is cropped so you see only part of it.

Mouse events, such as clicking and dragging, are the only events an Image component responds to; keyboard events just won't work with an Image component. (For more on mouse events, see Chapter 2.)

When you include an Image component as part of your program, C++Builder also includes the image data as part of your program, which means you could end up with a very large .exe (executable) file. And, as you know, a very large .exe file takes a long time to load.

Making Your Forms Scroll

What happens when a user resizes an application and makes a form so small that he or she can't see all the components in the form? Not to worry — C++Builder forms can display scroll bars automatically to allow users to scroll to see the entire form's contents. Try this example to see how it works:

1. **Choose File➪New Application to begin a new form.**

2. **Click on the Panel component button on the Standard page of the Component Palette and drop the component into the form by clicking into it.**

3. **Use the Object Inspector to set the Align property of the Panel to** `alTop`.

4. **Click on the Speed Button component button on the Additional page and then click on the Panel.**

   Repeat this step three times to place a row of speed buttons within the Panel.

5. **Click on the Button component button on the Standard page and then click in the bottom right-hand corner of the form.**

6. **Select the form and move the mouse pointer to the bottom right-hand corner of the form until the pointer changes to a double arrow, and then click on and drag to downsize the form until the Button component can't be seen.**

   Once the button is no longer visible, scroll bars are shown above the panel with the speed buttons.

7. **Select the Button in the bottom right-hand corner of the form and then choose Edit⇨Cut from the main menu.**

   The button moves into the Clipboard.

8. **Click on the ScrollBox component button on the Additional page and then click on the form.**

9. **Set the ScrollBox component's Align property to** `alClient` **in the Object Inspector.**

   The ScrollBox expands to fill the form.

10. **With the ScrollBox selected, choose Edit⇨Paste to place the Button component onto the ScrollBox component.**

You won't see any difference in the form's appearance after placing the ScrollBox until you resize the form by clicking on one of the form's edges and dragging. Now when the user shrinks the form, scroll bars are contained within the panel and the speed bar can be seen.

Using Bevels Instead of Panels

At times you may want to create separate areas on a form but you don't want all the extra features of a panel. The component you want for simply creating defined areas within a form (without any other gadgets) is the Bevel.

The Bevel component gives you the 3-D look of a panel, but it can't act as a container for other components. In fact, a Bevel is one of the few components that has no events whatsoever, so if you select a Bevel and click on the Events tab on the Object Inspector, you won't find any entries.

This section describes the properties that you can set for a Bevel component whenever you need to create separate form areas but don't need all of the functionality of a Panel component.

Figure 6-7 (the box I call "Speak of the Bevel . . .") shows various sample Bevel settings that you can select by using combinations of the Bevel Component's Shape and Style properties. The *Style property* can be set to either bsRaised or bsLowered, making it appear grooved or bumpy. The *Shape property* provides boxes, frames, or just a single line along one edge of the Bevel.

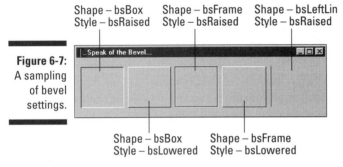

Figure 6-7:
A sampling of bevel settings.

Try these steps to create a sample bevel effect using the Bevel component and its Shape property:

1. **Select File⇨New Application to create a new form.**

2. **Click on the Bevel button on the Additional page and then click anywhere on the form to place a Bevel component.**

3. **With the Bevel component selected, set the Bevel's Align property to** alTop **using the Object Inspector.**

4. **Set the Bevel's Shape property to** bsBottomLine**.**

   You should end up with a horizontal groove dividing your form.

Drawing a Grid

The grid components DrawGrid and StringGrid that you find on the Additional page are somewhat like extended ListBox components (which are described in Chapter 3), but instead of housing just one column of information, you can have almost as many columns as you want, which makes them useful for presenting multiple items of information of the same type.

 To place a DrawGrid control onto a form, select the DrawGrid component by clicking on the DrawGrid button on the Additional page. Then click on a form where you want the DrawGrid control to appear.

Column and row properties

To determine how many rows and columns you want in a grid (after you place a DrawGrid component onto your form) you need to set the *ColCount property* and *RowCount property* in the Object Inspector (you probably want more than the default five rows and five columns).

You can set fixed rows and columns by using the *FixedCols* and *FixedRows properties.* You can use these properties to create headers that remain in place as the other cells in the DrawGrid are scrolled in and out of view. Fixed cells can be distinguished easily by you and the program user because they have their own color-setting property — FixedColor — and they run along the top and down the left-hand side of the DrawGrid.

To control of the height and width of the cells, use the *DefaultRowHeight* and *DefaultColWidth property* setting from within the Object Inspector.

DrawGrid events

The code that you place in the OnDrawCell event handler is accessed within your program for every cell in the grid, so it gets called many times in the course of using the program. (Try to keep the code that you place in the OnDrawCell event handler to a minimum. You can really slow down the drawing of the grid if you include code that does not directly relate to the DrawGrid design.)

The following steps contain a fair amount of code, but result in a DrawGrid application that'll have others asking, "How did you get it to do *that?*"

1. **Choose File⇨New Application to get a blank form.**

2. **Click on the DrawGrid component button on the Additional page and then click anywhere on the form.**

3. **With the Draw Grid selected and using the Object Inspector, set the following properties to the values shown in the table:**

Property	Value
ColCount	3
DefaultColWidth	30
FixedCols	0
FixedRows	0
Font.Type	MS Sans Serif
Font.Style	Bold

(continued)

(continued)

Property	Value
Font.Size	14
Height	78
RowCount	3
ScrollBars	ssNone
Width	96

4. **With the DrawGrid component selected, click on the Events tab on the Object Inspector and double-click on the empty** `OnDrawCell` **event-handler name field to get into the Code Editor.**

5. **Enter the following in the Code Editor:**

```
if (nGridArray[Col][Row] == 1)
 DrawGrid1->Canvas->TextRect(Rect, Rect.Left, Rect.Top,
      "X") ;
if (nGridArray[Col][Row] == 2)
 DrawGrid1->Canvas->TextRect(Rect, Rect.Left, Rect.Top,
      "O") ;
```

6. **Double-click on the empty** `onMouseDown` **event handler name field and enter the following in the Code Editor:**

```
long Col=0, Row=0 ;

DrawGrid1->MouseToCell(X, Y, Col, Row) ;

if (Counter%2)
 nGridArray[Col][Row] = 1 ;
else
 nGridArray[Col][Row] = 2 ;

Counter = Counter ++ ;

if (Counter == 9)
 {
 for (int i=0 ; i < 3; i++)
   for (int j=0 ; j < 3; j++)
   nGridArray[i][j] = 0 ;

  DrawGrid1->Invalidate() ;
 Counter = 0 ;
 }
```

7. **Select the form by clicking on its background.**

   The details of the form are loaded into the Object Inspector.

8. **Click on the Events tab of the Object Inspector and then double-click on the blank** `OnCreate` **event field and enter the following lines in the Code Editor:**

   ```
   for (int i=0 ; i < 3; i++)
     for (int j=0 ; j < 3; j++)
       nGridArray[i][j] = 0 ;
   Counter = 0 ;
   ```

   Next, I'm adding a couple of items to the form — a counter (to keep track of turns in the game) and an array of numbers to hold the game scoring. (Now you have an idea what this application is about.)

9. **Right-click anywhere on the Code Editor to bring up its speed menu and choose the Open Source/Header File option.**

   The code header opens up the header file for this form. This is where the "blueprint" for the form itself is held.

10. **Use the down-arrow key to move the cursor to the line that says** `private` **in the header file now displayed in the Code Editor.**

11. **Enter the following lines shown in bold into the header file:**

    C++Builder provides the other lines of code as part of creating the form for you.

    ```
    private:     // User declarations
      int nGridArray[3][3] ;
      int Counter ;
    public:      // User declarations
    ```

12. **Press the F9 key to play a lively game of tic-tac-toe (see Figure 6-8).**

    Plus, when the board is full, it automatically starts a new game for you!

Figure 6-8:
With some event-handling code, you can create your own tic-tac-toe game.

StringGrids: more powerful than DrawGrids

When you place a StringGrid component on a form, you've introduced a grid monster. The StringGrid is the most powerful of the grids and probably is the one you're going to use most often. StringGrids share many of the properties of DrawGrids but take organizing information in ordered cells one stage further.

Two properties differentiate the StringGrid from the DrawGrid — the *Cells property,* which refers to strings by referencing them by the Row and Column in which they appear in the StringGrid, and the *Objects property,* which can hold information as a reference. The reference can point to just about anything on the computer screen!

The following steps show you how to use the StringGrid component to construct an application that combines text and graphics in an orderly fashion.

1. **Choose File⇨New Application to get a new form.**

2. **Click on the Panel button on the Standard page and then click anywhere on the form to place a Panel component.**

3. **Using the Object Inspector, set the component's Align property to** alLeft **and remove the default text** Panel1 **from the Caption property of the Panel component.**

4. **With the Panel still selected on the form, click on the Button component button on the Standard page and then click in the middle of the Panel to drop in a button.**

5. **Use the Object Inspector to enter the word** Load **into the Button's Caption property.**

6. **Click on the System tab on the Component Palette, select the DirectoryListBox component button, and then click anywhere on the Panel to place a DirectoryListBox component.**

7. **Click on the StringGrid button on the Additional page and then click anywhere on the background of the form to place a StringGrid component.**

8. **Using the Object Inspector, set the Align property of the StringGrid to** alClient.

9. **With the StringGrid selected on the form, use the Object Inspector to set the properties to the values shown in the following table:**

Property	Value
ColCount	10
DefaultColWidth	80
DefaultRowHeight	40
FixedCols	0
FixedRows	0
RowCount	10

10. **With the StringGrid still selected on the form, click on the Events tab of the Object Inspector and then double-click on the empty name field of the** OnDrawCell **event.**

11. **You are now in the Code Editor, where you can enter the following code:**

```
if (StringGrid1->Objects[Col][Row]!= 0 )
  {
  StringGrid1->Canvas->Draw(Rect.Left + 10 , Rect.Top +
       20,(Graphics::TGraphic*)StringGrid1-
       >Objects[Col][Row]);
  }
```

12. **Click on the button that you placed on the Panel in Step 4 and double-click on the empty** OnClick **event handler name field in the Events page of the Object Inspector.**

13. **You end up back in the Code Editor, where you enter the following:**

```
int Col, Row ;
ffblk fbFileData ;
TPicture *picThis ;

String strPath = DirectoryListBox1->Directory + "\\";
String strWildCard = "*.bmp" ;
String strTemp = strPath + strWildCard ;

findfirst(strTemp.c_str(), &fbFileData, 0) ;

strTemp = strPath ;
strTemp += fbFileData.ff_name ;

for (Row=0; Row < 16; Row++)
  {
  for (Col=0; Col < 16 ; Col++)
    {
```

(continued)

(continued)

```
      StringGrid1->Cells[Col][Row] = fbFileData.ff_name ;

      picThis = new TPicture ;
    picThis->LoadFromFile(strTemp) ;

    StringGrid1->Objects[Col][Row] = (TObject*)picThis-
        >Graphic ;

    findnext(&fbFileData);
        strTemp = strPath ;
        strTemp += fbFileData.ff_name ;
    }    // for col
    }        // for row
```

14. Move to the top of this file in the Code Editor by pressing Ctrl+Home.

15. Enter the following lines that are in boldface:

```
//————————————————————————————
#include <vcl\vcl.h>
#include <Dir.h>
#include <Dos.h>
#pragma hdrstop
```

16. Press F9 to run the application.

17. Select the BUTTONS folder in which the button images are held.

Figure 6-9 gives you a big clue as to where that folder resides: It's in the Images folder within the Cbuilder folder.

18. Click on the Load button.

You've just built the form shown in Figure 6-9.

Figure 6-9:
StringGrids
can be used
to display
images as
well as
strings.

This form shows the contents of each of the files that you can use for button graphics in C++Builder applications — just in case you were wondering what the graphic behind each of these titles looks like. With the click of a button, this program shows both the name of the file and the graphic that's contained in the file — cool, huh?

Chapter 7

Dishing Up Menus

· ·

· ·

*M*enus of many sorts have been part of computer programs for as long as there have been restaurants (well, it *seems* that long). If you ever worked with DOS programming (think way back), you probably cringe at the memory of once having to create menus by using alphanumeric characters. Fortunately, that's all in the distant past now that you have neat and civilized Windows menus.

Menus provide the means to simplify complicated choices — especially when those choices constantly change according to where you are and what you are doing in a program. The Borland C++Builder main menu alone consists of almost 100 items. That menu would make for an intimidating panel of buttons if buttons were the only way a user could make computing choices (and there'd be little space left on the screen for the program to show anything else). Menus offer you not only a method of providing a great many program choices for the user, but also a way to use computer screen "real estate" efficiently.

Among the menu types you can find in C++Builder are

▸ The *main menu,* which is typically situated along the top edge of an application's main window (see Figure 7-1).

▸ The *popup menu,* so called because it pops up on the screen wherever you click the mouse (see Figure 7-2). You use C++Builder popup menus whenever you right-click and a *context-sensitive* menu appears that lists the most commonly used actions you can perform in a particular window. (I also refer to popup menus as *speed menus* because they appear on demand to help speed things along.)

The Popup Menu component is not displayed in any regular location on a C++Builder form. Popup menus are displayed wherever you specify them in your program — and typically appear at the current mouse pointer location.

Figure 7-1:
The C++Builder main menu.

Figure 7-2:
The C++Builder speed menu that appears when you right-click on the Code Editor.

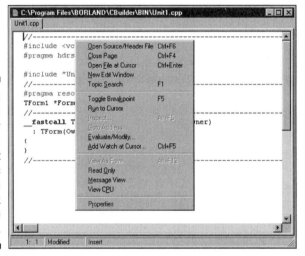

The First Course: Main Menu Ingredients

The MainMenu component resides in the Component Palette's Standard page. You select a MainMenu component by clicking on the MainMenu button and then clicking anywhere on a form.

You can use the MainMenu component to create MenuBars that appear at the top of your forms. The following are some sample steps to place a MainMenu component onto a new application:

1. **Choose File⇨New Application from the main menu to create a new C++Builder form.**

2. **Click on the MainMenu button on the Standard page of the Component Palette to select a MainMenu component, and then click anywhere on the new form to place the MainMenu component.**

3. Click into the background of the form.

If you look at the Object Inspector, you can see the form's Menu property is automatically loaded with a reference to the new MainMenu component (`MainMenu1`). This saves you from having to link the Menu component to the form yourself. (You can see these properties by clicking on the MainMenu component on the form and clicking on the Properties tab on the Object Inspector.)

The MainMenu component's *AutoMerge property* comes into play only when you develop a MDI-type application in which an application has one main form containing all the other application forms. (See Chapter 2 for more on MDI-type applications.)

The *Items property* houses the real action. This is where each of the menu items are held. (In the next section of this chapter, I tell you about the tools that C++Builder provides to visually manage the Items property.)

If you click on the Events tab of the Object Inspector with the MainMenu component selected on the form, you may be surprised to see that there are no events listed whatsoever. So how do you accomplish anything with the MainMenu? Think of the MainMenu component as a candy box that just holds the goodies, the goodies in this case being MenuItems that you add one by one.

Using the Menu Designer

To configure a MainMenu in C++Builder, click on the MainMenu component on the form, and then either click on the ellipsis button of the Items property in the Object Inspector or right-click on the MainMenu component to bring up the MainMenu's speed menu. Then choose the Menu Designer option from the SpeedMenu. Either way, you get the visual menu creation tool, the Menu Designer shown in Figure 7-3.

The name of the MainMenu component that you are viewing (in this example, it's `Form⇨1MainMenu1`) is shown in the title bar of the Menu Designer window.

Figure 7-4 shows the properties for a MenuItem object loaded into the Object Inspector.

The following steps show you how to add MenuItems to a MainMenu component:

1. Click on the MainMenu component on the form.

Figure 7-3:
Use the
Menu
Designer to
navigate
and manage
MenuItem
for the
MainMenu
component.

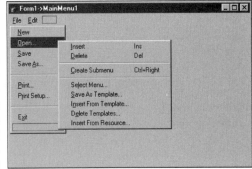

Figure 7-4:
Properties
for the
MenuItem
object
currently
selected in
the Menu
Designer
can be
viewed and
edited using
the Object
Inspector.

2. **Right-click on the MainMenu component to get the MainMenu component's SpeedMenu, and then select the Menu Designer option to open the Menu Designer window.**

   This also loads the Object Inspector with a new MenuItem and places the cursor on the Caption property for the new MenuItem.

3. **Using the Object Inspector, enter some text into the Caption property of the new MenuItem object.**

   This is the text that appears in the first MainMenu item located at the far-left side of the menu bar (for this example, I entered the word **File**, a logical choice).

4. **Press Enter.**

   You are ready to enter the text for the next menu item.

The Menu Designer automatically completes the *Name property* text for the MenuItem object by adding the numeral 1 to the end of the text that you enter into the Caption property. For example, if you enter the word **File** into the Caption property, C++Builder loads the text File1 into the MenuItem's Name property in the Object Inspector. This saves you the effort of having to compose and enter text for any of the Name properties in your MainMenu component's MenuItem objects.

 ✔ You can continue adding menu items by simply entering the text that you want to appear in the Caption property of the new MenuItem in the Object Inspector and then pressing Enter. This process can build up the menu section shown back in Figure 7-1 in a matter of minutes (or seconds, if you're really dexterous).

 ✔ You can insert a menu item into a main menu by selecting MenuItem in the Menu Designer and then pressing the Insert key. This action positions a new MenuItem in the Menu Designer before the selected MenuItem.

 ✔ To remove MenuItems from a main menu, just click on the MenuItem in the Menu Designer and press Delete.

 ✔ After you've added MenuItems, you can move any of them by clicking on a MenuItem and dragging it to another MenuItem's position. When you release the mouse button, the MenuItem is placed where you dragged it and the MenuItem that was under the mouse pointer when you released the button moves down one position in the MainMenu.

Adding action to a MainMenu

Naturally, you want your MenuItems to do something when selected by the user; however, MenuItems have only one event that can be accessed from the Events tab on the Object Inspector.

You can call on the trusty C++Builder Code Editor to add event code to the MenuItem by using the following steps:

1. **With the MainMenu component selected, right-click on the component for the speed menu and select the Menu Designer option to get the Menu Designer window.**

2. **Go to the MenuItem to which you want to add code.**

3. **Select the MenuItem component and then click on the Events tab on the Object Inspector.**

4. **Double-click on the empty field next to the OnClick event-handler to get into the Code Editor.**

You can now enter the code that is executed when the user selects the MenuItem.

Creating hot keys and shortcuts

By using the Object Inspector to insert an ampersand (&) before a letter in a MenuItem's Caption property, you can create a "hot key" the user can press to choose a menu option, rather than having to scroll through a list of options and click when the MainMenu is expanded. (The hot keys are identified by an underscore, so be careful not to use the same character twice in a single menu.) You can also add prefix characters to the MenuItems in the MainMenu on a form by editing the Caption properties in the Object Inspector.

You can easily link shortcuts into each MenuItem object in a MainMenu component. First, using the Menu Designer, navigate to the MenuItem that you want to access. This action loads the MenuItem into the Object Inspector. Then, by using the ShortCut property's drop-down list box on the Object Inspector, you can choose from among more than 80 key combinations, as shown in Figure 7-5.

Figure 7-5:
A list of
shortcut
key combi-
nations
for a
MenuItem
is available
in the
Object
Inspector.

Shortcut combinations

Be careful not to associate the same shortcut with more than one menu option, because the user can employ shortcuts at any time in the program, even when menu sections are not expanded. Figure 7-6 shows how the Menu Designer looks when shortcut keys have been associated with MenuItems.

Figure 7-6:
Shortcut
key combi-
nations
show up
alongside
the menu
items that
they trigger.

Grouping together menu items

At times, you may want to group menu items together, or to look at it another way, keep menu items apart.

Here's how you insert a dividing line into a form's MainMenu component to group or separate items:

1. **Click on the MainMenu component on a form.**

2. **Right-click to bring up the MainMenu SpeedMenu.**

3. **Select the Menu Designer option from the SpeedMenu to show the Menu Designer window.**

4. **Navigate to the menu item that you want to place a dividing line above.**

5. **Press the Insert key to create a blank MenuItem object above the currently selected item in the column of menu items.**

6. **Enter a minus-sign character (–) in the** Caption **property on the Object Inspector.**

   As soon as you move off of either the Caption property or the current MenuItem object in the Menu Designer by using the arrow keys or by clicking on another item, a separator is inserted in the new MenuItem space that was created when you pressed the Insert key in Step 5.

The MenuItem's *Break property* lets you determine when you want to start another column of MenuItems within the same top-level menu item. Three Break property options — mbNone, mbBreak, and mbBarBreak — are available in the Object Inspector.

By default, the Break property is set to mbNone, which has no effect. By changing the Break property to either mbBreak or mbBarBreak, the selected menu section is divided into two columns with the current menu item in the

Menu Designer shown at the top of the new column. You can create more than two columns, but then you would need to make the additional columns into subitems. (I cover subitems in the following section "Separating menu items.") If you select the mbBreak option, empty space is inserted between the two columns. If you select the mbBarBreak option, a vertical rule is inserted between the two columns.

Separating menu items

To separate MenuItems within a MainMenu component, follow these example steps:

1. **Select the MenuItem that you want to divide.**

2. **Follow Steps 1–4 from the section "Grouping together menu items" earlier in this chapter.**

3. **Select the desired Break property option from the Object Inspector.**

   I used mbBarBreak in the example shown in Figure 7-7.

4. **Press F9 to run the program, which puts the Break property into effect.**

With the steps outlined so far in this chapter, I created a menu that looks like the one in Figure 7-7 (in this example, I called the main menu item Fish, which expands to show you seafood entree items).

Figure 7-7:
Dividing a MainMenu component into two sections is a matter of changing only one property in the Object Inspector.

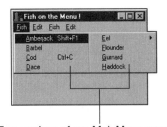

Two sections of one MainMenu component

When you have the Menu Designer displayed (refer to the section "Using the Menu Designer"), right-clicking on any item within the Menu Designer gives you the speed menu shown in Figure 7-8. Selecting the Create Submenu option from this speed menu results in a submenu that appears when you click on the associated menu option.

The right-pointing arrow next to the Eel menu option in Figure 7-9 indicates that a submenu exists within this item. If you add some submenu items to a menu selection (see the section "Using the Menu Designer" earlier in this chapter), the results look something like the submenu in Figure 7-9.

Figure 7-8:
When you right-click on a MenuItem within the Menu Designer window, a speed menu appears with additional options.

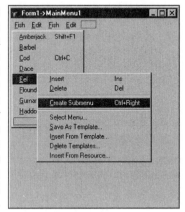

Figure 7-9:
Submenus help organize your menu items and save space in your windows.

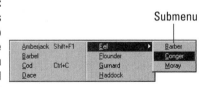

If a menu item that you are adding produces a dialog box or window of some sort when it's selected, indicate this to users by trailing an ellipsis (. . .) after the menu text. (Adding an ellipsis is a convention followed by most Windows programmers.)

Adding check marks to menu items

Each MenuItem object within a MainMenu component is capable of displaying a check mark next to its caption. The check mark is controlled by the MenuItem object's *Checked property.* Setting the Checked property to true (by using the drop-down list in the Object Inspector) displays a check mark; setting the Checked property to false removes the check mark.

The Checked property enables you to include true/false or on/off settings as part of a program's main menu. An example of this is in C++Builder itself. The last two option items in the View menu can be toggled to make the Toolbar and Component Palette visible or invisible.

Placing radio item buttons in a menu list

Windows menus can be made to behave like radio buttons, which means only one item at a time can be selected out of a menu group. The following steps show you how to use the MenuItem's *GroupIndex property* and *RadioItem property* to create a just-pick-one setup in your MainMenu components.

1. **Add a group of MenuItems to the MainMenu component by following the steps in the section "Using the Menu Designer" earlier in this chapter.**

2. **Divide the MenuItems into groups by following the steps in the section "Grouping together menu items" earlier in this chapter.**

3. **Use the Object Inspector to set the** `GroupIndex` **property to the same value (any whole number except 0) and each** `RadioItem` **property to** `true` **for each of the new MenuItems.**

Tick marks now show up as black dots similar to radio buttons to the left of the MenuItem caption. To determine which one of the MenuItems is selected, examine the Checked property in the Object Inspector.

Disabling menu items

At times you may want to disable menu items when their options aren't currently needed. You can switch MenuItem objects on or off within C++Builder by setting the MenuItem object's *Enabled property* in the Object Inspector to true or false. You can actually enable and disable MenuItems while the program is running by referencing MenuItem objects by name from anywhere in your code. The following line of code disables a MenuItem called `Options1`.

```
Options1->Enabled = false ;
```

With the MenuItem's Enabled property set to false, the MenuItem is grayed out and the user can no longer choose that selection.

Adding and removing menu items

In addition to changing MenuItems at runtime, you can also add or delete them. Because you have full access to the list of MenuItem objects via the MainMenu component's Items property, you can add the MainMenu component at runtime by using these steps:

1. **Click on the Button component button on the Standard page of the Component Palette, and then click anywhere on a form to place the button.**

2. **With the Button selected, click on the Events tab of the Object Inspector and then double-click on the empty field next to the** onClick **event handler.**

   You're then in the Code Editor, where you enter the following lines:

   ```
   TMenuItem *NewItem=new TMenuItem(this);
    NewItem->Caption = "New item";
    NewItem->Checked = True ;
    MainMenu1->Items->Add(NewItem);
   ```

3. **Press F9 to run the program and then click on the button that you added to the form.**

   Each time you click on the new button, menu items are added alongside the menu bar of the program.

If you want to add menu items within a File menu's drop-down list, just replace the last line of the code in Step 2 with the following line:

```
File1->Add(NewItem);
```

Make sure that you have a MenuItem named File1 in your MainMenu component. (In my example back in Figure 7-7, I actually called the File menu item Fish1!) As long as the reference to the MenuItem in the code matches the text entered in the Name property of the MenuItem on your form, you'll be okay.

Standardizing a menu

User-friendliness goes beyond creating versatile menus that are easy to figure out. Smart developers try to make all of their programs work the same way. For example, a user typically expects to exit a Windows application by pressing Alt+F, and then X. That's a shortcut convention to include in your program if you want to be a "friendly" developer.

As users move from program to program, common menu headings speed things along, as do uniform captions for menu options and standardized shortcut keys. The following table shows you some standard menu headings and the menu items that go with them.

Menu Heading	Menu Items
File	New, Open, Close, Save, Save All, Exit
Edit	Undo, Cut, Copy, Paste, Delete
Help	Search, Contents, About

Creating menu templates

Standardizing menu items across all your programs doesn't have to mean added work on your part — C++Builder menu templates allow you to store and retrieve menu sections for reuse with other applications. Talk about instant standardization!

You can gain access to the C++Builder menu templates by following these steps:

1. **Select a MainMenu component on a form and right-click on it to bring up its speed menu.**

2. **Choose the Menu Designer option from the speed menu to open the Menu Designer window.**

3. **Right-click on one of the MenuItems within the window to open the Menu Designer speed menu, and then choose the Insert From Template option.**

   The Insert Template dialog box shown in Figure 7-10 appears.

4. **Select the Window Menu option from the Insert Template list and click on OK.**

   C++Builder inserts a standard Windows menu section (with options such as New Window, Tile, and Cascade) into your main menu.

The C++Builder menu templates also allow you to store your own menu sections. So, now that you know where the menu templates live, you can add a menu template of your own. Just follow these steps:

1. **Activate the Menu Designer as described in Steps 1 and 2 in the previous list of steps.**

Figure 7-10:
Menu
templates
speed your
development
while giving
your users
recognizable
menu
formats.

2. **Right-click on a menu section to bring up the Menu Designer speed menu and choose** `Save As Template`.

3. **Enter a name for your new Template into the Template Description edit box.**

4. **Click on OK.**

That's all there is to it!

Before moving on from main menus, just remember: If you are not happy with the way your menu is working out, you can easily insert, delete, or drag MenuItems around, reorder them, or move them into completely different menu branches by using your mouse.

Placing PopupMenu Components

Unlike main menus, you can place as many PopupMenu components within a form as you desire. PopupMenus are triggered when a user right-clicks (or left-clicks with a left-handed mouse) into a form. The PopupMenu offers options that are relevant to the item that was clicked on (in techno-terminology it's called *context-sensitive help*).

Every control that's placed in a form has a PopupMenu property available. If you associate a PopupMenu property with a component, when users right-click on the component, they see that specific PopupMenu (but associating a PopupMenu with a component on a form is not mandatory). You can have a different PopupMenu property for each component in a form, but don't get carried away.

The following example steps demonstrate how you can build a program using a PopupMenu component:

1. **Drop a PopupMenu component into a form by clicking on the PopupMenu button on the Standard page of the Component Palette and then click anywhere on the form.**

2. **Right-click on the PopupMenu component to bring up its speed menu and then choose the Menu Designer option.**

   You can now add MenuItems to the PopupMenu component in the same way that you'd add them to a MainMenu component (refer to the section "Using the Menu Designer" earlier in this chapter for steps on how to add items to a main menu).

3. **Enter some text into the `Caption` property of each MenuItem.**

   For this example I entered "Amanita," "Boletus," "Coprinus," "Dermocybe," and "Entoloma" (see Figure 7-11).

4. **Select all the items in the Menu Designer by holding down the Ctrl key and clicking on each of them.**

5. **Click on the Events tab of the Object Inspector.**

6. **Double-click on the blank name field of the `OnClick` event in the Object Inspector to get into the Code Editor, where you enter the following:**

   ```
   if (Sender->ClassNameIs("TMenuItem"))
     Panel1->Caption = dynamic_cast<TMenuItem*>(Sender)-
           >Caption ;
   ```

   Each of the menu selections now points to a single event handler.

7. **Click on the Panel button on the Standard page, and then click anywhere on the form to drop in a Panel component.**

8. **With the Panel component selected, click on the Properties tab on the Object Inspector and then click on the `PopupMenu` property.**

9. **Select the PopupMenu component (PopupMenu1 created in Step 1) from the PopupMenu property drop-down list on the Object Inspector.**

10. **Press F9 to run the program.**

    You should see something like the example in Figure 7-11. When the program is running, right-click on the Panel component on the form to bring up the PopupMenu control. As you select items from the PopupMenu, the Caption property of the Panel changes according to the code that you entered into the `OnClick` event in Step 6.

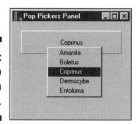

Figure 7-11:
A popup
menu in
action.

When you click on a component's PopupMenu property drop-down list, you get a choice of not only the popup menus that reside on the current form, but also any others in your current C++Builder project, which saves you from having to redefine some menus.

PopupMenu components can be modified at runtime in the same way that main menus are modified (refer to the section "Adding and removing menu items" earlier in this chapter). You are free to add or remove items to and from popup menus as the program is running.

Merging Menus with MDI Applications

Earlier in this chapter I warn against placing more than one MainMenu in the same form. Although that warning still stands, you may find that you have to work with multiple menus that are in different forms within the same application.

Suppose you're developing an application that involves both text entry and drawing. You could use an *MDI application* (MDI stands for Multi-Document Interface). The main form (the parent form) of a program contains all the other forms (the child forms) in a MDI. For example, one child form may handle drawing and another may deal with word processing. Each of these child forms can contain its own MainMenu component, and sections of the child main menus can be merged with the parent's as they are used in the application.

To see how MainMenus are used in MDI-type applications, follow these example steps:

1. **Create a new form in a new project by choosing File⇨New Application from the C++Builder main menu.**

2. Set the FormStyle property of the new form to fsMDIForm using the drop-down list in the Object Inspector.

3. Click on the MainMenu button on the Standard page of the Component Palette, and then click anywhere on the form to place a MainMenu component.

4. Right-click on the MainMenu component and then select the Menu Designer option from the speed menu that appears to open the Menu Designer.

5. Right-click on the Menu Designer window to bring up its speed menu and choose the Insert From Template option to get the Insert Template dialog box.

6. Choose File Menu from the list shown in the Insert Template dialog box.

   This places a File Menu section into the Menu Designer for your MainMenu component.

7. With the File Menu item selected in the Menu Designer, change the GroupIndex property in the Object Inspector to 2.

8. From the Menu Designer, double-click on <u>O</u>pen in the <u>F</u>ile menu to get into the Code Editor, where you enter the following:

```
TForm2 *form2 ;
form2 = new TForm2(this) ;
form2->Show() ;
```

9. Choose <u>F</u>ile⇨New <u>F</u>orm from the C++Builder main menu to add a second form to the project.

10. With the new form selected, choose fsMDIChild from the drop-down list of the FormStyle property in the Object Inspector.

    The new form becomes a subform of the form created in Step 1.

11. Click on the Events tab of the Object Inspector and then double-click on the empty field next to the OnClose event handler.

    You're then in the Code Editor, where you enter the following:

```
Action = caFree ;
```

12. Click on the form created in Step 1.

13. Select <u>F</u>ile⇨<u>I</u>nclude Unit Hdr from the main menu to show the Include Unit dialog box.

14. Select Unit2 from the list and then click on OK.

15. Click on the form created in Step 9, and then click on the Panel button on the Standard page.

16. Click on the form and then set the Align property of the Panel component to alTop using the Object Inspector.

17. Delete the text contents of the Panel's Caption property.

 18. Click on the Memo button on the Standard page and then click anywhere on the background of the form created in Step 9 to place a Memo component.

19. Using the Object Inspector, set the Align property of the Memo component to alClient.

20. Click on the MainMenu button on the Standard page and then click on the background of the form created in Step 9 to place a MainMenu component.

21. Add an Edit menu template to the MainMenu component using the method described in the "Creating menu templates" section earlier in this chapter.

22. Select the Edit Menu option from the Insert Template window list and click on OK.

23. With the new Edit MenuItem selected in the Menu Designer, change the GroupIndex property to 3 using the Object Inspector.

24. Click on the MainMenu component on the form and then set the MainMenu component's AutoMerge property to true using the Object Inspector.

 25. Click on the SpeedButton button on the Additional page of the Component Palette and then click on the Panel placed on the form created in Step 9 to add a SpeedButton component to the Panel.

26. You can also load a bitmap graphic into the Glyph property if desired.

    For this example, I use the graphic called FileOpen.bmp in the cbuilder\Images\buttons folder of C++Builder. (Loading graphics into SpeedButton components is covered in Chapter 4.)

 27. Click on the OpenDialog button on the Dialogs page, and then click on the Panel placed on the form created in Step 9 to add an OpenDialog component to the Panel.

28. Double-click on the SpeedButton that you placed on the form in Step 25 to get into the Code Editor, where you enter the following:

```
OpenDialog1->Execute() ;
Memo1->Lines->LoadFromFile(OpenDialog1->FileName) ;
```

29. Press F9 to run the application.

With the program running, click on Open from the main menu of the form to show the child form. As the child form appears, so does its main menu, but the menu options that you placed in the MainMenu component on the child form are shown as part of the main form's menu.

That's the *merge* part of this program. Auto-merging offers you an easy way to present consolidated menu options to the user and a low-maintenance way to create an uncluttered menu bar in an application.

The previous steps should produce a program that looks similar to the one shown in Figure 7-12. If you close the child form, you see that the menu options that you placed in the MainMenu component of the second form are no longer displayed on the menu bar.

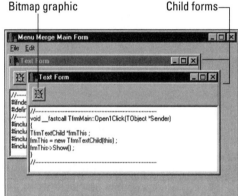

Bitmap graphic   Child forms—

Figure 7-12:
Parent and child form menus are merged in an MDI application.

The values placed in the *GroupIndex property* of the MenuItem (which can be accessed from the Object Inspector) determine the priority of each MenuItem when auto-merging is performed. The auto-merging process moves from left to right along the menu bar, and the GroupIndex of any menu item must never be less than that of the menu item to its left. If you have matching GroupIndex values for items on the menu bar in your program's forms, when you merge the forms the top-level menu item for the main form won't be visible.

To take a stab at prioritizing MenuItems when auto-merging, try these steps using the example program built in Steps 1–28:

1. Bring up the Menu Designer by double-clicking on the MainMenu component on the first form built in the previous list of steps.

2. **Select the** File **MenuItem in the Menu Designer and then change the** GroupIndex **property value to** 2 **in the Object Inspector.**

3. **Using the Object Inspector, double-click on the** MainMenuClick **event for the second form built in the previous list of steps and set the** Edit **menu value of the child form to** 2.

   When you run the application and start a child form, the main menu changes from File to Edit. It changes back to File again when the child form is closed.

If you start to get weird things going on during the merging of MDI menus, don't blame some supernatural menu monster; the culprit's more likely to be clashing GroupIndex values.

If you use the Object Inspector to set the *AutoMerge property* to true in the MDI parent form, you won't see the menu for that form in your program; you see the menu only at design time. Set the AutoMerge to true for the application's child forms only.

Chapter 8

Building with Win95 Components

● ●

In This Chapter

▶ Using the ProgressBar component to track program status

▶ Conveying information with the StatusBar component

▶ Managing text with the RichEdit component

▶ Adding images with the ImageList component

▶ Viewing and organizing data entries with the ListView and TreeView components

▶ Creating multipage forms with the PageControl component

● ●

*A*t the risk of stating the obvious, the Win95 page of the C++Builder Component Palette houses controls that make it easy to construct (surprise!) a Windows 95-style user interface.

In the interest of space, not every resident of the Win95 page gets coverage in this chapter. But I do make sure to include sample programs using the Win95 components that turn up most often in C++Builder applications. You find out how to create Windows mainstays such as progress bars, status bars, and "tree" structures for organizing files.

Adding a Progress Bar to an Application

Keeping end users informed of what's going on is more than just a matter of being polite, especially when users have to wait for one program operation to end before they can continue with another. Ideally, a user should never have to wait too long for anything, but some tasks just aren't done in a hurry. Some users even resort to the "three-finger salute" (Ctrl+Alt+Delete) when an application appears to be ignoring them, when in fact the program is simply finishing up a long procedure.

Whether you're loading files, saving files, performing calculations, or conducting any other operation that takes a while to finish, think about adding a ProgressBar component to your application. A progress bar displays exactly how much of a task is completed so the user isn't left wondering if the program will ever finish.

To add a ProgressBar component to an application, follow these example steps:

1. **Choose File⇨New Application to open a new form in a new project.**

2. **Click on the ProgressBar component button on the Win95 page of the Component Palette and then click anywhere on the form to drop in the component.**

3. **Click on the Label component button on the Standard page and then click directly below the ProgressBar to place a Label on the form.**

4. **Click on the Button component button on the Standard page and then click next to the Label component dropped into the into form in Step 3.**

5. **While the Button component is selected, change the** Caption **property of the Button to** Go To It! **in the Object Inspector.**

6. **With the Button component still selected, click on the Events tab on the Object Inspector and then double-click on the empty field next to the** OnClick **event handler.**

   This action puts you in the Code Editor, where you enter the following lines of code:

```
for ( ProgressBar1->Position = 0;
        ProgressBar1->Position < ProgressBar1->Max ;
   ProgressBar1->Position++)
   {
   Label1->Caption = String(ProgressBar1->Position) + "%"
        ;
   Application->ProcessMessages();
   Sleep(100) ;      // simulates some real work!
   }
```

7. **Press F9 to compile and run the program.**

   The end product should look like Figure 8-1. If you click on the "Go To It!" button, you can see the progress bar gradually fill as the program whizzes around the for loop created in the code.

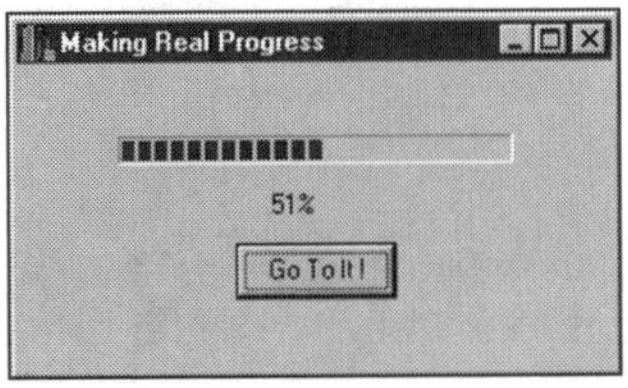

Figure 8-1:
Progress
bars, such
as this one,
tell users
how much
of a task is
completed.

Making Real Progress
51%
Go To It!

And While You're at It, Add a Status Bar

Status bars are a handy way to provide pertinent information about an application to the user. You can create separate message compartments in a status bar by using the Panels property to convey information to the user unobtrusively. Status bars normally sit along the bottom of a form. In fact, the StatusBar component automatically drops to the bottom of a form when you first place it.

StatusBar components aren't to be confused with ProgressBars. If a progress bar is running, the user has to wait for it to finish before doing anything else with the program. Status bars, on the other hand, provide information about the whole application in general and not just a single operation (for example, if you click on the C drive icon in the Window Explorer, a status bar tells you how much free disk space is available, what files are selected, and such).

The following steps use a StatusBar component to create an example status bar that both welcomes users and tells the time.

1. **Click on the StatusBar button on the Win95 page, and then click anywhere on a form (created using Step 1 in the previous section) to drop a StatusBar component onto the form.**

2. **Using the Object Inspector, double-click on the** `Panels` **property of the StatusBar component.**

   The StatusBar Panels Editor dialog box appears.

3. **Click on the New button in the dialog box to add a panel to the form.**

4. **Type the text HH:MM:SS in the Text box of the StatusBar Panels Editor dialog box to show the time, set the** `Width` **property in the Panel's properties to** `60`**, and then choose the** `Raised` **setting from the Bevel drop-down list in the** `Panel` **properties.**

5. **Add a second panel to the form by clicking on the New button, and then enter some text into the** `Panel` **properties Text box.**

   In this example, I entered **Welcome...** into the text box.

6. **Click on the Timer component button on the System tab and then click anywhere on the form to drop in a Timer component.**

7. **Click on the Events tab on the Object Inspector, then double-click on the empty field next to the** `onTimer` **event handler.**

   This puts you in the Code Editor, where you enter the following:

```
StatusBar1->Panels->Items[0]->Text = Now().TimeString()
        ;
```

8. Press F9 to run the application.

You should end up with a form similar to the one shown in Figure 8-2. The left-hand panel contains the clock, which keeps time through the Timer component, and the Welcome... text sits in the second panel to show how easily you can display a message for users.

Figure 8-2:
Panels made with the StatusBar component can be used to convey information to the user at a glance.

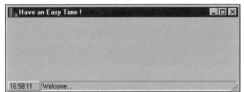

Adding Text with the RichEdit Component

By using the RichEdit component, you can allow the user to not only enter an unlimited amount of text, but also make changes to the style of that text. In fact, the RichEdit component goes even further and provides paragraph formatting and built-in printing.

Much of the functionality in the RichEdit component shines through at runtime, which the following steps show you. Use these steps to build a simple word-processing form of your own:

1. Choose File⇨New from the main menu to get the New Items dialog box.

2. Select the Projects tab in the dialog box and then click on the SDI Application icon.

3. Click on OK and the Select Directory dialog box appears next.

4. In the Directory treeview box, select the folder that you want the files for this new project to be saved in, and then click on OK.

5. Click on the RichEdit component button on the Win95 page and then click anywhere on the form to drop in a RichEdit component.

6. Using the Object Inspector, set the `Align` property of the RichEdit component to `alClient`.

7. Click on the SpeedButton component button on the Additional page of the Component Palette, and then click on the speed bar at the top of the form to place the newly selected SpeedButton; repeat this step six more times.

8. Click on and drag the SpeedButton components dropped on the form in Step 7 to cluster the buttons in two groups of three and one individual button.

9. Using the Object Inspector, set the SpeedButton property values to those shown in the following table, using a different property name for each button.

Property name	GroupIndex	Caption	AllowAllUp setting
btnBold	1	B	true
btnUnderline	2	U	true
btnItalic	3	I	true
btnLeftJust	4	|<	false
btnCenter	4	=	false
btnRightJust	4	>|	false
btnPrint	0	None	false

10. Select the first three SpeedButton components on the form as listed in the table in Step 9 (`btnBold`, `btnUnderline`, and `btnItalic`) by clicking on each while holding down the Shift key.

11. Click on the Object Inspector's Events tab and then double-click on the empty `OnClick` event name field.

You're now in the Code Editor, where you enter the following lines:

```
TFontStyles fsThis ;

if (btnBold->Down)
 fsThis << fsBold ;
if (btnUnderline->Down)
 fsThis << fsUnderline ;
if (btnItalic->Down)
 fsThis << fsItalic ;

RichEdit1->SelAttributes->Style = TFontStyles(fsThis);
```

These lines of code make sure that the RichEdit component's text style is set according to the user's button selection at runtime.

12. **Select the second group of three buttons listed in the table in Step 9** (btnLeftJust, btnCenter, **and** btnRightJust).

13. **Click on the Events tab on the Object Inspector and double-click on the empty field next to the** OnClick **event handler, and then enter the following in the Code Editor:**

```
TAlignment taThis ;

if (btnLeftJust->Down)
 taThis = taLeftJustify ;
if (btnCenter->Down)
 taThis << taCenter ;
if (btnRightJust->Down)
 taThis = taRightJustify ;

RichEdit1->Paragraph->Alignment = TAlignment(taThis);
```

These lines of code ensure that the proper text alignment is assigned to the appropriate RichEdit component. For example, you set btnLeftJust so that the text aligns left-justified.

At this point, the core of the application is complete. But to make this application look more polished, you can make the buttons reflect the current style of the text at the cursor location as the cursor moves around the RichEdit component.

14. **Click on the RichEdit component, then click on the Events tab of the Object Inspector, and then double-click on the empty field next to the** OnSelectionChange **event handler.**

You're now in the Code Editor, where you enter the following:

```
btnBold->Down = RichEdit1->SelAttributes-
        >Style.Contains(fsBold) ;
btnUnderline->Down = RichEdit1->SelAttributes-
        >Style.Contains(fsUnderline) ;
btnItalic->Down = RichEdit1->SelAttributes-
        >Style.Contains(fsItalic) ;
switch (RichEdit1->Paragraph->Alignment)
  {
  case taLeftJustify :
     btnLeftJust->Down = true ;
  break ;
  case taCenter :
     btnCenter->Down = true ;
  break ;
  case taRightJustify :
     btnRightJust->Down = true ;
  break ;
  }
```

Each button now reflects the font style and paragraph-alignment properties of the RichEdit componehl at the current cursor location as the user moves around the text.

To continue with the RichEdit example, you can add a printing feature to your program and save the text from the RichEdit component to a text file on your hard disk, and vice versa.

15. Press F9 to run the program.

16. Double-click on the Print SpeedButton component on the form (the last button that you added in Step 7).

You're now in the Code Editor, where you enter the following line:

```
RichEdit1->Print(Caption) ;
```

Now you can add file-opening and file-saving features.

17. Press F12 to move from the Code Editor to the Form Designer.

Next, you're adding some functionality to one of the program's menu options.

18. Choose File⇨Open from the main menu in the Form Designer (not from the C++Builder main menu).

You are now in the Code Editor and ready to modify the code that the C++Builder template provides for you.

19. Add the following lines (shown in bold) to the event handler in the Code Editor:

```
OpenDialog->Execute();
if (OpenDialog->FileName!= "")
  RichEdit1->Lines->LoadFromFile(OpenDialog->FileName) ;
```

Adding this code takes care of loading text from disk files into the program's RichEdit component. The user can select the file that he or she wants to load (open) by using the Open File dialog box that has been included in the OpenDialog component in the forms part of the application template.

20. Click on the form and choose File⇨Save.

Again, you go directly to the menu option's OnClick event handler in the Code Editor.

21. Add the following line that's shown in bold:

```
SaveDialog->Execute();
if (SaveDialog->FileName!= "")
  RichEdit1->Lines->SaveToFile(SaveDialog->FileName) ;
```

22. Press F9 to run the program.

Enter any text that you like into the RichEdit control's area and then use the program's speed buttons to change the appearance (bold, underline, and so on) and alignment of the text. Watch how the speed button settings change as you move the cursor from one style of text to another by pressing the arrow keys.

Figure 8-3 shows you what the program should look like. Choose File⇨Save and File⇨Open to save text to disk and then read the text by opening the file from the disk again. Don't forget that you can also print your text. How's that for functionality!

Figure 8-3:
Use the
C++Builder
project
template
and the
RichEdit
component
to create
speed
buttons that
change the
appearance
of text.

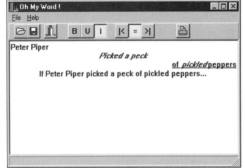

Getting the Picture with the ImageList Component

As its name implies, the ImageList component holds a collection of images — all of which are the same size. But you, the developer, won't see the images when using this component because ImageList is a nonvisual component (which means that the program's end user won't see the component directly either). However, the end user does see the actual images, which are usually small bitmap and icon files. These image files must be placed on a form in order to be used by the components covered next — ListView and TreeView.

Use the following steps to load some sample graphics into an ImageList component:

1. **Click on the ImageList component button on the Win95 page, and then drop the component into the form by clicking anywhere on the form.**

2. **Right-click on the ImageList component and choose the ImageList Editor option from the speed menu that appears.**

   The ImageList Editor dialog box shown in Figure 8-4 appears. By using the Add, Delete, and Clear buttons in the ImageList Editor, you can manage the images held in the ImageList component.

Figure 8-4:
The
ImageList
Editor
refines the
appearance
of graphic
images.

You can add a few images to the ImageList by clicking on the Add button and then selecting image files using the Open dialog box that appears. (Most of the graphics that I use in Figure 8-4 are available in the C++Builder subfolder images\icons.)

You can use the Delete button to remove the currently selected image within the ImageList Editor, or if you want to completely start over, you can remove all images from the ImageList by pressing the ImageList Editor's Clear button.

If you choose a graphic that clearly shows the background color the image is displayed on, you can hide the background color by selecting it from the Transparent Color drop-down list. Your image then looks more natural once it's used in your program.

Organizing Data Items with the ListView and TreeView Components

The ListView and TreeView components allow your end user to browse information visually to make your applications even more user-friendly.

The ListView component

The ListView component provides a way of presenting a list of data items to the user. You can associate a list of images with the data items in the ListView by using an ImageList component. The images are shown alongside each item in the ListView component.

Component properties

The descriptions for each data item in the ListView component are held in the *Items property,* which has its own property editor (the ListView Items Editor). This property editor, shown in Figure 8-5, allows you to view TListItems at design time.

Figure 8-5:
Use the
ListView
Items Editor
to add
items and
associate
graphics
with them.

TListItems contain a caption and data defined by your application. The caption contains a string, and the data (which can be an image) contains a pointer to a data structure associated with each list item.

To make sure the ListView operates as intended, each item in the list needs a picture. Enter the ImageList index number of the associated image into the Image Index EditBox (refer to Figure 8-5).

The graphic part of a ListView component is handled by an ImageList component that's loaded with the images that you want to use in a ListView (see the section "Getting the Picture with the ImageList Component" earlier in this chapter).

The ImageList component serves as an image container for the ListView component and is associated with the ListView component by either the *LargeImages property* or *SmallImages property.* Both of these properties have drop-down lists on the Object Inspector from which you can select any ImageList component that has previously been set up on the form. Which of these two properties you use depends on the ViewStyle property setting from the Object Inspector.

The *ViewStyle property* has four settings — vsIcon (which uses the LargeImages property), and vsList, vsReport, and vsSmallIcon, all three of which use the SmallImages property. LargeImages shows items in the ListView as complete icons, while SmallImages shows columns of entries with a less-detailed icon next to the item's text.

If you want the user to be able to select an entry in the ListView but not make any changes to data items in a ListView component, set the *ReadOnly property* of a ListView component to true using the Object Inspector. The user won't be able to change the caption of a selected data item.

Component events

The ListView component's *onChange event* can be used to find out which item the user selected, and the *onChanging event* can be used to hold code that you want executed prior to moving from the currently selected data item to the new data item.

Try these steps to construct a working program that shows three different ways of using a ListView component:

1. **Select File➪New Application from the main menu to open a new application.**

2. **Use the steps outlined in the "Getting the Picture with the ImageList Component" section of this chapter to drop an ImageList component onto the new form.**

3. **Click on the ListView component button on the Win95 page, and then click anywhere on the form to drop a ListView component onto the form.**

4. **Click on the Panel button on the Standard page, and then click anywhere on the form to drop a Panel component onto the form.**

5. **Using the Object Inspector, select** alBottom **from the Panel's** Align **property drop-down list.**

6. **Click on the ListView and using the Object Inspector to select the** ImageList1 **value from the** SmallImages **property drop-down list.**

7. **Using the Object Inspector, select the** vsList **option from the** ViewStyle **property drop-down list.**

   Now to create the data items that will populate the ListView.

8. **Still using the Object Inspector, double-click on the ListView component's** Items **property to open the ListView Items Editor dialog box.**

9. Click on the <u>N</u>ew Item button in the dialog box and then type any text you like for the caption of the new data item being created.

10. Enter a number in the I<u>m</u>age Index text box in the ListView Items Editor dialog box according to the index of the graphic that you want to display.

    The graphic appears next to the text entered in Step 9 in the corresponding ImageList component.

    When you add images to an ImageList, the image is assigned a number according to its order in the list. That number is the *index* of the graphic. When you add the images to the ListView, you can click on the Apply button to see which image you're associating to the list.

11. Repeat Steps 9 and 10 for as many items (such as text that corresponds to the image or data) that you want to add to your ListView component.

12. With the ListView component selected, press Ctrl+C to place a copy of the component on the C++Builder Clipboard.

13. Press Ctrl+V twice to place two copies of the component in the form.

14. Click on and drag the ListView components and arrange them in a horizontal row on the form.

15. Click on the middle ListView component in the row; then, using the Object Inspector, select vsReport from the ViewStyle property's drop-down list.

16. Add one column header to the second ListView component by double-clicking on the Columns property on the Object Inspector to activate the ListView Columns Editor dialog box.

17. Click on the New button in the ListView Columns Editor dialog box and type Items into the Caption text box; then click on the Header Width RadioButton before pressing the OK button to close the Columns Editor dialog box.

18. Click on the far-right ListView component in the row, and then use the Object Inspector to select the vsIcon option from the ViewStyle property's drop-down list.

19. Use the Object Inspector again to choose the ImageList component from the LargeImages property drop-down list.

20. Select all three ListView components and click on the Events tab of the Object Inspector, and then double-click on the blank event name field for the OnChange event.

This action takes you into the Code Editor, where you enter the following line:

```
Panel1->Caption = Item->Caption ;
```

21. Press F9 to see the ListView components in action.

You should end up with a form like the one in Figure 8-6.

Figure 8-6:
C++Builder lets you add graphics to ListView components.

The TreeView component

The TreeView component expands on the ListView component by allowing you to also visually organize program data. If you examine the Windows 95 Explorer, you can see that it uses a branching "tree" structure that allows users to navigate to folders within folders, and files within folders, with just a click (this functionality is what the TreeView component adds to your applications). By building these trees into your applications, you can visually represent hierarchical relationships to make it easy for users to choose and manipulate any type of data item.

TreeView component properties

The TreeView component boasts 36 properties, so I'm limiting myself to discussing the most important ones here. But first, follow these example steps to add a TreeView component to a program:

1. Select File⇨New Application from the main menu to create a new application with a blank form.

2. Click on the TreeView component button on the Win95 page and then click anywhere on the form to drop in a TreeView component.

3. Use the steps in the section "Getting the Picture with the ImageList Component" earlier in this chapter to populate an ImageList component with images associated with the TreeView component.

4. **To load the ImageList with three images associated with the TreeView component, first click on the** Images **property of the TreeView component on the Object Inspector, and then click on the down arrow to select** ImageList1.

You can find the images you need in the C++Builder Cbuilder\images\ icons folder.

5. **Double-click on the TreeView's** Items **property on the Object Inspector in order to enter data into the TreeView.**

This action displays the TreeView Items Editor shown in Figure 8-7.

Figure 8-7:
The
TreeView
Items Editor
enables you
to manage
TreeView
items.

6. **Click on the New Item button in the TreeView Items Editor dialog box to add a blank item to the Items ListBox.**

7. **Enter the text associated with the new tree item into the Text box.**

For the example in Figure 8-7, I entered **England** at the highest level of the tree. (If this tree item has an image, the Image Index setting should be 0; if no image is assigned to the tree item, it should be –1. The negative value is used to indicate that no image is associated with this item; a value of 0 refers to the first image in the ImageList component list.)

8. **Click on the New SubItem button in the TreeView Items Editor dialog box.**

This action creates a blank field below the item that you have just created.

9. **Enter a name for the blank field in the Text box, and then enter 1 in the Image Index box.**

In this example, I entered **London** and typed **1** in the Image Index because I want the city item to display a different graphic than the country item. (You would not necessarily enter 0 for the first level image setting, and 1 for the next branch; it depends on how the images are organized in the ImageList.)

10. **Once again, click on the New SubItem button in the TreeView Items Editor dialog box.**

   This action takes you down to the next item level, where you can enter a name for the blank SubItem. For this example, I entered a street name.

11. **Repeat Steps 6–10 to add more TreeView items to the TreeView component on the form.**

   You can add more items and set different properties as you like from the TreeView Items Editor dialog box.

12. **Press F9 to run the program.**

Once you've made a start with the preceding steps, you can examine some of the more important TreeView component properties in greater depth.

When you set the SortType property to true, the tree is sorted in alphabetical text order. If you use the drop-down list in the Object Inspector for this property (as opposed to setting the property in your code), your options are stNone, stText, stData, and stBoth. Selecting one of these choices triggers the TreeView component to check that the tree is in alphabetical order.

The *StateImages property* allows you to associate an ImageList component with the TreeView so that you can display an image with an item's text that reveals the status of that TreeView item. Suppose that you have a customer whose account has been placed on hold. You can use a suitable image to reveal that this customer's account needs attention.

Figure 8-8 shows how setting TreeView component properties can dramatically change the look of the TreeView in your programs.

Figure 8-8:
By using the Object Inspector and TreeView Items Editor, you can vary the presentation of TreeView components.

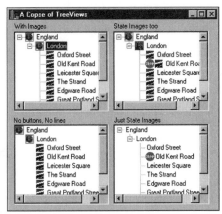

The *Selected property*, which is available only at runtime, holds the TreeView item that is currently highlighted or selected by the user's having clicked on it. (You need to know which item the user has chosen at runtime when you are using the TreeView event handlers, which I discuss in the next section.)

TreeView component events

Select a TreeView component and then click on the Events tab on the Object Inspector. More than 25 TreeView event handlers appear. You can read about some of these event handlers in this section.

The OnChange event

The *OnChange event* is triggered any time the user changes anything in a TreeView component. One example of how this event can be used is for code that loads text in other components on a form, such as EditBoxes and Labels. You can also use this event to place the contents of a data table field into other components on a form according to the selected item on the TreeView component.

The following steps use the form created in the "TreeView component properties" section earlier in this chapter to show you how the onChange event can be used to control other components on a form:

1. **Click on the Label component button on the Standard page of the Component Palette, and then click anywhere on the form to place a Label component.**

2. **Click on the TreeView that placed on the form created in the "TreeView component properties" earlier in this section.**

3. **Click on the Events tab of the Object Inspector and then double-click on the empty field next to the** OnChange **event handler.**

   You end up in the Code Editor, where you enter the following line:

   ```
   Label1->Caption = Node->Text ;
   ```

4. **Press F9 to run the application.**

   As you move from item to item in the tree, the text in the Label component that you just placed on the form changes to the text of the currently selected TreeView item.

The OnChanging event

Another useful TreeView event is the *OnChanging event*. The OnChanging event is called prior to leaving a TreeView item after the user has selected another TreeView item.

You can use the argument AllowChange inside the OnChanging event handler to decide if the program will allow the user to move from the current TreeView item. The following code example shows how you can use the OnChanging event handler to enforce *user-entry validation.* (If a user clicks on one item in a tree and then wants to click on another item, before C++Builder highlights the second item it checks to see if the user is allowed to select the item. This safety feature is accomplished by entering code in the OnChanging event.)

```
//————————————————————————————————
void __fastcall TForm1::TreeView1Changing(TObject *Sender,
          TTreeNode *Node,
   bool &AllowChange)
{
   if (Edit1->Text == "")
   AllowChange = false ;
}
```

The OnExpanded event

The *OnExpanded event* can be invaluable for building trees "on demand" — that is, when the user decides to expand a particular TreeView item. TreeViews can be slow if they load up all the many branches of the tree, especially when just a few are going to be used. Loading subitems on demand through the OnExpanded event can save time when the program initially loads your TreeView data.

If you want to add items to your trees on the fly, you can use the following steps:

1. **Click on the Button component button, and then click on the form that was created under "TreeView component properties" earlier in this chapter to drop a new Button component into the form.**

2. **Click on the Events tab on the Object Inspector and then double-click on the empty field next to OnClick event handler.**

3. **Enter the following lines in the Code Editor:**
   ```
   TreeView1->Items->Add(TreeView1->Selected, "New Node");
   TreeView1->Items->AddChild(TreeView1->Selected, "New
         Child Node");
   ```

4. **Press F9 to run the program.**

   Every time you click on the new button, two new items are added to the TreeView component. One TreeView subitem is added to the currently selected item and one new item is added on the same level and directly after the currently selected item.

Creating a Multilayer Form with the PageControl Component

The PageControl component gives you the means to create multiple-layer forms so that you can pack far more components onto a form than you could otherwise. You can access these form layers, called *pages,* by selecting a *tab* or label at the top of the component. (This is something you've done numerous times already; the pages of a Component Palette are accessed this way.)

Components can be added to each PageControl page in the same way that you add components to any form. By using a PageControl component, you can neatly pack the functionality of many forms into a single, easy-to-use form.

The following set of steps shows you how to use a PageControl to add a number of pages to a single form:

1. **Choose <u>F</u>ile⇨New Appli<u>c</u>ation from the C++Builder main menu to get a blank form.**

2. **Click on the PageControl component button on the Win95 page, and then click anywhere on the form to drop in a PageControl component.**

   Initially, the PageControl looks just like a panel.

3. **Using the Object Inspector, select** alClient **from the** Align **property's drop-down list, and then right-click on the PageControl component.**

4. **Select the New Page option from the speed menu that appears.**

   A new page is added to the PageControl component. The Object Inspector is now loaded with TabSheet1, which is a component with its own properties and events.

5. **Using the Object Inspector, change the text in the** Caption **property to something more meaningful than the default name** TabSheet1.

   For this example, I labeled the page **Page 1**.

6. **Repeat Steps 4 and 5 twice to add a couple more pages to the form.**

7. **Click on the PageControl component.**

   When a PageControl contains pages, you must click in the top section of the PageControl component next to the tab headers to select the component.

8. Press F9 to run the application.

Now you can click from page tab to page tab to view the contents of various pages on the form. In Figure 8-9, you can see how I make use of this multipage application.

Figure 8-9:
Figure 8-9:
The
PageControls
component
lets you
build
multiple
pages in a
form to
make the
most of
limited
screen
space.

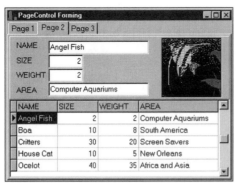

Part III
Wiring Your Building with More Components

The 5th Wave   By Rich Tennant

THE FIRST GRAPHICAL USER INTERFACE COPYRIGHT LAWSUIT.

OH HEY-GREAT STUFF, MERLIN! SWIRLING VORTEX, FLAMING SKULL, HARBINGER TOAD— JUST LIKE THE CALDRON USED BY THOSE THREE WITCHES UP ON THE HILL.

In this part . . .

C++Builder offers even more components that you can use "right off the rack" to turbocharge your programs. Continuing with the step-by-step example format, you find out how to choose the right components for the job and then how to link them together to create a robust application.

This part tells you how to build dialog boxes and applications for managing files and folders (then you'll really feel like a Windows programmer) and explores the powerful Borland Database Engine to visually integrate databases into your programs. Once you've accessed your data, you need to present the information to the end user. C++Builder's integrated QuickReport components provide a smooth path to constructing reports that you can connect to databases. Want to add some multimedia files to your programs? That's covered here, too, plus you can find out how to link and embed OLE objects (some high-end developing for when you get really brave).

Chapter 9

Talking about Dialog Box Components

In This Chapter

▶ Using dialog box components in file-management programs

▶ Adding a dialog box for font selection

▶ Offering the user color choices in a program

▶ Setting up a print options dialog box

*T*he Dialogs page of the Component Palette is home to eight components that won't knock you out when you place them on a form at design time, but watch out — these performers have talents that really shine come runtime when you activate them.

Dialog box components not only speed up your application development, but also provide consistency in your program operation and user interface. When your users need to perform a task of some kind using a dialog box, they won't have to wonder how Box A works versus how Box B works. Plus, the dialog box components let you to create intuitive programs that allow your end users to manipulate files without a lot of fumbling around.

Accessing Dialog Box Components

When you place a dialog box component in a form, you need a way of telling the dialog box when to make its appearance in the program. You can display a dialog box at any point in your program; you just need to execute it by placing a line of code such as the following in your program:

```
OpenDialog1->Execute() ;
```

All dialog boxes have the same call — `Execute()`. The name of the dialog box component in the call varies, of course, depending on the type of dialog box involved (for example, a Font dialog box call is `FontDialog1->Execute();`).

Most applications involve a user accessing data from a disk, making changes to the data in some way, storing the work back to a disk again, and then keeping the whole conglomeration organized through a system of files and folders. The OpenDialog and SaveDialog components provide an easy way for you, the programmer, to provide file access in your programs for the end user of your application.

Adding an OpenDialog Component to a Form

Most Windows applications follow a standard layout in order to open files, so it just makes sense that yours should, too. C++Builder already provides you with a dialog box component, so you may as well make good use of it. Figure 9-1 shows you what an OpenDialog component looks like when it's running.

Figure 9-1:
An
OpenDialog
component
in action.

To try out an OpenDialog component in a program, create this sample application using the following steps:

1. **Click on the OpenDialog button on the Dialogs page of the Component Palette.**

2. **With the OpenDialog button selected, click anywhere on a form to place an OpenDialog component onto the form.**

The OpenDialog component is the first in the line of components on the Dialogs page. If you select the Events tab on the Object Inspector, you can see that no events exist for this component, so you can forget about the events and concentrate on the properties of this component.

3. **With the DialogBox component still selected, and using the Object Inspector, enter** txt **into the** DefaultExt **property of the OpenDialog component.**

   This step determines the file extension that you want to be automatically appended to any filename that your program user enters. If the user gets specific enough to add a file extension, then the user's calling the shots — the file extension the user enters overrides whatever you had originally.

The *Filter property* allows you to stipulate a list of file types that an OpenDialog component is most likely to be used for in the context of your program. You can set up a list of the most likely file type candidates by using the following steps:

1. **With the OpenDialog component selected on a form, click on the Filter property and then click on the ellipsis (. . .) button on the Object Inspector.**

   You get the Filter Editor dialog box as shown in Figure 9-2, which is the editor for the Filter property.

Figure 9-2: Open only the files that you want by using the Filter Editor.

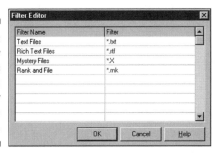

Filter Name	Filter
Text Files	*.txt
Rich Text Files	*.rtf
Mystery Files	*.X
Rank and File	*.rnk

You have room for a brief description of the file type in the Filter Name column of the Filter Editor dialog box, and you enter the actual filter in the right column. (For more details on how to use filters, see Chapter 12.)

2. Add the following filters to the Filter list and then click on OK.

Filter Name	Filter	Index
Text Files	*.txt	1
Rich Text Files	*.rtf	2
Mystery Files	*.X	3
Rank and Files	*.rnk	4

The user can choose from one of the listed filters in the OpenDialog component while the program is running. The OpenDialog then displays only the files of the selected filter type.

3. Set the FilterIndex property value to 2 in the Object Inspector.

After you fill up the Filter Edit dialog box in Step 2, the FilterIndex property is set to a value of 1 — the default filter that is used initially by the DialogBox at runtime. But in this example, I set the FilterIndex property to 2, so the filter with an Index of 2 becomes the Rich Text Format files as declared in the table in Step 2.

Just to keep you on your toes, the FilterIndex property index starts at 1 (the default) and not 0, as you may expect.

 4. Click on the Memo button on the Standard page of the Component Palette, and then click anywhere on the form to drop in a Memo component.

5. Using the Object Inspector, set the Align property of the Memo component to alBottom.

 6. Click on the Button component button on the Standard page, and then click on the form above the Memo component that was placed in Step 4.

This step places a Button onto the form.

7. Using the Object Inspector, set the Caption property of the Button component to Open.

8. Click on the Events tab of the Object Inspector and then double-click on the empty field next to the OnClick event handler.

You're then in the Code Editor, where you enter these lines:

```
if ( OpenDialog1->Execute() )
  Memo1->Lines->LoadFromFile(OpenDialog1->FileName) ;
```

The first line of the previous snippet of code shows the OpenDialog component to the user. If the user clicks on OK in the OpenDialog dialog box, a return value of true is passed back from the dialog box (it's checked using the if statement). To explain this example code in plain English (or *pseudo-code,* as it's called):

```
If the OpenDialog returns true then
    load the memo component with the file named in the
        OpenDialog
```

9. **Press F9 to run the program.**

10. **Click on the Button component to kick the OpenDialog component into action, and then select any file and click on OK on the OpenDialog component.**

The contents of the OpenDialog's chosen file are loaded into the Memo component.

Adding a SaveDialog Component to a Form

The SaveDialog component button sits next to its partner, the OpenDialog button, on the Dialogs tab page of the Component Palette and is used in much the same fashion.

In this section, I build on the example program steps listed in the previous section of this chapter. The steps that follow demonstrate how you can add file-saving capability to your programs using the SaveDialog component.

1. **Click on the SaveDialog button on the Dialogs page of the Component Palette, and then click on the form created in the previous section to drop a SaveDialog component into the form.**

2. **Using the Object Inspector, set the SaveDialog component's properties as shown in the following table:**

Property	Setting
DefaultExt	txt
Filter	Text Files, *.txt
Options ofOverwritePrompt	true
Title	My Save Dialog

3. **Click on the Button component button on the Standard page, and then click next to the Button on the form created in the previous section to place a new Button on the form.**

4. **Using the Object Inspector, enter** Save **into the** Caption **property of the new Button component.**

5. **Click on the Events tab of the Object Inspector and then double-click on the empty field next to the** OnClick **event handler.**

You end up in the Code Editor, where you enter the following:

```
if ( OpenDialog1->Execute() )
Memo1->Lines->SaveToFile(SaveDialog1->FileName) ;
```

6. **Press F9 to run the program.**

You now have a simple text editor. Figure 9-3 (a dialog box called "Simply Text") shows an example of how your program may look with some text entered into it. Have a go at loading and saving some files.

Figure 9-3:
You can
create a
basic text
editor
almost as
fast as you
can say
"Open" and
"Save"!

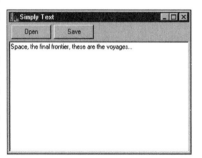

Styling Text with a FontDialog Component

The third button on the Dialogs tab page of the Component Palette leads you to the FontDialog component. A FontDialog box gives users the ability to choose from any of the available Windows fonts to incorporate font changes into your applications. Figure 9-4 shows you how much action is packed inside one little dialog box.

The FontDialog component loads the fonts that are available for your particular Windows installation. Where does it get this list of fonts? That depends on the setting of the *Device property.* The fonts the user can select varies according to the device where the font is viewed — a screen, a printer, or both. You can place some restrictions on the fonts that users may select by employing the *MaxFontSize* and *MinFontSize* properties. (Or, check out the property Options that are available in the C++Builder online help system.)

Sixteen font setting options can be included in the Font dialog box, such as check boxes to turn type styles on and off and options to show or hide the font example window.

Figure 9-4:
The Font dialog box is a familiar sight to Windows users.

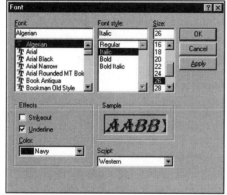

When you set the `fdApplyButton` subproperty of the Options property to `true` using the Object Inspector, you enable a runtime Apply button in the FontDialog component. You can then use the `OnApply` event in the Events page of the Object Inspector to place some code. Then when you click on the Apply button, a relevant action occurs according to the settings that are available. The `OnApply` event is typically used to make the font of a component or set of components the currently selected font for the FontDialog.

Use the following example steps to put the FontDialog component to work to build a simple font-selection application.

1. **Choose File⇨New Application from the main menu to open a new form.**

2. **Click on the FontDialog component button on the Dialogs page of the Component Palette, and then click anywhere on the form to place a FontDialog component.**

3. **Click on the Panel component button on the Standard page and then click anywhere on the form to drop in a Panel component.**

4. **Using the Object Inspector, set the** `Align` **property of the Panel component to** `alTop` **and enter some text in its Caption property.**

   In Figure 9-5, I chose to enter that popular adage about "Mad dogs and Englishmen . . .".

5. **Using the Object Inspector, change the Button component Caption to** `Set Font`.

6. **Click on the Events tab on the Object Inspector and then double-click on the empty field next to the** `OnClick` **event handler. Once you're in the Code Editor, enter the following lines:**

   ```
   if (FontDialog1->Execute())
     Panel1->Font = FontDialog1->Font ;
   ```

7. **Click on the FontDialog component, then double-click on the** `Options` **property to expand the list within the Object Inspector, and then set the** `fdApplyButton` **and** `fdEffects` **subproperties to** `true`.

8. **Click on the FontDialog component, then click on the Events tab on the Object Inspector, and then double-click on the empty** `OnApply` **event field.**

   You're then in the Code Editor, where you enter the following line:

   ```
   Panel1->Font = FontDialog1->Font ;
   ```

9. **Press F9 to run the program.**

   The program in this example should end up looking something like mine in Figure 9-5.

You can try out all the fonts and color combinations that you like from the Font dialog box that appears when you click on the Set Font Button, but don't forget to try out the Apply button in the dialog box and see what effect that has.

Figure 9-5:
It's much easier to change a font in C++Builder components than it is to change old habits.

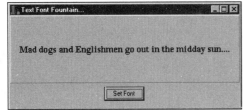

Adding a ColorDialog Component to a Form

What's your favorite color? If you said green, do you mean jade green, lime green, or the color of the Chicago River?

Whenever you need to offer a color choice within a program, you can allow your end users to pick their favorite tint by offering them the fully functional ColorDialog component.

 The button for the ColorDialog component (shown in the margin) sits next to the FontDialog button on the Dialogs page of the Component Palette. It spawns the rather fabulous ColorDialog box, shown in Figure 9-6.

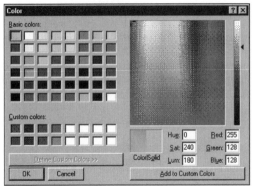

Figure 9-6:
The ColorDialog component shows its true colors.

The ColorDialog component has no events, so you have only properties to inspect on the Object Inspector. The *Color property* designates one color setting in the dialog box, and a handful of options is available through the Options property — the most interesting of which are listed in the following table:

Option	Description
cdFullOpen	Gives the ColorDialog component access to an extended color palette (the custom color selector in Figure 9-6).
cdPreventFullOpen	Restricts the ColorDialog component to a set palette of colors.
cdShowHelp	Adds a Help button to the ColorDialog component.

Custom colors and hexadecimals

The CustomColor property controls all those tints, tones, and shades that have no names but seem to be limitless in number.

The color information is stored in the CustomColor property using a string format with one line holding one Color. Here's how you create the string format:

Enter the name of the string, and then an equal sign (=), followed by the color's six-character *hexadecimal* equivalent.

The hexadecimal is broken down into three groups of two numerals with each group representing the amount of blue, green, and red (respectively) that when mixed together result in the desired color. To make these combinations easier for the computer to process, each number is held in a hexadecimal format (base 16). The numerals 10 through 15 are represented by the letters A through E and certain letter and color combinations equate to a numeric value that stands for a color. It would take pages of this chapter to explain the many details of the base-16 numbering system, but you can try using the following hexadecimal CustomColor property colors:

```
white=FFFFFF
blue=FF0000
green=00FF00
red=0000FF
black=000000
```

The right-hand section of the Color dialog box is where the user can concoct custom colors at runtime (refer to Figure 9-6). You can set up 16 custom colors at a time, indicated in the grid in the bottom-left corner of the Color dialog box.

To see how applications can perform with pigments, use the following example steps:

1. **Choose File⇨New Application from the main menu to open a new form.**

2. **Click on a Panel, a Memo, and a Button component button (on the Standard page of the Component Palette) and then click anywhere on the form after clicking on each button to place these components.**

3. **Click on the Memo component, click on the scrollbars in the Object Inspector, and then click on the down arrow and select** `ssVertical`.

4. **Click on the ColorDialog button on the Dialogs page and then click anywhere on the form.**

5. **Click on the Panel component and in the Object inspector set the** `Align` **property to** `alTop` **and clear the Panel's Caption property.**

6. **Click on the Memo component and then set its Align property to**
   a1Top **in the Object Inspector.**

7. **Click on the Button component and then change the Caption of the**
   Button to Set Color Object Inspector.

8. **With the Button component selected, click on the Events tab on the**
   Object Inspector and then double-click on the empty field next to the
   OnClick **event handler to get into the Code Editor, where you enter**
   the following lines:

```
if ( ColorDialog1->Execute() )
  {
  Panel1->Color = ColorDialog1->Color ;
  Memo1->Lines->Assign(ColorDialog1->CustomColors);
  }
```

9. **Click on the ColorDialog component, and then expand the Options**
   property in the Object Inspector by double-clicking on it, and set
   cdFullOpen **within the Options property to** true.

10. **Press F9 to run the program.**

    The form's custom color information is contained in the Memo compo-
    nent, which I called "Favorite Color Form..." for this example (see
    Figure 9-7).

11. **Click on the Set Color button in the form to invoke the Color dialog**
    box, and then choose a color.

12. **Click on the Define Custom Colors button (grayed out in Figure 9-6)**
    to select several custom colors on the right side of the Color dialog
    box, and then click on the A̲dd to Custom Colors button.

13. **Close the Color dialog box by clicking on OK.**

Figure 9-7:
The behind-
the-scenes
code for
creating
some
custom
colors.

Printing with the PrintDialog and PrinterSetupDialog Components

Before Windows came along, adding another printer to a DOS program could be a developer's worst nightmare. You were forced to deal with all the nuances and quirks of each printer yourself!

Two components in the Dialogs tab — PrintDialog and PrinterSetupDialog — make printer setup torture a thing of the past. Neither of these components has any associated events, so the design of these dialogs is achieved through their properties.

Using the printer components in an application

The following example steps make use of the PrintDialog and PrinterSetupDialog components within an application:

1. **Choose File⇨New Application from the main menu to open a new form.**

2. **Click on the Panel component button on the Standard page, and then click anywhere on the form to drop in a Panel.**

3. **Click on the SpeedButton component button on the Additional page, and then click on the Panel you just placed; then repeat this step to place a second SpeedButton onto the Panel.**

4. **Click on the PrinterSetupDialog component button on the Dialogs page, and then click anywhere on the form.**

5. **Click on the PrintDialog component button on the Dialogs page, and then click anywhere on the form.**

   You could also add a graphic to each of the SpeedButtons by assigning their Glyph properties (see Chapter 5 for more information on Glyphs).

6. **Click on one of the SpeedButton components, then click on the Events tab on the Object Inspector, and then double-click on the empty field next to the OnClick event handler.**

   This step puts you in the Code Editor, where you enter the following line:

```
PrinterSetupDialog1->Execute() ;
```

7. **Click on the other SpeedButton, then click on the Events tab on the Object Inspector, and then double-click on the empty OnClick event handler field. Then enter the following line in the Code Editor:**

```
PrintDialog1->Execute() ;
```

8. **Press F9 to run the application.**

When you run the program, you can start each of the dialog boxes by clicking on their corresponding SpeedButton. For example, when you click on the SpeedButton associated with the PrinterSetupDialog component, you get the dialog box shown in Figure 9-8.

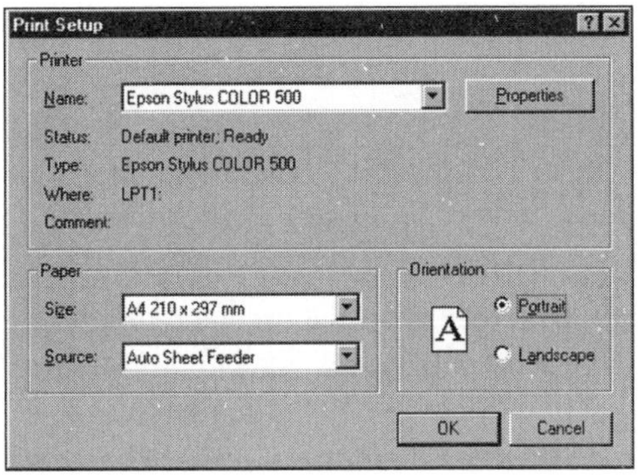

Figure 9-8:
The
PrintSetup-
Dialog
component
is the place
to pick a
printer.

After the PrinterSetupDialog component is added to your program, the user gets the Print Setup dialog box shown back in Figure 9-8, which displays the name of a printer currently selected as the target printer for any file the user outputs. The Name drop-down list shows the choice of available printers. (If you're connected to a network, a number of printers is shown on the list.)

Clicking on the Properties button in the Print Setup box produces a configuration dialog box for the printer that you selected. This dialog box can change according to the current target printer. Other options allow the user to set the size of the paper and the orientation (tall or wide) of the printed image.

More options with the PrintDialog component

After the trial run with the PrintDialog component in the previous section, you may be in the mood for another example of how to put this component to work. If you have a taste for more Print programs, continue on with the example application built in the previous section.

Click on the SpeedButton that you associated with the PrintDialog component — the dialog box shown in Figure 9-9 appears. This dialog box is used for setting up a print job before it's handed over to the Windows 95 Print Manager.

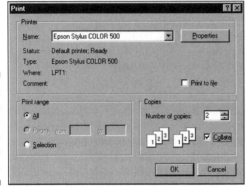

Figure 9-9:
Here's
where the
Print job
setup takes
place.

The top section of the dialog box shown in Figure 9-9 refers to the printer itself, so if you need to redirect a print job at the last minute, you can do so. (The Properties button is also thrown in for good measure for a more-complete printer dialog box configuration.)

The various subproperties of the Options property of a PrintDialog component, which you can view on the Object Inspector at design time, define how the dialog box appears to your program users. These subproperties are listed in the following table:

Option	Action
PrintToFile	Shows the Print To File check box.
PageNums	When set to true from the Object Inspector at design time, provides a Pages RadioButton (refer to Figure 9-9). From and To edit boxes are enabled to allow the user to set a page range for printing on the Print dialog box.
Selection	Enables the Selection radio button for printing only highlighted text.
Warning	Generates a warning message if you try to print to an uninstalled printer.
Help	Displays a Help button in the Print dialog box.
DisablePrintToFile	If PrintToFile is set to true, you can temporarily disable the check box by using this setting.

The PrintDialog component's *PrintToFile property* is set to true whenever the Print to file check box is selected by the end user.

The drop-down list of options available in the Object Inspector for the *PrintRange property* refer directly to the All Pages, Page Nums, or Selection radio buttons on the PrintDialog box that the user sees. You as a programmer would need to know the setting of this property (if the user has selected all pages or a range of pages) when the user closes the PrintDialog box. To determine the status of these properties, you can use code such as

```
if ( PrintDialog1->PrintRange == prAllPages )
   {
   // Take appropriate action to print all pages here
   }
```

The *FromPage* and *ToPage* properties refer to the corresponding edit boxes of the PrintDialog box. Use these properties according to which pages of a document are to be output or printed. Once the user has closed the PrintDialog, you can use the FromPage and ToPage properties in your code as follows to handle the current printing job:

```
for (int i=PrintDialog1->FromPage; i < PrintDialog1-
          >ToPage+1; i++)
   {
   // Code to print each page here
   }
```

The following steps extend the example program created earlier in this section to get some actual text on paper:

1. **Click on the RichEdit component button on the Win95 tab of the Component Palette, and then click anywhere on the form.**

2. **Using the Object Inspector, set the RichEdit component's Align property to** `alClient`**.**

3. **Click on the button associated with the PrintDialog component, then click on the Events tab on the Object Inspector, and then double-click on the** `OnClick` **event-handler name and change the code to the following:**

   ```
   if ( PrintDialog1->Execute() )
     RichEdit1->Print(Caption) ;
   ```

4. **Press F9 to run the program and then enter some text in the Rich Text Editor.**

   After you enter text into the RichEdit component on the form, and then set the print options in the PrintDialog in the program, when you close the PrintDialog box a printed page of the text you entered is output.

Chapter 10

Creating Database Applications

. . . .

. . . .

*T*he data components in C++Builder offer you an easy way to retrieve, manipulate, and store data in a robust application that knows its way around databases. More than a dozen database-related components fill two whole pages of the Component Palette — Data Access and Data Controls. In the interest of space, I picked out the "workhorse" data components — Table, DataSource, DBLabel, DBTable, DBMemo, and DBNavigator — to cover in this chapter.

C++Builder's data controls not only speed your development but also supply all-important functionality to applications that include database tables. Components that your program users work with directly, such as the Labels, DataGrids, and EditBoxes, are located on the Data Controls page. Those components depend on certain other components from the Data Access page to provide the actual data from the databases.

A distinction first needs to be made between two groups of components. Data Control components are *visual* components — you actually see them at design time and your end user sees them when working with your application. Data Access components are *nonvisual*. When you drop one into a form, what you see is an icon in place of the component; your end user doesn't actually see the component, but the program gains some behind-the-scenes functionality from the addition of the component (I discuss this topic a bit more later on in this chapter).

Before you can dive into building database applications, I first need to give you a brief introduction to the Borland Database Engine and the C++Builder Database Explorer.

Revving Up the Borland Database Engine

In the bad old days of programming, your program had to know the exact format that its data was in to gain access to that data. Then the program was restricted to using only that particular data format, unless you wanted to do a major rewrite of your program!

The Borland Database Engine (BDE) liberates you from this data communication confinement. The BDE acts as a go-between for your applications and databases. Essentially, it's a set of files that enables C++Builder to access databases. It doesn't matter if your data is held in Paradox or dBASE tables, or any other type of format; all of that data is basically just fields that contain raw data that are held in records that are held in tables.

The BDE needs to know which types of tables that you want to access, however, and for this purpose, it requires a *driver* (a single piece of software that can access a certain type of data file format). Most of the drivers that you're ever going need are provided with C++Builder, especially those drivers for accessing data stored locally on your hard disk, which is what I talk about throughout this chapter.

So how do you get to see these drivers? You can easily configure the BDE for the databases that you want to access from your application. In order to access database objects from C++Builder, you need to define BDE *alias.* The alias acts as an intermediary between your program and your database tables. (An alias can also be used by more than one program on your machine.)

The following steps show how you can configure the BDE to use a database:

1. **Choose Start⇨Programs⇨Borland C++Builder from the Windows 95 taskbar.**

   You then see a program called BDE Configuration.

2. **Click on the name of the program to run it.**

   You get a window similar to one shown in Figure 10-1.

3. **Click on the Aliases tab.**

   An *alias* represents a particular folder where your data is stored. Instead of having to remember long path names that reference databases, you can simply refer to the alias, which will connect you to the database. Figure 10-2 shows the Aliases tab page in the BDE Configuration Utility for managing your own aliases. (The PATH entry, for instance, tells you which folder holds the tables.)

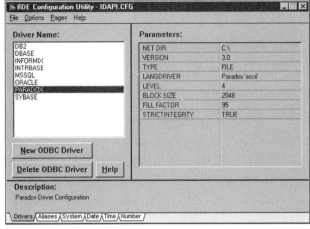

Figure 10-1:
The BDE
Configuration
Utility
provides
you with
ready-to-
use drivers.

Path with location of table folders

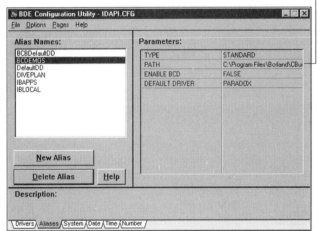

Figure 10-2:
Aliases help
make your
database
table
locations
easier to
find.

4. Click on the <u>N</u>ew Alias button to bring up the Add New Alias dialog box, and then add the name of your choice for the alias in the <u>N</u>ew Alias name edit box and leave the Alias type as STANDARD.

5. Click on <u>O</u>K to close the Add New Alias dialog box.

6. Select the newly created alias by clicking on it, and then on the opposite page click on Path and enter the path where your dBASE or paradox database files reside.

7. From the main menu, choose <u>F</u>ile➪<u>S</u>ave and then <u>F</u>ile➪E<u>x</u>it to finish up.

Discovering the Explorer

To experience the most powerful data viewing and manipulation tool that C++Builder has to offer, just follow these steps:

1. **Choose Database⇨Explorer from the main menu.**

    The Database Explorer allows you to access, modify, test, and in general manage data held in tables that you use within your application *while* you're developing (see Figure 10-3).

2. **Click on the Databases tab of the Explorer, and then double-click on the Databases item in the tree beneath it.**

    The aliases shown back in Figure 10-2 are also presented in the Database hierarchy of the Explorer.

When you click on the plus sign next to an item's icon, you can see all the details of the tables within an alias. You can view and modify the information about the tables by clicking on the tables and then selecting one of the three pages on the right-hand side of the Database Explorer screen. You can modify the information shown just by clicking into the appropriate edit boxes and then adding or removing the information.

Table name   Field name   Button bar for navigating table data

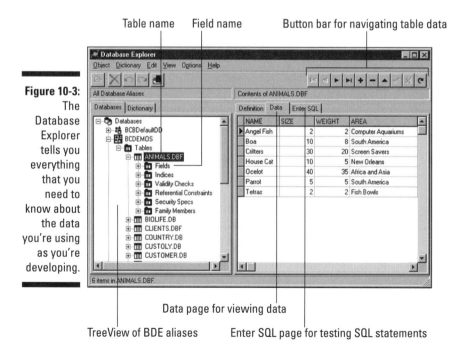

Figure 10-3: The Database Explorer tells you everything that you need to know about the data you're using as you're developing.

Data page for viewing data

TreeView of BDE aliases   Enter SQL page for testing SQL statements

Conjuring Up the Database Form Wizard

C++Builder comes equipped with some productivity tools called *Wizards*. One in particular, the Database Form Wizard, almost does the form creation for you by automatically placing and linking the components on a form to the fields and tables in a particular database. This supplies you with an instant form for editing and saving data that's ready for use in your program.

Before getting into some of the details of database-application development, I want to show you just how easily you can get a data-editing application off the ground using C++Builder. Just follow these steps to create an example program.

1. **Choose File⇨New Application to create a blank form in a new application.**

2. **Choose Database⇨Form Wizard.**

   The first screen of the Database Form Wizard appears.

3. **Click on the Next> button.**

4. **In the next screen, select** BCDEMOS **as the Drive or Alias name and** BIOLIFE.DB **as the Table Name (as shown in Figure 10-4).**

   C++Builder supplies a ready-made data file.

Figure 10-4: The Database Form Wizard makes it easy to choose a database table.

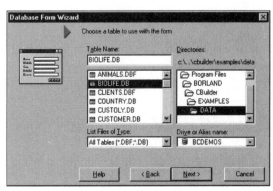

5. **Click on Next>.**

6. **Click on the >> button (in between the two list boxes on the third screen of the Database Form Wizard) to select all fields for the BIOLIFE table selected in Step 4.**

7. **Click on Next> and then click on Next> again.**

8. **Click on the Finish button.**

9. **Choose Project⇨Remove From Project, and then select** Form1 **and click on OK.**

10. **Press F9 to run the program you just created.**

Yes, you have just created your first database application. Easy, wasn't it? Figure 10-5 shows the sample program that C++Builder automatically titled "Form2."

Figure 10-5:
You can conjure up database forms such as this one almost as fast as you can say "Follow the Yellow Brick Road."

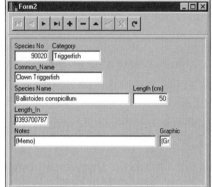

Have a play with this program; it does everything that you need to manage a single table. Try out the button bar (this is a Navigator component) at the top of the form. It allows you to navigate through, edit, add, and remove records. ("The DBNavigator component" section later in this chapter has more information on this control.)

Accessing Data Modules

One type of form that handles data access in your programs is called a *Data Module*. Your program users won't ever see a Data Module at runtime, because it is a nonvisual component. The *Data Module* can hold any type of other nonvisual components that a program requires. Don't bother trying to place a visual component in one of these because you'd waste your time; C++Builder won't allow it!

To see what a data module looks like, choose File⇨New Data Module from the main menu. A data module looks just like a form except that it has far fewer properties and events. With the data module selected, if you click on the Events tab on the Object Inspector, you see two events that you can use: the OnCreate event to place code for opening tables and connecting to the databases that are used in your program, and the OnDestroy event to close tables that may have been used in the Data Module.

Components fall into the category of *visual* or *nonvisual.* A visual component is visible or can be made visible on a form at runtime; you know what the component will look like when the program runs. A nonvisual component doesn't reveal itself at runtime, but helps other visual components to do their job when the end user uses visual components. Examples of visual components include the Edit, Label, and Memo components. Examples of nonvisual components include all the components from the Data Access and Dialogs pages on the Component Palette. A nonvisual component is represented by an icon at design time so that you're not flying blind as you're building — you can still change the nonvisual components' properties by using their icons.

Building an Application with the Table Component

The Table component resides on the Data Access page of the Component Palette and can be accessed by clicking on the Table button. The Table component represents a single data table and it's with this component that you control all aspects of using data file tables in your programs.

The following steps demonstrate how to drop a Table component into a form, associate it with a data table file, and then open the table ready to use.

1. **Click on the Table button on the Data Access page of the Component Palette, and then click anywhere on a form to drop in a Table component.**

   You can now see some of the Table component's properties if you examine the Object Inspector.

2. **Click on the Object Inspector's Properties tab and using the drop-down list from the DatabaseName property, select the ready-made BCDEMOS value.**

   Next, you need to select the table that you want the Table component to represent in your program.

3. **Using the Object Inspector, select the CUSTOMER.DB value from the drop-down list in the TableName property.**

4. **Again using the Object Inspector, set the** `Active` **property of the Table component to** `true`.

Step 4 opens the ready-made customer table in the Table component; the table can now be used.

✔ The Table component's *Exclusive property* prevents programs that might be running on other computers from using a table while you have it open. The Exclusive property is used primarily when you store your tables on a network drive where multiple users may be trying to access the table at the same time. The Active property must be set to false before setting the Exclusive property to true, otherwise you get an error message saying `Cannot perform this operation on an open dataset` when you try to set the Exclusive property to true while the Active property is true.

✔ The *ReadOnly property* needs to be set before setting the Active property to true (setting the Active property to true is also called *opening* the table). As its name suggests, the ReadOnly is property prevents any data changes that the user may make from being written to the table.

✔ The *Filter property* provides a quick way to restrict the view of the data in a table. For example, if you are interested in the records for just one customer in particular, you can assign the Filter property to something like **CustNo = 5.** Then when you set the Filter property to true, you can restrict your view of the table to those records that have a value of 5 in the CustNo field.

The following example program shows you how to use some of the built-in methods of the Table component to navigate through a data table. Just run through these steps:

1. **Select File➪Application from the main menu to create a blank form in a new application.**

2. **Follow Steps 1–5 described earlier in this section of the chapter.**

3. **Hold down the Shift key and click on the Button component button on the Standard page of the Component palette, and then click four times in a horizontal row at the top of the form to drop in four Button components.**

You're aiming to have four buttons in a row at the top of the form, such as in Figure 10-6.

4. **Click on the Memo button on the Standard page of the Component Palette, and then click anywhere on the form to place the component.**

5. **Click on the far-left Button component that you placed on the form in Step 3 and then enter** |< **into the** `Caption` **property on the Object Inspector.**

6. **Click on the Events tab of the Object Inspector and then double-click on the empty** `OnClick` **event-handler name field.**

You're then in the Code Editor, where you enter the following:

```
Table1->First() ;
LoadMemo() ;
```

Clicking on the far-left button (with the |< caption) now moves the
Table1 component (created in Steps 1–5 in the previous example) with
the function call First() to look at the first record in the table, which
shows you the Memo component that was dropped on the form.

7. **Click on the second button from the left and then enter < into the
   button's** Caption **property on the Object Inspector.**

8. **Click on the Events tab on the Object Inspector, then double-click on
   the empty name field next to the** OnClick **event handler, and then
   enter the following in the Code Editor:**

```
Table1->Prior() ;
if (Table1->Bof)
  ShowMessage("You're at the start!") ;
LoadMemo() ;
```

Clicking on the second button in the program now moves the component to the previous record in the table.

9. **Next, click on the third button from the left and using the Object
   Inspector enter > into the** Caption **property.**

10. **Click on the Events tab on the Object Inspector and then double-click
    on the empty field next to the** OnClick **event-handler, and then enter
    the following in the Code Editor:**

```
Table1->Next();
if (Table1->Eof)
  ShowMessage("You've hit the end!") ;
LoadMemo() ;
```

Clicking on the third button now moves the component to the next
record in the table.

11. **Using the Object Inspector, set the right-hand button's Caption
    property to** >| .

12. **Click on the Events tab of the Object Inspector, double-click on the
    empty** OnClick **event handler field, and then enter this code in the
    Code Editor:**

```
Table1->Last() ;
LoadMemo() ;
```

Clicking on the far-right button now moves the Table1 component to
look at the last record in the table.

13. **While still within the Code Editor, press Ctrl+End, and then press Enter to drop to the end of the file. Now enter the entire** LoadMemo **function, as follows, into the Code Editor:**

```
void TForm1::LoadMemo()
{
  Memo1->Clear() ;
  for (int i=0; i < Table1->FieldCount-1; i++)
  Memo1->Lines->Add(Table1->Fields[i]->FieldName +": "+
       Table1->Fields[i]->Text) ;
}
```

14. **Right-click on the Code Editor and choose the Open Source/Header File option from the speed menu that appears.**

15. **Use the arrow keys to cursor down the file and enter the following boldface line where shown:**

```
  .

  .
private:     // User declarations
   void LoadMemo();
public: // User declarations
  .

  .
```

16. **Press F9 to run the program.**

The field details displayed in the Memo component change as you click on the buttons on the form to navigate through the customer table. A message appears to tell you when you've reached the last record. This program should look something like the one shown in Figure 10-6.

Figure 10-6:
You can navigate a table's records by using buttons to access the table component's methods.

Linking a DataSource Component to a Table

Before you let yourself loose on the components in the Component Palette's Data Controls page, you should know about another control on the Data Access page — the DataSource component.

The data held within the Table components must be accessed by the Data Controls components so that the end user can interact with your programs. But Data Controls components can't be linked directly to Table components without the help of the DataSource component. The DataSource functions as a "matchmaker" of sorts between a Table and any Data Controls components that you drop into a form.

The following steps show you how to place a DataSource component onto a form and how to link it to a Table component:

1. **Using the form constructed in Steps 1–16 in the previous section of this chapter, click on the DataSource button on the Data Access page of the Component Palette, and then click in the form next to the Table component form to drop in a DataSource component.**

2. **Using the Object Inspector, select the existing Table component name from the drop-down list of the** DataSet **property of the DataSource component.**

   The Table component name is already there, waiting to be selected, so do it!

Setting a DataSource component's Enabled property to false blanks out the Data Controls component's contents, which in effect puts the "big freeze" on any Data Controls components that are linked to the DataSource.

Creating Applications with Data Controls Components

Data Controls components rely on the components from the Data Access page (described in previous sections of this chapter) to provide the data from a database. Then the Data Controls components allow the user to view and manipulate the data on a form.

Data Controls components feature a *DataSource property* that links them to a database. Most of the components covered in this section also have a *DataField property* that links them to a particular field within a table. These components are sometimes known as *data-aware controls.* These controls are linked to database tables and are rigged so they can send and receive data to and from those tables. Every component on the Data Control page is data aware because it has a *DataField* property that inherently knows about all data types. When you set the DataField property to any field in a table, the property gets the data type from the table without writing any code.

The DBGrid component

The DBGrid is a powerful data-aware component that enables your program to view many rows in DBGrid component table at once. As you can see in the set of steps that's coming up next, you can use a grid to create an instant table-maintenance program with a handful of mouse clicks with no coding whatsoever.

The following steps show you how to create a data-aware program:

1. **Select File⇨New Application from the main menu to create a blank form in a new application.**

2. **Follow Steps 1–5 from the first set of steps in the section "Building an Application with the Table Component" earlier in this chapter to place and open a Table component onto the form.**

3. **Click on the DBGrid component button on the Data Controls page of the Component Palette, and then click on the form to place it.**

4. **Click on the DataSource component button on the Data Access page and then click in the form next to the Table component that was dropped into the form in Step 2.**

5. **With the DataSource component still selected, select the** `Table1` **value from the drop-down list of the** `DataSet` **property on the Object Inspector (make sure you've clicked on the Properties tab first).**

6. **Click on the DBGrid component on the form, and then select the** `DataSource1` **value from the** `DataSource` **property's drop-down list on the Object Inspector.**

7. **Press F9 to run the application.**

   You can use the DBGrid to move around the records in the table and even edit them, as long as the AutoEdit property of the DataSource is set to true.

You don't have to leave this example program yet. DBGrids offer far more than a view of a data table. You can add more pizzazz to the grids that you use in your programs.

The next couple of steps show you how you can select which columns the user sees.

1. **Continuing from the steps in the previous section of this chapter, make sure the DBGrid component is selected and double-click on the** Columns **property on the Object Inspector.**

   You get the DBGrid Columns Editor dialog box, which is initially shown with no entries.

2. **Click on the Add All Fields button in the dialog box.**

   The Columns list box fills with all the fields for the table linked to the DBGrid via the DBGrid component.

   To remove a field from the DBGrid, select the field by name in the Columns ListBox and then press Delete.

   You can change the way that each column in your DBGrid looks in the program by selecting the field by name in the Columns ListBox on the Columns Editor and then setting the values that you want in the EditBoxes and drop-down lists in the Column and Title pages. (The Columns Editor should end up looking something like the one in Figure 10-7.)

Figure 10-7:
Use the
DBGrid
Columns
Editor to
customize
your grids.

3. **When you're finished customizing the DBGrid, click on OK to close the Columns Editor.**

✔ By default, DBGrid columns are displayed according to the order in which the fields that they represent are held in the linked table. To reorder columns, open the DBGrid Columns Editor (as shown previously in Steps 1–3) and then click on and drag the field names within the Columns ListBox and then drop the names into their new positions.

✔ Click on the PickList button in the Column Properties page of the DBGrid Columns Editor (refer to Figure 10-7). You get the String List Editor dialog box, which you can use to enter a list of items that can be selected for a particular field.

✔ Experiment with the different settings in the Columns Editor, such as the Font button and the Color drop-down list on both properties pages. You may end up with some interesting design effects like those in Figure 10-8.

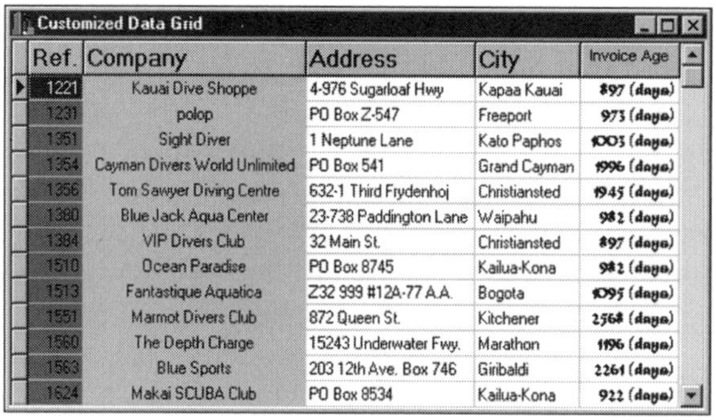

Figure 10-8:
Try experimenting with the settings in the DBGrid Columns Editor to change the appearance of the grid.

Ref.	Company	Address	City	Invoice Age
1221	Kauai Dive Shoppe	4-976 Sugarloaf Hwy	Kapaa Kauai	897 (days)
1231	polop	PO Box Z-547	Freeport	973 (days)
1351	Sight Diver	1 Neptune Lane	Kato Paphos	1003 (days)
1354	Cayman Divers World Unlimited	PO Box 541	Grand Cayman	1996 (days)
1356	Tom Sawyer Diving Centre	632-1 Third Frydenhoj	Christiansted	1945 (days)
1380	Blue Jack Aqua Center	23-738 Paddington Lane	Waipahu	982 (days)
1384	VIP Divers Club	32 Main St.	Christiansted	897 (days)
1510	Ocean Paradise	PO Box 8745	Kailua-Kona	982 (days)
1513	Fantastique Aquatica	Z32 999 #12A-77 A.A.	Bogota	1095 (days)
1551	Marmot Divers Club	872 Queen St.	Kitchener	2568 (days)
1560	The Depth Charge	15243 Underwater Fwy.	Marathon	1196 (days)
1563	Blue Sports	203 12th Ave. Box 746	Giribaldi	2261 (days)
1624	Makai SCUBA Club	PO Box 8534	Kailua-Kona	922 (days)

DBGrid components can be used to convey loads of information and are useful for showing an entire table all in one shot, but you may want to focus on a single field. That's when some of the other data-aware components can come in handy.

The DBLabel component

The DBLabel component, like other Data Controls components covered in this chapter, has a *DataField property* in addition to a *DataSet property*. The DataField property enables the DBLabel component to be linked to a single field or column in a table. (The DBLabel component has similar properties and exactly the same events as the regular Label component on the Standard page of the Component Palette, which is discussed in Chapter 4.)

The following steps show you how the DBLabel component operates:

1. **Continuing with the example program created in "The DBGrid component" section earlier in this chapter, increase the size of the form by clicking on it and dragging to allow room for another component.**

2. **Click on the DBLabel button on the Data Controls page of the Component Palette, and then click anywhere on the newly created space on the form to place a new DBLabel component.**

3. **Select the** DataSource1 **value from the DBLabel component's DataSource property drop-down list in the Object Inspector.**

4. **Select a field name from the** DataField **property's drop-down list. (The DataField property is directly above the** DataSource **property on the Object Inspector.)**

5. **Click on the Table component on the form and then, using the Object Inspector, make sure the** Active **property is set to** true.

   You can see the data in the field that you chose in Step 4 for the first record in the table.

6. **Press F9 to run the application.**

   Use the arrow keys on the DBGrid component to move down through the records of the table and you can see that the contents of the DBLabel component correspond to the contents of the field for the currently selected row on the DBGrid.

The DBLabel automatically updates its contents when the row in the table changes. It's fine for showing data, but what component do you use to change values in fields? That's covered in the next section.

The DBEdit component

The DBEdit component's properties and events are much the same as those of the Edit component on the Standard page of the Component Palette (which is covered in Chapter 4). This section focuses on how to link the DBEdit component to a data table. As with the DBLabel component, you link a DBEdit component to a single field within a record.

Add the following set of steps to the previous example to see how you can put the DBEdit component into operation:

1. **Continuing with the example in the previous section, click on the DBEdit component button on the Data Controls page of the Component Palette, and then click anywhere on the empty space on the form to drop in a DBEdit component.**

2. **Use the Object Inspector to select the** `DataSource1` **value from the drop-down list of the** `DataSource` **property of the DBEdit component.**

3. **Using the Object Inspector again, select a field name from the** `DataField` **property's drop-down list of the DBEdit component; then press F9 to run the application.**

   Use the arrow keys to scroll down through the DBGrid and you can see the contents of the edit control change. Try entering some different text into the contents of the DBEdit. As you leave the field (you can do this by pressing the Tab key), the same value in the DBGrid also changes. All these components are now linked by the DataSource component.

The DBMemo component

Like the components on the Standard page of the Component Palette, a DBEdit component is not always capable of displaying multiple lines of text — it's designed to handle only a single line of text at a time. What you need is a DBMemo component to give the user memo fields (multiple lines of text).

To see the DBMemo component in action, use the following steps, building on the example program created in the previous section of this chapter:

1. **Select File⇨Application from the main menu to create a blank form in a new application.**

2. **Follow Steps 1–5 described in "The DBLabel component" section earlier in this chapter.**

3. **Click on the Table component on the form and use the Object Inspector to set the** `Active` **property to** `false`.

4. **Click on the DBMemo component button on the Data Controls page of the Component Palette, and then click anywhere on the form to drop in a DBMemo component.**

5. **Using the Object Inspector, set the** `DataSource` **property of the DBMemo component to** `DataSource1` **and its** `DataField` **property to** `Notes`.

6. **Click on the Table property and, using the Object Inspector, set the** `Active` **property to** `true`; **then press F9 to run the application.**

   When you run this example program, multiple lines of text are automatically read in from the `Notes` field in the `BIOLIFE` table and displayed in the DBMemo component on the form.

The DBNavigator component

Using grids to navigate the records of a table may not offer you all control that you want. The DBNavigator component gives your programs navigational and editing control through an integrated set of speed buttons. To drop a DBNavigator component into the form built with the steps in the previous sections of this chapter, just follow these couple of steps:

1. **Continuing with the steps in "The DBEdit component" section earlier in this chapter, click on the DBNavigator component button on the Data Controls page, and then click anywhere on the form to drop in a component.**

2. **Set the DataSource property of the DBNavigator component to** DataSource1 **using the Object Inspector; then press F9.**

   See Figure 10-9 for the results.

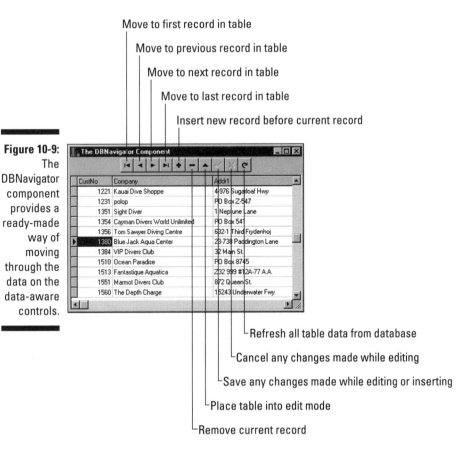

Move to first record in table

Move to previous record in table

Move to next record in table

Move to last record in table

Insert new record before current record

Figure 10-9: The DBNavigator component provides a ready-made way of moving through the data on the data-aware controls.

Refresh all table data from database

Cancel any changes made while editing

Save any changes made while editing or inserting

Place table into edit mode

Remove current record

The buttons on the DBNavigator component resemble the buttons you'd see on a VCR or CD player, with a few extra buttons thrown in for added functionality (refer to Figure 10-9). You can decide which buttons you want available in this component by setting them to either true or false within the expandable VisibleButtons property in the Object Inspector.

Filtering Data with the Query Component

At times you may need to analyze data from multiple tables simultaneously to acquire information that a single table just can't provide. By using a Query component instead of a Table component, you can not only filter information from a single table, but also merge columns from many tables to give you the view of the data you need to solve your problem.

Query components have a number of properties and methods in common with the Table component. Queries have both records and fields, but a Query is more dynamic than a Table component, thanks to its *SQL* (Structured Query Language) *property*. *SQL* is an industry-standard language specifically designed to let users create databases, add new data to databases, maintain the data, and retrieve selected parts of the data.

So how do you go about setting up a Query? You can use the following steps to manufacture an example program that uses the Query component.

1. **Select File⇨New Application from the main menu to create a blank form in a new application.**

2. **Click on the Query component button on the Data Access page of the Component Palette and then click anywhere on the form.**

3. **Click on the DataSource component button on the Data Access page and then click next to the Query component just dropped onto the form.**

4. **Click on the DBGrid button on the Data Controls page and then click anywhere on the form to drop in a new DBGrid component.**

5. **Click on the DataSource component on the form and select** Query1 **from the** DataSet **property's drop-down list on the Object Inspector.**

6. **Click on the DBGrid component and then use the Object Inspector to select** DataSource1 **from the drop-down list in the** DataSource **property.**

7. **With the DBGrid still selected, use the Object Inspector to set the** Align **property of the DBGrid to** alBottom.

The Query is now linked to the DataSource in exactly the same way that you hook a DataSource to a Table (as shown in the "Linking a DataSource Component to a Table" section earlier in this chapter).

8. **Click on the Query component and, using the Object Inspector, set the** DatabaseName **property to** BCDEMOS.

9. **Double-click on the** SQL **property on the Object Inspector to start the String List Editor for the SQL property, and then enter the following line of SQL into the Code Editor:**

```
SELECT * FROM EVENTS
```

This single line of SQL code results in the Query component displaying every field from the Events table (the asterisk is a *wildcard,* or substitute, that stands for "all fields" when placed in this position in an SQL statement).

10. **Click on OK to close the String List Editor.**

11. **Using the Object Inspector, set the Active property of the Query component to true.**

These steps place a Query component onto a form and link the Query, via a DataSource component, to a DBGrid. When you set the Active property to true, an exact match for the Events table (in the BCDEMOS database) appears in the DBGrid that you placed on the form.

At the beginning of this section, I explain how to use a Query to filter data from a table. In the next set of steps, I show you how to specify criteria that data fields in a record must match before the record is included in the set of records for the Query.

1. **Continuing with the previous set of steps, double-click on the** SQL **property on the Object Inspector to open the SQL String List Editor.**

2. **Extend the SQL code in the editor to the following:**

```
SELECT * FROM EVENTS WHERE VENUENO = 5 ;
```

3. **Click on OK to close the String List Editor.**

4. **Reactivate the Query component by using the Object Inspector to set the** Active **property to** true.

C++Builder closes the query when you close the String List Editor because you can't change an active Query. You then see a subset of the Events table data in which only the records that have a venueno field value of 5 are shown in the data set.

The previous example program provides you with an introduction on using the TQuery component in conjunction with other components on the form (such as the DBGrid, in this case). The secret behind successful use of Query components is to get the most out of the SQL language. For more information, you may want to pick up *SQL For Dummies,* 2nd Edition, by Allen G. Taylor (IDG Books Worldwide, Inc.).

Chapter 11

Constructing Reports

· ·

· ·

*Y*ou really have your hands full when it comes to creating a report program. The whole process involves retrieving information stored in a database, presenting the information in a concise and meaningful way, and then formatting the information so that the end user can understand what all those rows, columns, fields, entries, and labels in a report are all about.

C++Builder has gone a long way to help you manage your report generation by dedicating a chunk of the Component Palette entirely to report-building controls. You can find the QuickReport components stashed away on the QReport page of the Component Palette. By using the QReport components in your application development you can create all kinds of quality reports (in full color, too). Most, but not all, of the QReport components get some coverage in this chapter. But you can still get a feel for how to incorporate these components into your applications.

Adding a QuickReport Component to a Form

QuickReport components by and large control your reports and any print and preview methods that go along with them. The fact is, you can't create reports in C++Builder without reaching for a QuickReport component.

Dropping a QuickReport component onto a form changes the nature of the form so that its sole purpose is to hold report components. The form is no longer a regular application form. It becomes, in effect, a read-only reporting and browsing program because you're limited to reading data rather than adding, removing, or changing data in the form.

To add a QuickReport component to a form, just follow these steps:

1. **Choose File⇨New Application from the main menu to create a blank form in a new application.**

2. **Click on the QuickReport button on the QReport page of the Component Palette, and then click anywhere on the new form to drop in a QuickReport component.**

The QuickReport component houses an army of properties that, once you have placed the QuickReport component onto a form, can be accessed through the Object Inspector. Here's a rundown of some of those properties:

✔ The *ReportTitle property* holds the text (which you enter using the Object Inspector) that's used to identify a report when it's sent to either the Print Manager or a network printer queue. So try to make this text meaningful and relatively polite!

✔ If you want to display the standard Windows printer dialog box before you print a QuickReport report, set the *DisplayPrintDialog property* to true using the Object Inspector (the default setting is false).

✔ The *Orientation property* settings determine whether the report prints out tall (the Portrait setting, which is the default) or wide (the Landscape setting).

✔ The *PaperLength* and *PaperWidth* properties are set to 0 by default. With that setting, the properties use one of three standard paper-size dimensions in the *PaperSize property.* If you want to specify a custom paper size (by using the Object Inspector) you need to set both the length and width properties.

✔ Use the *Columns property* when you need to specify multiple-column reports (once again, using the Object Inspector). Here's an example of when this comes in handy: If you need to print out addresses for a mass mailing onto sheets of adhesive labels, you can increase the *Columns* property setting to account for the number of labels that you're printing across a page.

To load a QuickReport labels form (just to get a look at a multicolumn report template), select File⇨New from the main menu to get the New Items dialog box. Click on the Forms page tab and then click on the QuickReport labels icon to load up the QuickReport labels report example.

✔ The *ColumnMarginMM* (the MM stands for millimeters) and *ColumnMarginInches* properties take effect when the Columns property is set to greater than 1. For example, to make sure that your printed report text doesn't run off the edges of your expensive adhesive mailing labels, you can set a gap between rows of labels by changing either of these properties. You need to change the value for only one of these properties; the value is automatically converted into the other measurement and loaded into the corresponding property on the Object Inspector.

✔ The *LeftMarginMM* and *LeftMarginInches* properties determine the width of the nonprinting area on the left side of the sheet being printed.

Creating a Data Module to Hold Data Controls

Later on in this chapter, I show you how to create report applications. But first you need to know how to create a *data module* that contains the Table and DataSource components used in the examples in the sections "Building a Report with QuickReport Components" and "Mastering Master-Detail Reports." (Chapter 10 has more information on data modules and Table and DataSource components.) A data module is a special type of form designed to hold your nonvisual data controls in one handy place, making them easy to access and manage.

The data module in this example includes two tables — one table contains records for vendors of widget parts and the other table contains the widget parts that can be bought from the vendors. A relationship is then created between the two tables that makes them capable of operating together. This can happen because the code for each vendor is added to the record for each part that the vendor supplies. With that said, you can begin to build the example program.

The following steps guide you through creating a sample data module:

1. **Continuing with Steps 1–2 in the previous section, choose File⇨New Data Module from the main menu.**

   You get what looks like a blank form, but it's actually a data module.

2. **Click on the Table button on the Data Access page of the Component Palette and then click anywhere on the data module form. Then repeat this step one more time.**

3. **Click on the DataSource button on the Data Access page, and then click next to either of the Table components placed onto the data module form in Step 2. Then repeat this step one more time.**

4. Using the Object Inspector, set the values for the properties listed in the following table for each of the components in the data module:

Property	Value
First Table Component	
DatabaseName	BCDEMOS
Name	tblVendor
TableName	VENDORS.DB
Active	True
First DataSource Component	
DataSet	tblVendor
Name	dsVendor
Second Table Component	
DatabaseName	BCDEMOS
MasterSource	dsVendor
Name	tblPart
TableName	PARTS.DB
Active	True
Second DataSource Component	
DataSet	tblPart
Name	dsPart

5. Double-click on the blank field next to the MasterFields property in the Object Inspector and set it to the table tblPart value.

You get the Field Link Designer dialog box (see Figure 11-1).

6. Select VendorNo from the Available Indexes drop-down list in the Field Link Designer dialog box.

VendorNo (which stands for Vendor Number in this example) then appears in the Detail Fields list box.

7. Click on VendorNo in both the Detail Fields and the Master Fields list boxes, and then click on Add.

The text VendorNo->VendorNo will be added to the Joined Fields list box (the two tables are now "joined" by their both having a VendorNo field). In this example, all the parts records in the Parts table contain a

VendorNo field. C++Builder can then use the fields from the Vendor table to automatically display records from the Parts table that match the VendorNo field of the current record in the Vendor table. Now parts can be grouped by the vendor who supplies them.

8. **Click on OK to close the Field Link Designer.**

9. **Click on the background of the data module and use the Object Inspector to set the** Name **property of the data module to** dmVendorPart.

   The initial build of the data module is done; now it has to be saved to disk.

10. **Select File⇨Save As from the main menu for the Save As dialog box, and then enter** udmVendorPart **in the File name text box and click on OK.**

That completes the data module. Now back to the job of generating reports, which is why you created this data module in the first place.

Figure 11-1:
Use the
Field Link
Designer to
create a
master-
detail
relationship
between
tables.

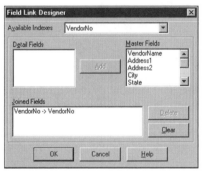

Connecting a QuickReport Component to a Database

After the data module is created, you need to connect a QuickReport component to the data in the report to display the data on the form. A QuickReport component accesses data through its *DataSource property*.

(***Note:*** The following steps continue from the first set of steps listed earlier in this chapter in the section "Adding a QuickReport Component to a Form.")

1. **Choose File⇨Include Unit Header from the main menu to get the Include Unit dialog box.**

2. **Double-click on** udmVendorPart **and then click on the QuickReport component.**

3. **Using the Object Inspector, set the** DataSource **property of the QuickReport component to** dmVendorPart->dsVendor.

4. **Again using the Object Inspector, type** frmSimpleReport **into the** Name **property of the Form.**

5. **Select the File⇨Save As to invoke the Save As dialog box, then type** ufrmSimpleReport **in the File name text box and then click on OK.**

You've connected the QuickReport component to the Vendor table in the data module and saved your work to disk. Now the user can see the data from the two tables in readable format, thanks to the DataSource component working with other components on the form.

Striking Up the QuickReport Band Properties

If you ever wanted to play with a band, here's your opportunity (you don't have to be able to play a musical instrument and it doesn't matter if your singing's off-key). QuickReport components feature *bands* — not the country or heavy-metal kind — but rather strips of space within a report form that hold form headers or details about the report. The QRBand component plays an important role in formatting reports, so I focus on that for a bit here.

 If you drop a QRBand onto a form (by clicking on the QRBand button on the QReport page of the Component Palette and then clicking anywhere on the form) you can get a look at how this component works.

The most important property for the QRBand component is *BandType,* which determines where and when the band is printed (use the drop-down list in the Object Inspector to select the contents of the BandType property). The following table lists the most commonly used BandType properties and what they do.

BandType Property Setting	*Description*
rbTitle	Prints at the start of the report automatically. You can place more than one title band onto a QuickReport form; the bands are printed sequentially in the order that you place them on the form.
rbPageHeader	Used for placing specific information such as the date or time.
rbPageFooter	Used for page footers, such as report page numbers. Appears at the base of every page.
rbGroupHeader	Used to set up master-detail relationships within reports (master-detail reports are covered later in this chapter).
rbGroupFooter	Used for placing subtotals or report flags as group trailers within table master-detail relationships.
rbColumnHeader	Similar to a page header; used for multiple-column reports because it can be repeated for each column across the width of a page.
rbDetail	Used for each detail record in a report that holds the actual table data; several can be used at a time. (A report can have multiple bands and each can hold anything from actual data to the title of the report.)
rbSubDetail	Holds the fields shown in a report for a detail table's records when a master-detail arrangement is used. In the example built in the "Mastering Master-Detail Reports" section of this chapter, a subdetail band is used to hold the order table fields for each vendor.
rbOverlay	Used to create bands that "float" over the report page independent of the positions of other bands on the page.
rbSummary	Used for summaries tagged onto the end of a report (this band typically contains fields and text that helps to explain the contents or helps to draw conclusions from the report).

With the *Ruler property,* you can set horizontal, vertical, or grid rulings on the area of a QRBand component in either inches or centimeters. Having on-screen rulers at design time enables you to see exactly how much room you're using on a report page and for ensuring that you can squeeze that extra field in when you need to.

The *Frame property* adds boundary areas to your band components. The Frame property is expandable, with a bunch of subproperties you can use to set attributes such as width, color style, and boundary placement. For reports with multiple columns, use this property to provide separators between the report fields.

Building a Report with QuickReport Components

The previous sections of this chapter have paved the way for this section — the steps to building a sample report using components on the QReport page of the Component Palette.

1. **Using the form called "SimpleReport" created in the two previous sections of this chapter, click on the QRBand button, and then click on the form to drop in a new QRBand component.**

2. **Click on the QRLabel button and then click on the QRBand component that was placed on the report in Step 1.**

   The QRLabel component is used to place text onto a QuickReport Band component.

3. **Using the Object Inspector, type** C++Builder Vendor List **into the** Caption **property of the QRLabel component.**

   You may also use the Object Inspector to adjust the Font property to change the caption's size, color, or style.

4. **Click on the QRBand button, and then click anywhere on the form to drop in another QRBand component.**

5. **Using the Object Inspector, set the** BandType **property to** rbColumnHeader.

6. **Click on the QRLabel button and then click on the QRBand component that was placed on the report in Step 4.**

   Perform this step four more times, placing QRLabel components in a horizontal row along the bottom of the QRBand component.

7. **Using the Object Inspector, enter the following values in the** Caption **property of the five components:**

```
Vendor No
Vendor Name
City
Phone
Fax
```

Enter **Vendor No** in the Caption property of the first component, enter **Vendor Name** in the Caption property of the second component, and so on, to create the report headings.

8. **Drop another QRBand component onto the form and, and using the Object Inspector set the** BandType **property to** rbDetail.

9. **Click on the QRDBText button, and then click on the QRBand component that was dropped on the report in Step 8.**

Perform this step a total of five times, placing QRDBText components in a horizontal row along the QRBand component.

The QRDBText component is a data-aware text component that can be associated with a single field in a table through its DataSource and DataField properties.

10. **Using the Object Inspector, set the DataSource property of each of the QRDBText components to** dmVendorPart->dsVendor.

You can perform this step on all five components at once by first holding down the Shift key before clicking on each QRDBText component.

11. **For each of the QRDBText components, use the Object Inspector to set the** DataField **properties to the following values:**

```
Vendor No
Vendor Name
City
Phone
Fax
```

Enter **Vendor No** in the DataField property of the first component, enter **Vendor Name** in the DataField property of the second component, and so on for all five DataField values.

You can use the Object Inspector to increase the Size subproperty within the Font property for the QRDBText components if you think that would make the report easier to read.

12. Right-click on the QuickReport component to get the QuickReport speed menu and choose the Preview Report option.

The QuickReport component then gives you a *WYSIWIG* (what you see is what you get) report preview on your screen. (The report should look similar to the one shown in Figure 11-2.) Reports are typically output to a printer, but many of today's Windows applications offer users a sneak peek of how a report's going to look before it hits the page. This option saves on paper as you don't have to keep on printing out a report to get it right.

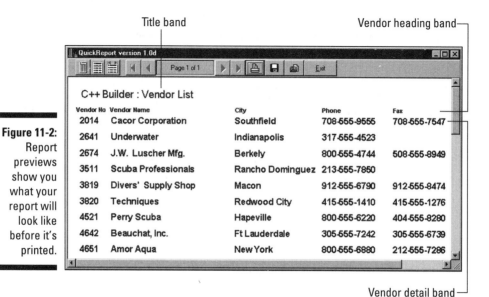

Figure 11-2:
Report previews show you what your report will look like before it's printed.

The rows of information in the report shown in Figure 11-2 are courtesy of the rbDetail component that you dropped onto the form in Step 8 in this section. Each column refers to the data-aware QRDBText components associated to a column of the vendor table through their DataField components.

Running the Report Applications

The following steps show you how to create a simple application that you can use to run the reports created in this chapter.

Begin by using the project built in the previous section, "Building a Report with QuickReport Components."

1. **Choose File➪New Form from the main menu for a new form.**

2. **Using the Object Inspector, change the** Name **property of the new form to** frmControlForm.

3. **Click on the CheckBox button on the Standard page of the Component Palette, and then click on the new form to drop a CheckBox component onto the form.**

4. **Using the Object Inspector, set the** Name **property of the CheckBox to** cbPreview **and set the** Checked **property to** true.

   As you'll soon see, this check box component is going to save you some paper!

5. **Click on the Button component button on the Standard page, and then click on the form to place a new Button component.**

   Repeat this step twice for a total of three buttons.

6. **Using the Object Inspector, set the** Caption **property of the first Button component that you placed on the form to** Simple Report.

7. **Double-click on this same Button component to get into the Code Editor, where you enter the following lines:**

   ```
   if (cbPreview->Checked == true)
     frmSimpleReport->QuickReport1->Preview() ;
   else
     frmSimpleReport->QuickReport1->Print() ;
   ```

   The next two steps add a header file to the report form because this form needs to have access to the report form created in the "Building a Report with QuickReport Components" section earlier in this chapter.

8. **Choose File➪Include Unit Header from the main menu to get the Include Unit dialog box.**

9. **Select the unit name** ufrmSimpleReport **from the list box of the Include Unit dialog box and then click on OK.**

   This is the form file that contains the first example report in this chapter constructed with QuickReport components.

   Next, you want to make the form created in this set of steps the main form of the application.

10. **Choose Options➪Project from the main menu to get the Project Options dialog box and then choose** frmControlForm **from the Main form drop-down list in the dialog box.**

11. **Click on OK to close the dialog box and then press F9 to run the program.**

If you have a printer connected to your computer, you can deselect the Preview CheckBox on the main form of your example program and click on the "Simple Report" button. You then get a printout of your first C++Builder report. Congratulations!

If you don't have a printer connected to your computer, that's okay. Select the Preview CheckBox and then click "Simple Report" anyway and you can see exactly what the report would have looked like on paper.

Mastering Master-Detail Reports

If you read the section "Creating a Data Module to Hold Data Controls" earlier in this chapter, little did you know that a master-detail relationship was created in those example steps. The vendor table in the example program in that section essentially functions as the "master" and the parts table functions as the "detail." In this case, the *master/detail form* browses two related tables, displaying one table in one portion of the form and the second table in another portion.

The following section of this chapter leads you through the steps to construct an example master-detail QuickReport form. (If you haven't already read the previous sections of this chapter, you may want to do so now before tackling the following project.)

Setting up the beginnings of a master-detail report

The following steps provide the groundwork for a complete report that's built by the end of this section:

1. **Continuing with the example steps in the previous section, choose File⇨New Form from the main menu to add a new form to the application.**

2. **Using the Object Inspector, change the** Name **property of the newly created form to** frmMasterDetail.

3. **Choose File⇨Include Header from the main menu to show the Include Unit dialog box.**

4. **Choose** udmVendorPart **from the list box and then click on OK to close the dialog box.**

5. **Click on the QuickReport button on the QReport page and then click anywhere on the new form.**

6. Using the Object Inspector, set the `DataSource` property of the QuickReport component to `dmVendorPart->dsVendor`.

   If you already created the example form in the section "Building a Report with QuickReport Components" earlier in this chapter, then continue on to the next step; otherwise you may get stuck at this point.

7. Select the QRBand components dropped in the form in the earlier example by holding down the Shift key while clicking on each, then copy the components by pressing Ctrl+C, and finally insert them into the new form by clicking into the form and pressing Ctrl+V.

   If you want to change the shape or position of the bands after they are placed, you can click and drag them to size, and then drag and drop them to the desired location.

8. Click on the title QRBand component and, using the Object Inspector, change the `Name` property of the component to `bndTitle`.

   (Three bands are currently on the form — BandTypes `rbtitle`, `rbColumnHeader1`, and `rbdetail`.) This step helps you identify which band is which as you accumulate additional bands in the report.

9. Click on the QRLabel component on the title QRBand component and using the Object Inspector, change the `Caption` property of the Label to something appropriate.

   For this example, I entered the title of this book and **Master Detail Report**. Next, add some graphic appeal to the report.

10. Click on the Image button on the Additional page of the Component Palette and then click on the title QRband of the report.

11. To load an image into the Image component, double-click on the Image component to open the Picture Editor dialog box.

    For this example, I selected the Technlgy.ico file in the cbuilder\images\icons folder.

12. Click on the QRShape button on the QReport page of the Component Palette, then click on the title QRBand component, and then click and drag the QRShape component to create a colored underline for the QRLabel component.

13. Click on the second QRBand component from the top of the form (the QRBand that contains the headings for the vendor table column headers) and, using the Object Inspector, set the `Name` property to `bndVendorHeader`.

14. Click on to the third QRBand component from the top of the form (the vendor table detail band itself) and use the Object Inspector to set the contents of the `Name` property to `bndVendorDetail`.

Turning the form into a working master-detail report

So far, the steps in the "Mastering Master-Detail Reports" section duplicate the functionality of the report constructed in the "Building a Report with QuickReport Components" section earlier in this chapter. After laying down the groundwork, you're ready to extend the report into a master-detail report.

1. **Select the form created in Steps 1–14 in the previous section.**

2. **Click on the QRBand component button on the QReport page and then click below the last QRBand component placed in the form to add another QRBand component.**

3. **Using the Object Inspector, set the** Name **property of the new QRBand to** bndPartHeader **and its** BandType **property to** rbColumnHeader.

4. **Click on the QRLabel component button on the QReport page and then click on the new QRBand component that was placed on the report in Step 2.**

   Perform this step a total of five times, placing QRLabel components in a horizontal row next to the new QRBand component.

5. **Using the Object Inspector, set the** Caption **properties of the QRLabel components as follows (one setting for each caption in order):**

   ```
   PartNo
   Description
   # On Hand
   # On Order
   Cost
   ```

6. **Click on the QRBand button on the QReport page, and then click below the last QRBand component dropped into the form to add another QRBand component.**

7. **Using the Object Inspector, set the new QRBand component's** Name **property to** bndPartDetail **and its** BandType **property to** rbSubDetail.

8. **Click on the QRDBText component button on the QReport page and then click on the QRBand component that was dropped in the report in Step 6.**

   Perform this step a total of five times, placing QRDBText components in a horizontal row along the QRBand component added in Step 6.

9. **Group-select the QRDBText components and using the Object Inspector, set their** DataSource **property to** dmVendorPart->dsPart.

10. **Again in the Object Inspector, set the** `DataField` **properties for the five new QRDBText components on the new QRBand component as follows (one setting for each in order):**

```
PartNo
Description
On Hand
On Order
Cost
```

11. **Click on the QRDetailLink button on the QReport page and then click anywhere on the form to place a QRDetailLink component.**

The QRDetailLink component controls how the master-detail relationship operates within the report.

12. **With the QRDetailLink component still selected, use drop-down lists on the Object Inspector to set the** `DataSource` **property to** `dmVendorPart->dsPart`, **the** `DetailBand` **property to** `bndPartDetail`, **the** `HeaderBand` **property to** `bndPartHeader`, **and the** `Master` **property to** `QuickReport1`.

13. **Add one more band (using the process in Step 6) and use the Object Inspector to set its** `BandType` **property to** `rbPageFooter`.

14. **Click on the QRSysData button on the QReport page and then click on the QRBand component that you dropped in the form in Step 8.**

15. **Using the Object Inspector, set the** `Data` **property of the QRSysData component to** `qrsPageNumber` **and type** `Page` **in its** `Text` **property.**

The report is done! Now to call the new master-detail report from the report control form (the one with two buttons and a check box built earlier in this chapter).

Calling a master-detail report from a program

The following set of steps lead you through the process of calling the master-detail report from the example program constructed in this section, "Mastering Master-Detail Reports."

1. **Select** View⇨Project Manager **from the main menu, and then double-click on the name of the unit** `ufrmReportControl` **in the Project Manager dialog box to bring the frmControlForm to the front.**

2. **Click on the Button2 component on the frmControlForm and then, using the Object Inspector, change the** `Caption` **property to** `Master-Detail Report`.

3. **Double-click on the Master-Detail Report button from the frmControlForm to get into the Code Editor, where you enter the following:**

```
if (cbPreview->Checked == True)
  frmMasterDetail->QuickReport1->Preview() ;
else
  frmMasterDetail->QuickReport1->Print() ;
```

4. **While in the Code Editor, choose File⇨Include Unit Header from the main menu to get the Include Unit dialog box.**

5. **Select the unit name** `ufrmMasterDetailReport` **from the Include Unit dialog box.**

6. **To see your handiwork, press F9 to run the program.**

7. **Click on the Master-Detail Report button to summon your master-detail report.**

Figure 11-3 shows the report produced for this example. You can see that the parts are listed by the vendor who supplies them. The master-detail report can either be printed to a printer or shown on the screen as a preview according to the setting of the CheckBox component on the control form.

┌Part detail band   Part header band┐

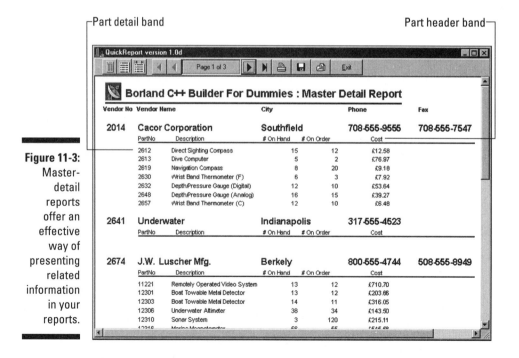

Figure 11-3:
Master-
detail
reports
offer an
effective
way of
presenting
related
information
in your
reports.

Adding a QRSysData component

Back in Step 14 of the section "Turning the form into a working master-detail report," a QRSysData component is dropped into the report. This component offers some very useful reporting features that are listed in the following table. If you place the QRSysData component in a band and use the Object Inspector to set up some properties, the QRSysData needs no further intervention from you. (The *Data property,* which has seven choices in its drop-down list, is probably the one you use most often.)

The QRSysData component's Data property has the following functional settings:

Setting	*Function*
qrsDate	Shows the current date in short format (for example, 5/20/97), depending on your Windows setting.
qrsDateTime	Provides both date and time in the same component.
qrsDetailCount	Provides a count of all the records that appear in a band, group, or report.
qrsDetailNo	Provides a number that increases as the report outputs the detail records (useful if you want a counter alongside each detail record).
qrsPageNumber	Prints out the current page number of the report.
qsReportTitle	Outputs the string from the QuickReport component's ReportTitle property wherever you place a QRSysData component with the Data property set to this type.
qrsTime	Outputs the time in a hh:mm:ss (hours, minutes, seconds) format onto the report when the Data property of the QRSysData component is at this setting.

If you want to include some text to identify a QRSysData component placed on a report, enter the text in the *Text* property using the Object Inspector. The text is then always used as a prefix to the actual field value, whether it's the current time, date, or whatever else you set the Data property to output.

Creating Groups with the QRGroup Components

What's the difference between a Band and a Group? Not much, if you're a talent scout for a record company, but on your Desktop, you don't want to get the two mixed up. In C++Builder terms, Groups are used in master-detail reports for adding headers and footers to groups of records. As this section shows you, Groups are implemented through Bands.

To find out what Groups have to offer, just place a Group component onto the master-detail form created in the previous section. To do that, click on the QRGroup button on the QReport page and then click anywhere on the form.

The QRGroup component has some interesting properties. A pair of those properties, *DataSource* and *DataField,* are used to link the QRGroup component with a field in a table. When the value of the field changes, the QRGroup component is aware of it through the DataField property setting. You can also place your own code into the event handlers that are triggered. The event handlers may, for example, provide subtotals, add spacing between elements, or show an image in a report.

The following steps add some automatic calculations grouped by vendor to the master-detail report constructed in the "Mastering Master-Detail Reports" earlier in this chapter.

1. **Select the QRGroup component dropped onto the master-detail example report form created earlier in this chapter and, using the Object Inspector, set the** DataSource **property to** dmVendorPart->dsVendor **and the** DataField **property to** VendorNo.

2. **Click on the QRBand component button on the QReport page and click below the part detail band (the one with the** bndPartDetail Name **property) on the master-detail report form to drop in a QRBand component.**

3. **Using the Object Inspector, set the** Name **property of the new QRBand component to** bndVendorGroupFooter **and the** BandType **property to** rbGroupFooter.

4. **To insert a border, click on the + button in the Object Inspector to expand the** Frame **property of the new QRBand component and set the** DrawBottom **subproperty to true.**

5. **Click on the QRGroup1 component and use the Object Inspector to select** bndVendorGroupFooter **from the** FooterBand **property's drop-down list.**

   The next step introduces the QRDBCalc component. The most important property of this component is the *Operation property,* which determines how a field is processed. The property offers five options: sum, average, maximum, minimum, and counting. You can build in an automatic calculation capability for any columns included in a report. You determine which column you want to process by designating it in the DataSource and DataField properties.

6. **Click on the QRDBCalc button on the QReport page, and then click on the group footer QRBand component added in Step 2 of the section "Turning the form into a working master-detail report" to drop in a QRDBCalc component.**

   Perform this step three times — the first time click below the "On Hand" column, the second time click below the "On Order" column, and the third time click below the "Cost" column.

7. **Using the Object Inspector, set the `ResetBand` property for all three QRDBCalc components to `bndVendorGroupFooter`.**

   This step assure that the automatically calculated group values are cleared each time one of these group bands is printed.

8. **While still in the Object Inspector, set the values of the properties for the three QRDBCalc components added in Step 6 to those shown in the following table (the components are identified by their labels):**

Property	Value
On Hand	
DataSource	dmVendorPart->dsPart
DataField	OnHand
Operation	qrcSUM
PrintMask	####0
On Order	
DataSource	dmVendorPart->dsPart
DataField	OnOrder
Operation	qrcSUM
PrintMask	####0
Cost	
DataSource	dmVendorPart->dsPart
DataField	Cost
Operation	qrcAVERAGE
PrintMask	"Average" ###,##0.00

9. **To sneak a peek at what the report is going to look like, right-click on the QuickReport component on the master-detail form to get the speed menu and choose the Preview Report option.**

The report should turn out looking like the one shown in Figure 11-4.

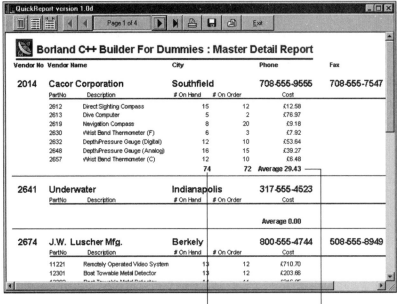

Figure 11-4:
Subtotals
added to a
master-
detail
report.

Subtotals   Group footer band

Chapter 12

On the Right Path: Using File and Folder Components

In This Chapter

▶ Placing file and folder components on a form

▶ Using the Drive property

▶ Integrating the Directory property

▶ Filtering files

▶ Displaying and navigating folders and files

*T*he components covered in this chapter have a common mission — to allow you to quickly get at controls needed to manage drives, folders, or files whenever and wherever you need them in your applications. By using the components introduced in this chapter, you can provide your programs with a standard interface for any task that requires the user to choose a file.

Using File Components

I like to call these components the "F-team" (the *F* can stand for *file* or *folder;* that's up to you). Each of the file components has properties that allow the team to stick together. When combined, each component plays its part to make your file-accessing plans happen.

The file components include the

✔ **FileListBox** — Provides a list box specifically for listing files.

✔ **DirectoryListBox** — Shows the folders for the currently selected drive.

✔ **DriveComboBox** — Displays all of the drives available to your computer.

✔ **FilterComboBox** — Allows you to apply filters to the files that are listed in the FileList Box.

The file components reside on the System page of the Component Palette (see Figure 12-1). As with the other components in the C++Builder palette, you can place them onto a form by clicking on any corresponding button and then clicking in the form at the location where you want the component.

Figure 12-1:
The F-Team: the C++Builder file component buttons on the Component Palette.

DriveComboBox

FileListBox

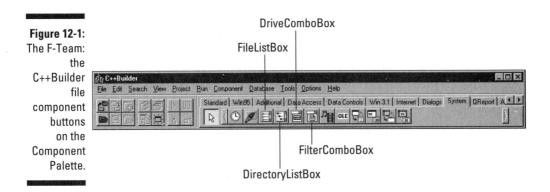

FilterComboBox

DirectoryListBox

The DriveComboBox component

The first step in selecting a file is figuring out which disk drive you have to access to find it. The following steps are designed to help you do that:

1. **Choose File⇨New Application from the main menu to create a new form for a new program.**

2. **Click on the DriveComboBox component button on the System page of the Component Palette and then click anywhere on the new form.**

3. **Press F9 to run the program.**

4. **Click on the downward-pointing arrow on the DriveComboBox component.**

   A list of drives available on your machine is displayed in the DriveComboBox's drop-down list (see Figure 12-2).

   If you are on a stand-alone machine, you more than likely have three drives — the A drive being your floppy-disk drive, C being your hard disk drive, and D being your CD-ROM drive. You can have quite a few more if you're connected to a network.

5. **Choose the desired drive from the drop-down list (refer to Figure 12-2).**

This looks all well and good, but there's not much doing yet. The DriveComboBox's *Drive property* changes that (it contains the letter of the drive that's chosen by the user). You won't find the Drive property in the Object Inspector; it's a run-time property only.

Figure 12-2 :
You can
select a
drive by
employing
the Drive-
ComboBox
component.

The Drive property enables you to determine from your program code which drive has been chosen from the DriveComboBox drop-down list. So it stands to reason that you use the Drive property when users are making selections from a DriveComboBox. The following line of code shows how you can access the Drive property:

```
ShowMessage("You selected drive " + String(DriveComboBox1-
            >Drive) ) ;
```

You can place your own code for the OnChange event handler of the DriveComboBox (accessed from the Events tab on the Object Inspector) to set values when the user selects another drive from the drop-down list.

Another property worth knowing about for the DriveComboBox component is the *TextCase property.* If you set the TextCase property to tcUpperCase, the drives are displayed in all uppercase letters.

The DirectoryListBox component

The previous section shows you how to select a drive from within a program; this section takes the next step to show you how to select a folder within a drive by using the DirectoryListBox component.

You can expect to use the DirectoryListBox component most often in conjunction with a DriveComboBox component. With that in mind, I designed the following steps to give you an example of how to link together a DirectoryListBox and a DriveComboBox in a program.

1. **Click on the DirectoryListBox component button on the System page of the Component Palette, and then click onto the form created in the previous section of this chapter.**

2. **Select the DriveComboBox component by clicking on it.**

3. **Using the Object Inspector, select** DirectoryListBox **from the drop-down list of the** DirList **property.**

   This action links together the DriveComboBox and the DirectoryListBox.

4. **Press F9 to see how the program built in the earlier steps is transformed.**

   Now you can click on all the folders for the drive that is currently selected in the DriveComboBox.

The DirectoryListBox is an important team player, and now you can see why: Select another drive (if you choose the A or CD-ROM drive, make sure that you have a disk or CD-ROM inserted into your computer or you get an error message). The DirectoryListBox follows the selection in the DriveComboBox by updating itself with the list of folders in the newly selected drive.

When you need to know which folder the user selected in a DirectoryListBox, use the *Directory property.* This is a run-time property, so you won't see it on the Properties tab on the Object Inspector; you need to access it in your program code.

The Directory property contains a string that holds the full directory path of the selected folder, so you don't have to worry about entering the drive letter.

The following steps show you how to integrate the Directory property into the example program described earlier in this chapter.

1. **Click on the Label button on the Standard page of the Component Palette, and then click anywhere on the form that's been built in the previous steps in this chapter.**

2. **Using the Object Inspector, select the DirectoryListBox component on the form by clicking on its name, and then select** Label **from the drop-down list in the** DirLabel **property.**

   The Label component is then loaded with the contents of the directory that's chosen in the DirectoryListBox.

3. **Press F9 to kick your program back to life.**

   The DriveComboBox and DirectoryListBox can be linked together so that the DirectoryListBox reflects the folder structure for the currently selected drive (see Figure 12-3).

Figure 12-3:
The
components
added to
this form
exhibit C++
teamwork.

When you set the Label's *AutoSize* property to false, if the path name doesn't fit within the Label, a middle portion of the pathname is substituted with an ellipsis (. . .).

The FileListBox component

After you've dealt with applications for choosing drives and folders, you can get down to the actual selection of files within those folders. This section introduces you to FileListBox, another component that's used in conjunction with the other F-team components. The FileListBox component shows users the list of files available within a selected folder.

The following steps can be used to incorporate a FileListBox component into the example program built in the previous steps of this chapter.

1. **Click on the FileListBox button on the System page, and then click anywhere on the form.**

2. **Click on the FileListBox on the form, and then drag it to position it directly below the DirectoryListBox component on the form.**

3. **Click on the DirectoryListBox component and using the Object Inspector select** `FileListBox` **from the drop-down list of the** `FileList` **property.**

The *FileList property* acts as the link for the "F-team" components. You now have a FileListBox powered by a DirectoryListBox that's controlled by a DriveComboBox.

To check out the *FileEdit property* of the FileListBox component, drop an EditBox component (from the Standard page) onto the form created in previous sections of this chapter. You find the EditBox ready to be selected in the FileEdit drop-down list on the Object Inspector. The FileEdit property lets you filter out the type of files you want to select.

The *FileName property* in the next example provides you with the full path of the file that's selected from the FileListBox component (it's a run-time property, by the way). This saves you from having to do lots of up-front work before your program can use the file that the user selects.

Filtering Files

The FilterComboBox component offers users a choice of file *filters*. (A filter lets users exclude any file types they're not interested in seeing listed in the FileListBox).

The following steps demonstrate how to add a FilterComboBox to the example program that has been developed in previous sections of this chapter.

1. **Click on the FilterComboBox button on the System page, and then click anywhere on the form to drop in a FilterComboBox component.**

2. **Using the Object Inspector, select** FileListBox **from the drop-down list in the FilterComboBox component** FileList **property.**

3. **Click on the ellipsis button in the** Filter **property on the Object Inspector.**

   Now you've put the Filter property into service — the most important FilterComboBox property. You can enter a list of file types and you can restrict the view to these file types shown in the FileListBox.

4. **Enter a brief description of the Filter name in the left column of the Filter Editor (as shown in Figure 12-4).**

5. **In the right column of the Filter Editor, enter the wildcard that you want to apply (see the sidebar on wildcards later on in this chapter).**

6. **Click on OK to close the Filter Editor.**

Figure 12-4:
Use the
Filter Editor
to set up
filters.

Filter Name	Filter
All files (*.*)	*.*
Text Files	*.txt
Incremental Link Files	*.il?

Once you've been introduced to the idea of filtering, you can more fully integrate the EditBox component into your programs. The following steps allow the user to employ the EditBox to add their own file filters at run time. (In this example, I'm sticking with the sample form that's been developed throughout earlier sections of this chapter.)

1. **Select the EditBox component in the form by clicking on it.**

2. **In the Events tab of the Object Inspector, double-click on the empty field next to the OnExit event handler.**

   This puts you into the Code Editor, where you enter the following lines of code:

   ```
   FileListBox1->Mask = Edit1->Text ;
   FileListBox1->Invalidate() ;
   ```

   This action loads the FileListBox with the contents of the EditBox whenever the user leaves the EditBox while using the program.

   You can now enter a file filter at run time. The filter is applied whenever you enter any file details into the EditBox while using the program and then move to another component on the form.

3. **Press F9 to run the program.**

You now have a whole load of functionality in a small area of form real estate. Your program should look something like the form called "The F Team" shown in Figure 12-5.

Play around with this application to get the feel of how it works. Notice that as you select filters from the FilterComboBox the FileEdit changes, too.

Figure 12-5:
Multiple
functions
can be
packed into
a compact
form.

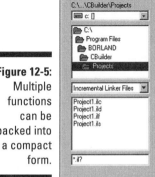

Dealing wildcards

A *wildcard* is not the King of Diamonds in a rage over catching the Jack of Hearts with the Queen. It's a term used describe a method of filtering out a group of files according to selected criteria.

Consider the example program found in the "Filtering Files" section earlier in this chapter. When the FileListBox initially has the EditBox hooked to it, the EditBox contains the string *.*. This string is a *universal wildcard.* The asterisks on either side of the period refer to any characters that could be entered in their place. The period between the two asterisks serves the same purpose as the period between any other filename and extension.

If you use the wildcard ***.cpp,** you're going to get a list of every C++ source file that has a .cpp file extension. If you use the wildcard ***.?pp,** you are including every file with an .hpp extension as well as any file with a .cpp extension.

The question mark in a wildcard substitutes for any single character. You can use the * and ? characters as stand-ins for other characters, as you would a joker in card games. In the example programs in this chapter, the files that match the filter (or wildcard) are the only files that are visible and that can be chosen from the FileListBox component.

Chapter 13

It's in Your System: Using System Components

- -

In This Chapter

▶ Building timed applications using the Timer component

▶ Embedding and linking files with the OLEContainer component

▶ Adding sound and video with the MediaPlayer component

- -

*I*n the coming pages of this chapter, I delve into the deep, dark secrets of applications that are timed to run themselves in the middle of the night, applications that link files created in separate applications, and techniques for adding video and sound to your otherwise still and silent programs.

The components used to manufacture the sample applications in this chapter are all located on the System page of the Component Palette. They're nonvisual components, which means you see them at design time, but your users won't see them when the programs are run. For the example programs in this chapter, I picked out the System components that I have found to have the most impact in my development.

Because these components are nonvisual, exactly where you drop them into the form doesn't really matter because the component works *behind* the scenes at runtime.

Making Applications Tell Time with the Timer Component

Wouldn't it be nice if you could get your PC to wake you up in the morning or tell you when an egg is done cooking? If that sounds just too frivolous, how about if you could arrange for office systems to perform housekeeping tasks when no one is around. (Who wants to hang out at the office until midnight to start a backup routine or run out daily reports?) These automatic operations, whether silly or serious, can all be accomplished by means of the Timer component.

To find out what makes the Timer component tick, you have to put it to use. In the following example, the Timer component is used to create a digital clock and to animate objects on a form.

1. **Choose File⇨New Application from the main menu to open a blank form in a new application.**

2. **Click on the Timer component button on the System page of the Component Palette, and then click anywhere on the form to place a new Timer component onto the form.**

   Use the *Interval property* of the Timer component to state how often you want the OnTimer event to be triggered (enter the code you want the Timer component to execute in the `OnTimer` event handler of the Object Inspector). The default value for the Interval property is 1,000 milliseconds; that means that the OnTimer event is triggered once a second.

   The smaller the value you place in the Interval property, the more frequently the `OnTimer` event executes. If you set the Interval property value too low, it can make your program appear sluggish to the user. That's because the program spends a major part of its time running the `OnTimer` event code.

3. **Using the Object Inspector, set the value in the `Interval` property to 500 (just for purposes of this example) to trigger the event twice a second.**

4. **Click on the Shape component button on the Additional page of the Component Palette, and then click anywhere on the form to place a new Shape component onto the form. Then repeat this step once.**

5. **Using the Object Inspector, set the Shape component's `Shape` property to `stCircle`.**

   You can also make the Shapes component different colors by using the `Color` subproperty of the `Brush` and `Pen` properties (expand the Brush and Pen properties by clicking on the + button in the Object Inspector).

6. **Click on the Timer component that was dropped in the form in Step 2.**

7. **Click on the Events tab of the Object Inspector and then double-click on the empty field next to the `OnTimer` event handler.**

   You're then in the Code Editor, where you enter the following lines:

```
Label1->Caption = Now().TimeString() ;
if (Shape1->Visible)
    {
Shape1->Visible = False ;
Shape2->Visible = True ;
}
 else
    {
Shape1->Visible = True ;
Shape2->Visible = False ;
}
```

8. Press F9 to run the program.

You should see that you created a digital clock (as shown in Figure 13-1) with the added bonus of a flashing light (trust me, in real life that black dot is mesmerizing).

Figure 13-1:
Digital
clocks are
easy to
program
with the
Timer
component.

Embedding and Linking Objects Using the OLE Component

The OLEContainer component allows you to link or embed *OLE objects* into your applications. OLE stands for *Object Linking and Embedding,* an activity carried out in Windows. OLE allows you to insert a document or part of a document (termed an OLE object) created by one application inside a document created by another application and maintain a live link between the two. For example, you can store a report and a graph in the same file (known as *embedding*) or in separate files (that's *linking*).

Although OLE makes it easy for programs to share files, many developers avoid OLE coding for the sake of their sanity. Fortunately, the OLEContainer component makes your life much simpler by protecting you from the complexities of OLE programming by already having done much of the work for you.

Building a basic OLE program

Use the following example set of steps to build a program that employs an OLEContainer component.

1. **Choose File⇨New Application for a new form in a new application.**

2. **Click on the OLEContainer button on the System page of the Component Palette, and then set the component's** Align **property to** alClient **using the drop-down list in the Object Inspector.**

   The component expands to fill the whole form.

3. **Click on the MainMenu button on the Standard page and then click anywhere on the form to drop a MainMenu component onto the form.**

4. **Right-click on the MainMenu component to get the speed menu, and select the Menu Designer option.**

   This gives you a Menu Designer form with a caption of Form1->MainMenu1.

5. **Type** &File **to get into the Caption property of the Object Inspector automatically and press Enter; then click on the new submenu item, type in** E&xit, **and press Enter.**

   Two menu items are now added to the MainMenu component (the & character in front of a menu item letter adds an underline to that character to make it a "hot key").

6. **Double-click on the Exit menu item on the Menu Designer form to get into the Code Editor; then enter the following line in the menu item's event handler:**

```
Close() ;
```

7. **Click on the dotted square next to the "File" menu item added to the Menu Designer in Step 5.**

8. **Type the text** &OLE **and C++Builder takes you automatically to the** Caption **property of the Object Inspector; then press Enter.**

   A second top-level menu item called "OLE" is added to the main menu.

9. **Add four subitems to the "OLE" menu item in the Menu Designer by typing the following text into the** Caption **property of the Object Inspector, and then pressing Enter after entering each of the four items:** Insert &Object, Object &Properties, Paste &Special, **and** Change &Icon.

10. **From the Menu Designer, double-click on the "Insert Object" menu item to get into the Code Editor, where you enter the following line:**

```
OleContainer1->InsertObjectDialog() ;
```

11. **Double-click on the "Object Properties" menu item and enter the following line of code:**

```
OleContainer1->ObjectPropertiesDialog() ;
```

12. **Double-click on the "Paste Special" menu item and enter the following line of code:**

```
OleContainer1->PasteSpecialDialog() ;
```

13. **Double-click on the "Change Icon" menu item and enter the following line of code:**

```
OleContainer1->ChangeIconDialog() ;
```

14. **Press F9 to run the program.**

In these few steps you can create a surprisingly versatile program. OLE is very high-end feature in Windows that's mostly suited to advanced development. You can develop really cool applications with OLE, such as applications that run other applications and applications that talk to other applications on different computers.

Adding to the basic program

To put the example program built in the previous section through its paces, continue on with that program by performing the following steps:

1. **Choose OLE⇨Insert Object from the main menu of the example program.**

   The dialog box shown in Figure 13-2 appears. You can scroll through a list of numerous OLE object types in the Object Type list box.

2. **Click on** `Bitmap Image` **in the Object Type list box.**

3. **Click on OK.**

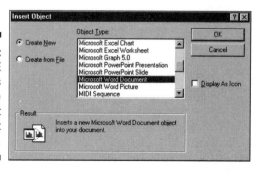

Figure 13-2: Choose OLE object types from the Insert Object dialog box.

4. **Double-click on any part of the OLEContainer object on the form built in the steps in the previous section of this chapter.**

   The simple menu created in the steps in the previous section expands to include another five top-level items, and the color palette, tool palette, and status bar appear. This functionality is all associated with the application — with no code required. If you're feeling arty, you can use your mouse to sketch out a graphical masterpiece inside the OLEContainer component.

5. **To see how truly fab the OLEContainer component really is, choose OLE➪Insert Object again to get the Insert Object dialog box.**

6. **Select an Object Type other than Bitmap Image from the Object Type list.**

   This time, you may choose a spreadsheet or word-processor object instead of the Bitmap Image.

7. **Click on OK.**

8. **Double-click on the OLEContainer object again.**

   Your application adjusts to show the new type of object. The toolbars and menu options change to reflect the object type you've chosen.

You can see that this simple example program can be changed with a few mouse clicks from a drawing package to a fully functioning word processor. All of this was accomplished by using the single line of code placed into the "Insert Object" menu item in Step 9 of the previous section of this chapter.

To check out the properties of the OLEContainer object, choose OLE➪Object Properties from the main menu of the example program. You get the dialog box shown in Figure 13-3 (for this example it's titled "Bitmap Image Properties"). This dialog box provides the details of the current type of OLE object for the OLEContainer; therefore, its title and contents change with the object type.

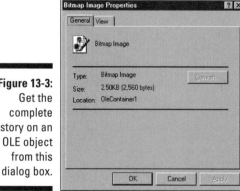

Figure 13-3:
Get the complete story on an OLE object from this dialog box.

The Change Icon option

The Change Icon option, found in the main menu of the example programs built in earlier sections of this chapter, lets you change the icon that represents the OLE object type. This comes into play when you opt for displaying the OLE object as an icon rather than in an editable format. This can be done by clicking the Display As Icon check box in the Insert Object dialog box (refer to Figure 13-2). If you opt to display the OLE object as an icon, that's exactly what you see.

The following steps extend the example program built in the previous section of this chapter — the program displays an error message if the user attempts to select the Change Icon menu option before assigning an OLE object type to the OLEContainer component.

1. **Using the Menu Designer for the Menu1 component (by right-clicking on the component and selecting Menu Designer from the speed menu that appears), select the Change Icon option from the example program's main menu OLE.**

   This step takes you to that menu item Change Icon OnClick event handler.

2. **Change the event handler code to the following:**

   ```
   if (OleContainer1->State!= osEmpty)
     OleContainer1->ChangeIconDialog() ;
   else
     ShowMessage("Please select an object type") ;
   ```

The *State property* has been incorporated into this changed code. Now you can find out what's going on with an OLE object just by checking the State property. Performing a simple check can save you from making function calls that are destined to fail!

The Paste Special option

The Paste Special option goes to work when you have data from another application stashed in the C++Builder Clipboard and want to place it in your OLE object.

To see how this works, continue on with the example program built in the previous sections of this chapter, and then run through the following steps:

1. **Open the Paint application that comes with Windows 95 by choosing Start➪Programs➪Accessories➪Paint from the Windows 95 taskbar.**

2. **Create your own graphic using Paint — feel free to draw whatever comes to mind.**

3. **Choose Edit⇨Select All from the Windows 95 main menu.**

4. **Press Ctrl+C.**

   This places your masterpiece in the Windows 95 Clipboard.

5. **After executing the OLEContainer example application built in the previous section, choose OLE⇨Paste Special from the application's main menu.**

   You should see the Paste Special dialog box, shown in Figure 13-4.

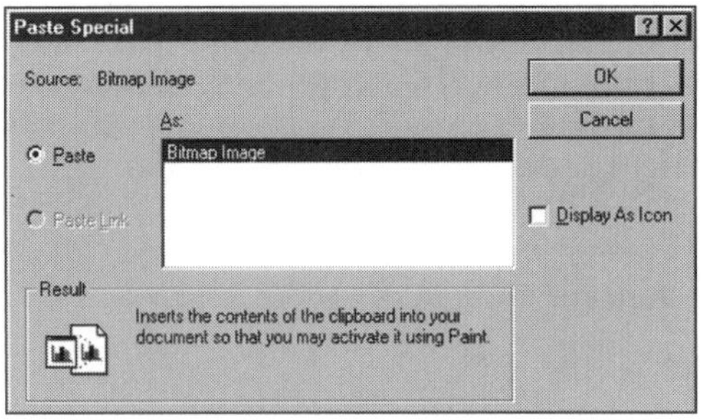

Figure 13-4:
You can choose how you want to paste an object into an OLEContainer component with the Paste Special dialog box.

6. **Click on OK.**

   The contents of the Clipboard are placed in the OLE container. You don't even need to choose the appropriate OLE Object type from the Insert Object dialog box (you can now see how the Paste Special option works). The line of code added to the event handler in Step 12 of the "Building a basic OLE program" section earlier in this chapter takes care of handling the object type for you.

7. **Double-click the OLEContainer component that was added in the section "Building a basic OLE program" earlier in this chapter.**

   Your application magically transforms into its very own Paint-type application and displays the graphic that you created using the Paint application in Steps 1 and 2 of this sequence. You can continue working on your masterpiece from within the OLEContainer component example program, as shown in Figure 13-5.

Figure 13-5:
You can change an OLE application (such as adding the Paint program shown here) at any point during runtime.

Curing the component disappearing act

A common problem plagues programmers using OLE objects in real-life programs. When a user activates an OLEContainer component, the other components in the program can disappear from view. The following steps extend the OLEContainer component examples set up in the "Embedding and Linking Objects Using the OLE Component" section in this chapter.

First I demonstrate how components disappear; then I tell you how to avoid this problem.

1. **Choose OLE⇨Insert Object from the main menu of the example program to get the Insert Object dialog box.**

2. **Select an Object type from the Object Type list (for this example, I chose Bitmap Image) and then click on OK.**

3. **Double-click on the OLEContainer component.**

   The speed bar that you placed into the application in the previous section disappears out of sight as the OLE object is activated!

4. **Select File⇨Exit from the main menu to shut down the program.**

Now you want to make sure that the speed bar remains visible at all times while the program runs. Follow these modifications to the example OLEContainer program built in this chapter.

1. **Click on the Panel component dropped in the form created in the section "Adding a speed bar."**

2. **Using the Object Inspector, set the** Locked **property of the Panel component to** true.

3. **Press F9 to run the example program again.**

4. **Choose OLE⇨Insert Object from the main menu of the example program to show the Insert Object dialog box.**

5. **Select an Object type from the Object Type list (for this example, I chose** Bitmap Image**) and click on OK.**

6. **Double-click on the OLEContainer component on the form.**

Now, with the Locked property set to true, the speed bar stays put when the OLEContainer component is double-clicked (Figure 13-6 illustrates this action).

Adding a speed bar

You can place a Panel component at the top of the form built throughout the "Embedding and Linking Objects Using the OLE Component" section to act as a handy roost for an application's speed buttons. Just follow these steps:

1. **Continuing with OLEContainer application built throughout the previous sections of this chapter, set the** Align **property of the OLEContainer component to** alBottom **using the Object Inspector.**

2. **Click on the top edge of the OLEContainer component and drag it down just enough so that you can see some of the form's background.**

3. **Click on the Panel button on the Standard page and then click on the background section of the form uncovered in Step 2.**

4. **Using the Object Inspector, set the** Align **property of the Panel component to** alTop.

   The Panel is going to act as a SpeedBar for the program.

5. **Click on the SpeedButton Component button on the Additional page, and then click on the Panel component added in Step 3.**

   Repeat this step five times to place a row of six SpeedButton components along the Panel to give it the appearance of a speed bar.

6. **To fill any gap between the Panel component and the OLEContainer component, use the Object Inspector to set the** Align **property of the OLEContainer component back to** alClient.

7. **Press F9 to run the program.**

   The end result should look something like Figure 13-6.

Panel component with Locked property set to true

Figure 13-6: You can keep your SpeedButton components in one handy place by building a speed bar.

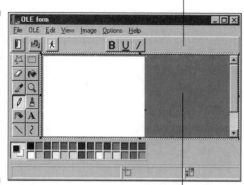

Activated OLEContainer component

Grabbing an OLEContainer component from a disk

Use these steps to load an OLE object from a file on disk into an OLEContainer component. (Just continue on with the example program developed throughout the "Embedding and Linking Objects Using the OLE Component" section of this chapter.)

1. **Right-click on the OLEContainer component to show the SpeedMenu.**

2. **Choose the Insert Object option from the SpeedMenu to show the Insert Object dialog box.**

3. **Click on the Create from File button on the dialog box.**

   This step allows you to select a file to load from disk. This step also changes the Dialog box by adding a Browse button and other options such as a Link check box and file path box.

4. **Click on the Browse button to show the Browse dialog box and then select a file to load.**

(I chose a Bitmap (.bmp) file from the cbuilder\images\icons folder for this example.)

5. **Click on Insert to close the Browse dialog box.**

6. **Click on the Link check box in the Insert Object dialog box.**

   Linking the file to the OLEContainer can save on memory resources. Otherwise, the contents of the bitmap file would be embedded inside the program no matter how large the file. This increases the size of the executable file generated by C++Builder, which really slows things down.

7. **Click on OK to close the Insert Object dialog box.**

You can see that the graphic you choose is displayed in the OLEContainer component on the form.

To embed or to link? OLE!

If you embed OLE objects into your application at design time (by *not* clicking on the Link check box in the Insert Object dialog box), a copy of the OLE object's data is added to the application, and the program's executable file then contains all the data for the OLE object. A simple program file can become very large, very quickly.

By linking instead of embedding, a pointer is created telling the client application which file to use; the data itself stays in the external file. That way, the program file isn't burdened with OLE object data. But remember to keep a copy of the linked file in the location stated when the file was linked into the program; otherwise, C++Builder won't know where to find it.

Seeing (And Hearing) Is Believing: Using the MediaPlayer Component

Multimedia applications add moving images and sounds to your programs. As a developer, you're probably itching to make your programs a super-sensory experience.

You probably first need to know a few things about multimedia files. Sound and video files are held on your PC's hard disk just like text or graphic files. These files have their own extensions and can consume large amounts of file space. A short video clip alone requires a significant amount of data.

With C++Builder, you don't have to run through a complicated maze of programming steps to juice up your programs with multimedia; you just need to drop the right kind of component onto a form and set a few properties.

To place a MediaPlayer component onto a form and get a good look at its properties, use the following steps:

1. **Choose File⇨New Application to create a blank form in a new application.**

2. **Click on the MediaPlayer button on the System page and then click anywhere on the form to drop a MediaPlayer component onto the form.**

   The MediaPlayer component appears on your form, as shown in Figure 13-7.

Figure 13-7:
The
MediaPlayer
component
is the easy
way to get
your
applications
dancing
and
swinging.

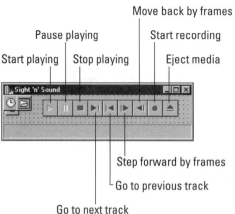

Move back by frames

Pause playing

Start recording

Start playing   Stop playing   Eject media

Step forward by frames

Go to previous track

Go to next track

The MediaPlayer component features three Auto properties:

✔ When the *AutoEnable property* is set to true, the component has logic built in to tell the component how to set its buttons according to the component's runtime status. In general, opt for the default setting of true.

✔ The *AutoOpen property* indicates whether the media file opens automatically at runtime or whether you have to open the media file yourself.

✔ If you set the *AutoRewind property* to true, the multimedia file always starts from the beginning of the file when its play or record option is selected. If it isn't set to true, the user must click on the component's "Prev" button to rewind it to the start before playing or recording.

The *DeviceType property* determines which type of multimedia file you want the component to control. If the DeviceType is set to dtAutoSelect (the default setting), the extension of the file that is specified in the MediaPlayer component's *FileName property* (.wav for a sound file, .avi for a video file) determines how the MediaPlayer component presents the file to the user.

If you're using a multimedia file for screen display, the MediaPlayer component can be associated with another component that can act as a projection "screen." Panel components, for example, make ideal C++Builder projection screens for video and animation files (you associate them with the MediaPlayer through the *Display property*).

The MediaPlayer component's *EnabledButtons*, *ColoredButtons,* and *VisibleButtons* properties (accessed from the Object Inspector) each offer the same set of nine buttons for a MediaPlayer component. The VisibleButtons property determines whether a certain MediaPlayer button is displayed or not. If a button is set to false in the EnabledButtons property, that button is deactivated and appears grayed out on the screen. If you set the ColoredButtons property to false for a particular MediaPlayer button, the button shows up only in black. (You can see the false settings make for a dull-looking component.)

The *FileName property* is arguably the most important property for this component. This holds the full path of the file that's going to be played.

Sounding good — adding sound to a program

This section shows you how the MediaPlayer component can introduce sound into your programs. Go ahead and create an example program of your own:

1. **Use Steps 1 and 2 in the previous section to place a MediaPlayer component onto a new form.**

2. **Using the Object Inspector, set the properties of the MediaPlayer component on the form to the following values:**

Property	Value
AutoOpen	true
DeviceType	dtWaveAudio
VisibleButtons.btStep	false
VisibleButtons.btBack	false

3. **Using the Object Inspector, click on the ellipsis (. . .) button inside the FileName property setting of the MediaPlayer component.**

   You get the Open dialog box.

4. **Select Wave Files on the Files of Type drop down-list.**

   If you are not sure where to look for a sound file, try the Windows folder or the Windows\Media folder. This saves you from having to hunt through a number of irrelevant files.

5. **Select a .wav file to play in this example program.**

6. **Click on the ProgressBar button on the Win95 page of the Component Palette, and then click in the middle of the form to drop in a ProgressBar component.**

7. **Click on the Timer button on the System page and then click anywhere on the form to drop in a Time component.**

8. **Click on the ProgressBar component and use the Object Inspector to set the Align property to alBottom.**

9. **Click on the Timer component and use the Object Inspector to set the Interval property to 100.**

10. **Click on the Events tab of the Object Inspector and then double-click on the empty field next to the OnTimer event handler.**

    You end up in the Code Editor, where you enter the following:

    ```
    ProgressBar1->Position = MediaPlayer1->Position ;
    ```

11. **Click on the background of the form that you're currently constructing.**

12. **Click on the Events tab of the Object Inspector, and then double-click on the empty** `OnCreate` **event-handler name field and then enter the following two lines in the Code Editor:**

```
ProgressBar1->Position = 0 ;
ProgressBar1->Max = MediaPlayer1->Length ;
```

13. **Press F9 to run the program.**

    You should see a form similar to the one shown in Figure 13-8 titled "Sight 'n' Sound." Click on the Play button (refer to Figure 13-7) and the sound file that you selected in the FileName property earlier emanates from your computer's speakers.

Figure 13-8:
Ready to
play:
MediaPlayer
component
for sound.

And, looking good, too — including video in a program

The previous section covers the aural side of MediaPlayer; now it's time for some visual treats. You can easily extend the sound program created in the previous section to convert it to a video screen. Build on Steps 1–13 in the previous section, continuing with the following steps:

1. **Click into the bottom right-hand side of the MediaPlayer program form and drag out to enlarge the form to allow for another Panel component.**

2. **Click on the Panel button on the Standard and then click into the lower part of the form to drop in a new Panel component.**

3. **Using the Object Inspector, set the** `Align` **property of the new Panel component to** `alBottom` **and remove the text from its** `Caption` **property.**

    Now turn your attention to the MediaPlayer component; you need to change a couple of property values.

4. **Click on the MediaPlayer component, and then using the Object Inspector change the** `DeviceType` **property to** `dtAVIVideo`.

5. **Select the new Panel from the Display property drop-down list in the Object Inspector.**

   The Panel component is going to act as the projection screen for the video file.

6. **Click on the ellipsis button in the** `FileName` **property value on the Object Inspector.**

   The Open dialog box appears.

7. **Select the Video for Windows option from the Files of type list box, then select a video file to view in the example program.**

8. **Press F9 to run the program.**

9. **Click on the MediaPlayer component's Play button (refer to Figure 13-8).**

   Now you have your own movie show. Figure 13-9 shows the viewing screen and a still image from a sample video file.

Video image being played on Panel component

Figure 13-9:
Adding
video to a
program
takes just a
few more
steps than
adding
sound.

Part IV
Advanced C++Builder Development

In this part . . .

All this visual programming stuff really rocks, but don't forget you have an industrial-strength C++ compiler working behind the scenes. This section shows you how C++Builder provides you with a code frame-work from which to launch your applications. You see first-hand the C++ language syntax and the code constructs you can use to add hidden mega-strength to your programs.

C++Builder also helps you with some custodial chores. To rid your building of any pests, there's a whole chapter on the integrated debugging capabilities of C++Builder. And, because no one's perfect (not even your end users), Chapter 18 covers exception handling to error-proof your programs.

Chapter 14

Setting Up Project Files

. . . .

In This Chapter

▶ Handling an event handler

▶ Checking out unit code

▶ Examining source code

▶ Changing a name property

▶ Using `include` statements to include code from another file

. . . .

Some developers out there may be happy to lope along with C++Builder, not caring too much about what's happening behind the scenes. But they're missing out on some valuable insights on not just C++Builder, but also how the C++ language works. (I will say, if you're one of those non-inquisitive types, you'd better unhand this book right now!) By delving into the nitty-gritty of exactly how C++Builder projects are constructed you can get the most out of your development work (I promise).

This chapter takes a close look at the contents of the files that C++Builder produces when you create a new application and shows you how those files relate to what's actually happening in your programs. You can also see how C++Builder applications are constructed, how program files work interdependently, and what you can and can't change yourself in the files.

Identifying Parts of a Project

When you choose File⇨New Application in C++Builder, what actually happens? C++Builder goes off to create a framework or skeleton of a project that becomes your new program. Before you can even scoot your mouse across the main form of a new application, C++Builder is already busy creating the basics of a Windows application for you automatically. I cover those basics — the form, the source code, the header file, and the source file — as well as the C++Builder project files in this section.

When you choose the New Application menu item from the C++Builder main menu, a new project with a blank main form called "Form1" (the default name for the new form that C++Builder opens for you) stands ready for components to be dropped into it.

If you choose View⇨Toggle Form/Unit, or Press F12, you switch to the Code Editor and can view the contents of the Unit1.cpp file that is associated with Form1.

Getting a handle on event handlers: checking out the Unit1.cpp file

The Unit1.cpp file holds the *event handlers* and other helper functions for your form. Event handlers are special functions that perform useful actions when something happens in a program (for example, when a user clicks on a button).

Here's how the code for the Unit1.cpp file looks as soon as C++Builder creates it for you (I added line numbers to the following code sample to make it easier to follow):

```
1 //----------------------------------------
2 #include <vcl\vcl.h>
3 #pragma hdrstop
4
5 #include "Unit1.h"
6 //----------------------------------------
7 #pragma resource "*.dfm"
8 TForm1 *Form1;
9 //----------------------------------------
10 __fastcall TForm1::TForm1(TComponent* Owner)
11 : TForm(Owner)
12 {
13 }
14 //----------------------------------------
```

This is most of what's going on in the preceding code example (I just touch on the "business end" of the code):

Line 2 — The #include statement is roughly equivalent to your pasting entire files of code at the top of the file (see the "Including #include statements" section later in this chapter). The file vcl.h gives you access to the most commonly used Visual Component Library (VCL) header files.

Line 3 — This contains a *pragma statement* (a compiler directive that performs useful or time-saving tasks for you). This statement marks the end of the list of header files that should be included in the precompiled header file. (A *header file* is a special file that contains declarations of functions and global variables the program requires.)

C++Builder uses the technique of precompiled headers to store header files in an already-processed format. This cuts down on the time that you have to spend waiting for C++Builder to compile and link your programs. (Not all headers are precompiled to save you some disk space.) If the header file is included after the #pragma hdrstop statement, then this file won't be included in the already-processed format and C++Builder takes longer to compile and link your program.

If you won't be making many changes to the header file, include the header file before the #pragma hdrstop statement to speed up the compiling and linking.

Line 5 — This line refers to the header file that acts as the partner to the source file in this example. In C++Builder it takes two source files to hold a form's component details and its event handlers (*source files* contain the main parts of your program). These two files are collectively referred to as the form's *unit source files.*

Line 7 — Here's another pragma statement. It includes the form resources and also states that the source file requires a corresponding form layout file. (A *form layout file* holds the details concerning how and where components have been placed onto a form. It is identified by a .dfm file extension.)

Line 8 — A variable of type TForm1 is declared here. This variable belongs to the new form type (you create a new form type every time you open a new form in C++Builder). For a new application, this variable goes by the default name of Form1.

Line 10 and 11 — The constructor for the form starts here. You place any initialization code that you need for your form in this ready-made function. The initialization code includes the variables that you declare and initialize when the variable is first used.

Examples in previous chapters of this book (such as in Chapters 5–7) show how the source unit file for a form grows as each event handler (which increases functionality) is tagged onto the end of the file.

Crawling inside C++Builder header files

This section focuses on the C++Builder form header file (identified by the .h file name extension) and what C++Builder creates and maintains for you in this file. I also explain how and where you can add your own lines of code to this file.

To check out a form's header file, follow these steps:

1. **Select the form by choosing View⇨Toggle Form/Unit.**

2. **If you are not currently in the Code Editor press F12 to go to the form's unit source file.**

3. **Press Ctrl+F6 to go into header file.**

   You can see the header file open in the Code Editor.

I have taken a copy of the default header file for the blank form (it has no components on it) that is created when C++Builder starts off a new application. By default, this file is named Unit1.h, which is detailed in the code section that follows. (I numbered the lines to reference them.)

```
1  //--------------------------------------------
2  #ifndef Unit1H
3  #define Unit1H
4  //--------------------------------------------
5  #include <vcl\Classes.hpp>
6  #include <vcl\Controls.hpp>
7  #include <vcl\StdCtrls.hpp>
8  #include <vcl\Forms.hpp>
9  //--------------------------------------------
10 class TForm1 : public TForm
11 {
12 __published: // IDE-managed Components
13 private:      // User declarations
14 public:       // User declarations
15 __fastcall TForm1(TComponent* Owner);
16 };
17 //--------------------------------------------
18 extern TForm1 *Form1;
19 //--------------------------------------------
20 #endif
```

Here's a line-by-line account of what this file is doing:

Lines 2 and 3 — These lines prevent the file from being included in the program more than once. It works as a form of protection, so even if the file is placed in many #include statements throughout a program, the actual contents of the file are only used once. (Repeated declarations of a global variable that has already been defined in a header file would cause redefinition errors on that global variable when you go to compile the program.)

The code in Lines 2 and 3 work on the principle that if the word Unit1H has already been defined, then this file has been used elsewhere in the program and, as such, none of the code between Lines 3 and 20 are needed again. If the definition of the word Unit1H has not yet been made, then #define Unit1H in Line 3 makes the definition (to prevent further redefinitions). The rest of the file is used as normal.

Line 5 — The inclusion of the Classes.hpp file provides some of the basic utility C++Builder class declarations.

Line 6 — The Controls.hpp file enables the program to access the C++Builder Visual Component Library.

Line 7 — The StdCtrls.hpp file has been included so that Standard form component declarations (TEdit, TCheckBox, and so on) can be accessed by the program.

Line 8 — The include statement for the Forms.hpp file tells the form what type it is.

A form is basically just another object at your disposal within C++Builder. Watch out for other program-level classes (such as Application and Screen) in the Forms.hpp file.

Lines 10–16 — The form's *declaration* (the code that tells the compiler what's in the form's structure) is found in these lines. Line 10 tells you that this form is type TForm1 and inherits from a TForm. (The TForm is the basic type of form from which all others spring in C++Builder.)

Lines 12 and 13 — As you build up a form by dropping components onto it, the components become *members* of your form. They are placed inside the form's declaration and are referenced as form variables. C++Builder places the references to these between Lines 12 and 13. If you drop some controls into the form, and go back to the form's header file, you see extra lines added in this section of the form declaration.

Lines 13 and 14 — These lines are *class section headers*. Here you place any extra variables and function declarations that you want to manually add to the form yourself.

Line 15 — Here you find the *constructor declaration*. (*Constructors* are routines that are automatically called when you create an object.) You need access to the constructor declaration from functions that are not actually part of the form. Any *private declarations* that you make can be referenced only from within member functions of the form. A class is not so secretive about its *public declarations;* public data members and functions are available to the rest of your application. (See Chapter 16 for more on classes.)

Even though you define the functions themselves in the unit source file (with the `.cpp` file extension), you need to declare the way that you want the rest of the application to view or access those functions. You can do this by placing an entry in the form's header file that states the name of the function, the return type, and the name and type of arguments that it takes, if any. Assume, for example, that you need to add a function of your own to a file that added two numbers. It would look like this:

```
int TForm1::AddNumber(int Number1, int Number2)
{
return(Number1 + Number2) ;
}
```

In the form declaration in the header file, you need to place a line, such as the following one, in either the private or public section to declare the function as a *member* of the form.

```
int AddNumber(int Number1, int Number2) ;
```

Understanding the Project Source file

In this section, you get a up-close-and-personal visit with the project's main source file — plus some insight on what makes it tick.

To gain access to the project's main source file, Choose <u>V</u>iew⇨Project <u>S</u>ource from the main menu.

You can see part of the "nerve center" in a C++Builder project in a file called Project1.cpp (this is the default C++Builder name for a newly created project).

You seldom need to access this file directly; maintaining this file is in C++Builder's territory. C++Builder makes changes to this file for you as you change options within its menu selections, such as the Options⇨Project menu selection. When you change Auto-Create Forms within the Forms tab, C++Builder modifies the project main source file accordingly.

To let you in on the secret life of the project's main source file (this almost sounds exciting!), the code to come for the source file is followed by a line-by-line description of its significance. (In this example, the project has just been created and the default names still apply. I numbered the lines to make code explanations easier to follow.)

```
1 //--------------------------------------------
2
3 #include <vcl\vcl.h>
4 #pragma hdrstop
5 //--------------------------------------------
6 USEFORM("Unit1.cpp", Form1);
7 USERES("Project1.res");
8 //--------------------------------------------
9 WINAPI WinMain(HINSTANCE, HINSTANCE, LPSTR, int)
10 {
11 try
12 {
13    Application->Initialize();
14    Application->CreateForm(__classid(TForm1), &Form1);
15    Application->Run();
16 }
17 catch (Exception &exception)
18 {
19    Application->ShowException(&exception);
20 }
21 return 0;
22 }
23 //--------------------------------------------
```

Line 3 — The #include statement is roughly equivalent to your pasting entire files of code at the top of the file (see the "Including #include Statements" section later in this chapter). The file vcl.h gives you access to most commonly used Visual Component Library (VCL) header files.

Line 4 — This line contains a *pragma statement,* which marks the end of the list of headers that should be included in the precompiled header files. (See Line 3 in the first code example in this chapter for more information on precompiled header files.)

Lines 6 and 7 — These lines contain two *macro calls,* which add form resources and units to your project. As the number of forms in your application increases, so does the number of lines in this set of lines.

Lines 9–22 — Here you find what's called the *application entry point.* This is the "boss" function of the program, which means it's always the first function to be executed when the application starts. In this example, the function is called `WinMain`.

Lines 11–17 — These lines contain the exception error control. (See Chapter 18 for more on this subject.)

Lines 13–15 — The program's "starting whistle" is actually sounded in these lines. First, the Application object is initialized, and then the application's main form (`Form1`, in this case) is created. When the main form has been created, the Application object itself runs.

Changing Name Properties

When you change the Name property of a form from the Object Inspector (see Chapter 1 for information on the Object Inspector), C++Builder automatically changes the references to the form. Always use the Object Inspector, as shown in Figure 14-1, to change Name properties — don't attempt to make the changes on your own. You may bite off more than you can chew if you try to amend the form's name inside code. The Object Inspector is far faster at replacing the necessary references than you can ever be!

Figure 14-1:
Always use
the Object
Inspector to
rename
forms —
unless you
enjoy
spending
countless
hours in
front of
your
screen.

You could use the Object Inspector to change the Name property of the Form1 example described earlier in the chapter to something like **JoeBloggs.** You would see that the references to the form in the Code Editor are changed for you in a twinkling.

C++Builder respects your privacy to a fault. As such, if you make any modifications to a form variable directly within one of your functions, you have to modify the form variable name references yourself.

Including #include *Statements*

If you examine the top of any C++Builder source files, you are likely to find *#include statements* (you may hear them called *include* or *pound include* commands). These statements are extremely useful code constructs. They tell the compiler to load an include file. Some header files are added by C++Builder or you can also add your own header files. In this case, the file that's being included is the header file. Just as a reminder, here's an example of what an include statement looks like:

```
#include <vcl\vcl.h>
```

Where does C++Builder expect the file that's referenced within the brackets of the #include statement to reside? Here are some simple steps to follow to find out yourself:

1. **Choose** **Options**⇨**Project from the main menu.**

   The Project Options dialog box appears. (See Figure 14-2.)

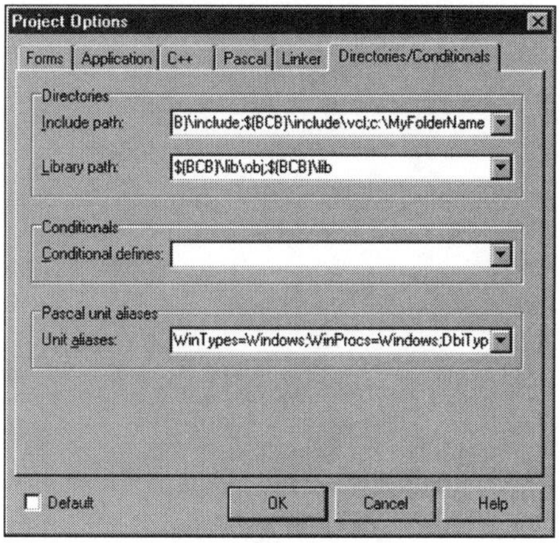

Figure 14-2:
The Project Options dialog box is where you can locate files referenced in #include statements.

Project Options

Forms | Application | C++ | Pascal | Linker | Directories/Conditionals

Directories
Include path: B\include;$(BCB)\include\vcl;c:\MyFolderName
Library path: $(BCB)\lib\obj;$(BCB)\lib

Conditionals
Conditional defines:

Pascal unit aliases
Unit aliases: WinTypes=Windows;WinProcs=Windows;DbiTyp

☐ Default   OK   Cancel   Help

2. Click on the Directories/Conditionals tab.

The Include path text box in the Directories group furnishes the answer to where C++Builder expects this file to be. It contains a list of folders in which the file can be located.

Refer back to Figure 14-2 for a moment and I tell you what some of those entries mean. The characters $(BCB) — BCB stands for Borland C++Builder — represent the full folder name where C++Builder is installed (for example `c:\program files\borland\cbuilder`). That shorthand $(BCB) is called an *environment macro*.

Knowing this, you may guess that the `#include` statement at the start of this section in effect says something like

```
#include "c:\program
          files\borland\cbuilder\include\vcl\vcl.h"
```

Notice that in this example, the angle brackets (< >) have been swapped for quotation marks. Because `"c:\program files\borland\cbuilder\include\vcl\vcl.h"` is the full path of the folder, the `include` statement does not need to be processed in order for the compiler to discover the actual location of the folder in question.

The benefit of using the environment macros is that they save you from having to create long lines at the top of every file. What if the files that you need to include in your programs have moved? That means that all of the folder references in the `#include` statements in your code have to be changed. Whatta nightmare! You'd find yourself plowing through all of your source files amending the `#include` lines, which wouldn't leave you much time for eating, sleeping, or discovering what's in the chapters in the rest of this book.

Chapter 15

Controlling Programs with Data Types

. . . .

In This Chapter

▶ Declaring variables to put data in its place

▶ Getting a line on character strings

▶ Using pointers to manage data

▶ Adding mathematical expressions

▶ Writing if, else, and switch statements

▶ Building loops to save time

. . . .

*A*t some point after writing quite a few programs and experimenting with the available C++Builder components, you start itching to move on to bigger, better, and more challenging projects. When you reach this moment of maturity (or madness), this chapter can provide you with the nitty-gritty details of how C++ code is constructed and empower you to take control over how your programs react to a variety of events.

Of all the chapters in this book, you're likely to find this one to be the heaviest going, but take heart. The amount of effort this chapter requires is directly proportional to the benefits you ultimately get out of it. Feel free to tuck the wisdom of this chapter under your belt piece by piece.

If you feel brain-burn coming on, bookmark your place and go grab yourself one of those sugar-loaded, high-caffeine drinks that constitute a major food group for most developers. Then you can come back ready to continue with another chunk of work and to take on the world (or at least the next C++Builder program).

Declaring Data Types: It's All Variable

When you really get into developing, you may find that you need to store, move, or change data. This data can be numeric, text, or graphical. For example, the values a program maintains to balance your bank account are a different kind of data from the text you use to write letters, and that text is a different sort of data from the scanned photos from your bachelor party that you keep meaning to e-mail to a few select friends.

As you create programs, you want to be able to reference various items of data by some sort of meaningful notation. That's where *variables* come into play. A variable is a name that you assign to a piece information of a certain type. You *declare* a variable (that is, note it properly in code so that the system recognizes it) and then use the variable's name to clear it, cram it with data, or anything else that the language enables you to do to it.

Entry-level variables

Before you give a variable a name, you need to decide what *type* of data the variable is going to hold. Certain basic data types are available to you in C++. You can make up more complicated types of your own built on the basic data types, as I explain in Chapter 16. Try the three types listed in Table 15-1 for starters, though.

Table 15-1	Basic C++ Data Types	
C++ Data Type	*What It Holds*	*Valid Values*
char	Exactly one character	Single letters (A, a, B, b, and so on) or punctuation (' or ; or even & and $) are valid.
int	A whole number	Examples of valid numbers are 0, 1, 190, or –10, but not numbers that require a decimal place, such as 1.5.
float	Decimal number	Values such as 3.6, 10.0, and –9.9 are valid float numbers.

Declaring variables

So once you know what variables you have to choose from, how do you go about using variables and their respective data types? Read on.

The first stage to using a variable is to *declare* (or create) the variable. A *variable declaration* consists of two parts, the variable type and the variable name. Variable declarations are normally one to each line. The following steps demonstrate how to create a variable:

1. **Enter the data type name (such as** char **or** int**) on a new line in your code.**

2. **Press Tab.**

3. **Enter the name that you want to give the variable and end the line with a semicolon (;).**

4. **Press Enter.**

   Way to go! You have one variable ready for action.

The following examples show you how you could declare one variable for each of the basic types of variables:

```
char     Letter ;
```

```
int      Counter ;
```

```
float    Payment ;
```

I choose the words Letter, Counter, and Payment as variable names because they indicate the function of the variable's data. You can name variables as you like, but don't forget that you may well have to make quick sense of your code at a later stage!

As mentioned earlier in this chapter, choose the names of variables so that they imply what the data refers to or what it is used for. That's just a piece of advice; however, some variable-name rules *are* set in stone. Here are the five don'ts of naming variables:

✔ Don't start variable names with numbers.

✔ Don't use spaces in variable names.

✔ Don't use certain special characters (+, –, and ! are some examples) in variable names. Use only letters, numbers, and the underscore character (_).

✔ Don't use words, such as *if* and *while,* that are reserved by the C++ language (explained later in this chapter).

✔ Don't use C++ library function names (for example, printf, scanf, getchar, and others)

Here are some examples of valid variable names (even if their appropriateness is questionable):

```
nice_one_deb_its_a_boy
```

```
Take5
```

```
HaveABeer
```

These are examples of variable names that the compiler will bounce back at you for sure:

1ForTheMoney — **starts with a number**

C++Builder! — **contains illegal characters**

switch — **a C++ reserved word**

No Way — **has a space in it**

If you plan to use a variable in more than one file, declare that variable in a header file (see Chapter 2 for more on header files). You can then reference the variable from any unit that includes that header file. Such variables are called *global* variables, because they potentially can be used in any of the program's other code units.

A variable's declaration offers an ideal opportunity to also set the starting value. This is called *initializing* a variable. If you don't set your own initial value for a variable, there's the danger that the variable can contain just about any old value which could cause some unexpected results for your program. The following code shows how you can extend the variable declarations listed earlier in this chapter so that the variables hold valid data.

```
char  Letter = 'X' ;
```

```
int   Counter, i = 0 ;
```

```
float Payment = 99.99 ;
```

Notice that in the second line I use a comma to declare multiple variables of the same type in one statement. It would be the same as entering

```
int Counter = 0;
int i = 0 ;
```

so you can save yourself a line of code. In this case, both variables are also initialized to zero — cool! (As you may know, initializing the variables to zero removes any "garbage" that may be left over in the variable, making it ready to be used.) If you want to initialize the variables to different values, you could use the following line:

```
int Counter = 1, i = 0 ;
```

The following steps give you an example of how to initialize a variable:

1. **Create a new application by choosing File⇨New Application from the main menu.**

2. **Drop one Button and three Labels components onto the form. (See Chapters 4 and 5 for steps on how to do this.)**

3. **In the OnClick event for the Button, add the following lines:**

```
char Letter = 'X' ;
int Counter = 0 ;
float   Payment = 99.99 ;
Label1->Caption = Letter ;
Label2->Caption = Counter ;
Label3->Caption = Payment ;
```

4. **Press F9 to run the application, and then click on the Button in the form.**

   The Labels display the variables' initialized values.

Advanced data types

You probably won't use the advanced data types listed in Table 15-2 as often as the basic types, but the following data types can help you to get more specific about how your program holds data.

Table 15-2	Additional Data Types
C++ Data Type	*What It Holds*
unsigned char	Values from 0 to 255 in 8 bits
short int	Values from –32,768 to 32,767 in 16 bits
unsigned int	Positive values from 0 to 4,294,967,295 in 32 bits
unsigned long	Positive values from 0 to 4,294,967,295 in 32 bits
long	Negative to positive values from –2,147,483,648 to 2,147,483,647 in 32 bits
double	Values from $1.7 \times 10{-}308$ to $1.7 \times 10{+}308$ in 64 bits
long double	Values from $3.4 \times 10{-}4{,}932$ to $1.1 \times 10{+}4{,}932$

Deciphering digi-dialect

The numbering method used by most humans is the decimal system, which is based on ten numerals with each digit in a numeral calculated in powers of ten. For example, the number 99 equates to 9 x 10 + 9.

This may seem incredibly obvious to you, but computers don't understand a system based on ten digits. They speak in a *binary* tongue that uses only the numerals 0 and 1, with each digit in a number calculated by a power of 2. This means the number 11 in the binary system equates to 1 x 2 + 1, or 3 in the decimal system. So, 99 in the decimal system becomes 1100011 in the binary system (1 x 64 + 1 x 32 + 0 x 16 + 0 x 8 + 0 x 4+ 1 x 2 + 1 x 1). Each of these binary digits is called a bit and it takes a full seven bits to store the decimal number 99.

Computers group bits into a set of 8 digits called a *byte,* and a byte has the capacity to hold up to a 255 decimal value. Two adjoining bytes are called a *word,* which can hold up to a 2,655,535 decimal value.

Keeping Things Constant

You are going to find that some values in your programs never change. For example, pi will always equal 3.141592 (plus an infinite number of other digits). In C++Builder, you can use a special kind of variable that, once assigned, acts like quick-dry cement and from then on can't be changed. These are called (you guessed it) *constants* and you create them by appending the keyword const in front of the variable name.

Here are some examples of constants in action:

```
const int MaxCount = 999;
```

```
const float pi = 3.141592;
```

```
char * const Str1 = "Jason is a dude!";   // no heckling
            from the back, please!
```

(The importance of the '*' character in the last line is explained later in this chapter.)

Stringing Characters Along

One of the basic data types introduced at the start of this chapter is char. It is capable of holding a single character. But what about when you need to store whole words, or even complete sentences?

Fear not, you can soon take care of this by building upon the humble char type. Characters are grouped together to form a *string* that is stored in an *array*. This is a way of saying that you can refer to a bunch of single characters by using just one variable. You can determine how many characters are in your array (that is, how many letters your word can contain) by adding a whole number enclosed in square brackets at the end of the variable name.

The following declaration provides a variable that is capable of holding a word up to ten characters long:

```
char cPlaceName[10] ;
```

You don't have to use all these characters all the time. This declaration simply sets aside a maximum number. I sense a looming question: How do you know when you've come to the end of a word contained in the array if the word is shorter than the number of characters the array can hold? *Null termination* (described in the nearby sidebar) tells you.

Null termination — not just for nothing

C++ uses a technique called *null termination* to indicate the last letter within a character array when the text within the array is shorter than the variable's capacity.

If, for example, you place a word four characters long inside an array that can contain ten characters, a special "null" character (\0) is placed in the fifth character position in the array.

This eliminates the need to store a word length inside the array. The null character indicates that the word has ended and the rest of the array is not in use. If you figured out that this means you can actually use only nine of your ten characters, well done! Go and get yourself a biscuit! You have only nine characters available to you because you must use the tenth one to prevent overrunning the end of the array.

You don't have to worry too much about all this null termination stuff, because C++Builder provides a special string class called `AnsiString`. This string manages a great deal of the run-of-the-mill string chores for you and allows you to use strings in conjunction with C++Builder controls in a much more natural way. That's because the components that you place in your forms also use `AnsiString` types for their Caption, Text, and other such string properties. You often see code like the following snippets in C++Builder applications.

```
AnsiString strTemp ;
strTemp = Edit1->Text ;
Label1->Caption = strTemp ;
```

The first line declares a variable called `strTemp` of type `AnsiString`. The second line loads the contents of an Edit box into the variable `strTemp` and the third line passes the contents of a Label component with the same string of characters.

Getting to the Pointer

In an earlier section of this chapter called "Keeping Things Constant," I used the * (asterisk) character in code. You use this operator to say that you want a particular variable to be a *pointer* type.

Computer programs hold their data in memory and variable names are labels humans can read to find the place in memory where the data is located. That seems like a reasonable way of going about things, but when amounts of data become greater, or when you have a group of items that are of the same data type, referring to items directly can become unwieldy. That's when you might look at using pointers instead to refer to data.

A pointer-type variable does not hold the data of a particular type; it holds the *address* for some data of a particular type. It's actually one step removed from the real thing. This characteristic provides pointer type variables with the flexibility to be redirected to point somewhere else in memory.

The giveaway syntax for a pointer is the * (asterisk) character, which is placed in between the variable name and the variable's data type.

The first two of the following lines are character array declarations; the character pointer variable is declared on the third line.

```
char str1[255] = "This is String One" ;
char str2[255] = "This is String Two" ;
char * cPtr ;
```

The cPtr pointer variable does not point at anything yet, but it can be made to access either of the character arrays by using this simple assignment:

```
cPtr = str1 ;
```

At any point in your program you could redirect the pointer to the other string by using the following code:

```
cPtr = str2 ;
```

This is a technique that can be used for any variable type and not just character arrays.

If you look inside a header file for one of your forms, you can see that all the C++Builder components you placed in the form at design time are actually held as pointers to objects.

Pointers are extremely useful when you're holding large amounts of data in your program. If you need to pass this data to a function that you are calling, the laborious process of sending over all the data as a copy becomes a real chore. Instead, you can use a pointer to the data. Essentially, C++Builder is saying, "I don't have it, but I know where you can get it!" to the function that you are calling. (See Chapter 16 for more on calling a function.)

The misuse of pointers is probably the single largest cause of problems in C++ programs. Things go awry, especially if you use a pointer that has not been properly initialized first. You can end up sending the program into the memory twilight zone. Be careful, and remember — if in doubt, check it out!

Expressing Operators

I don't suppose that you're going to declare variables without wanting to actually perform operations on them. Why, that would be like pumping up your bicycle tires and then taking the bus!

To perform an operation on variables in C++, you need to build an *expression* — something that looks like this example: surf_time = have_board + waves_high.

Doing the math

A simple mathematical expression that springs to mind is

```
a = 1 + 2 ;
```

Here you are using the + (plus sign) symbol to indicate that you want to perform the mathematical operation of adding the two integers. (The + character is called an *operator.*) Table 15-3 provides a rundown of the basic operators that you can use in your C++ code.

Table 15-3		Basic C++ Mathematical Operators
Operator	*Example*	*Action*
+	2 + 2	Add the two numbers.
-	2 - 2	Subtract one number from another.
*	2 * 2	Multiply the two numbers.
/	2 / 2	Divide the first number by the second number.
%	11 / 2	Provide the remainder after dividing the two numbers.

If you use an integer to represent an amount of money and hold the entire value in cents (for example, $79.50 represented as 7950 cents), you can easily isolate just the cents part by using an expression such as this:

```
Cents = Payment % 100
```

This expression discards the dollar amount and assigns just the coinage left over into the variable Cents.

C++ has a diverse and varied selection of operators to make your programming life more exciting. Table 15-4 lists some of the more-advanced operators you can use in your code.

Table 15-4		Advanced Operators
Operator	*In Action*	*Description*
++	i++	Increments the value of variable *i* by 1.
—	i—	Decrements the value of *i* by 1.
>>	i>>j	Performs a bitwise right shift, *j* bits.
<<	I<<j	Performs a bitwise left shift, *j* bits.

Comparatively speaking — Boolean operators

When you are faced with making a decision in your code, you may not be so concerned about the numeric result of an expression directly; you may be more concerned with whether the test that you are making is actually true or false. This situation leads you to what are called *Boolean operators,* a special kind of operator that you're sure to use in many of your if statements. With Boolean operators, you're mostly concerned with determining whether an expression is true or false. Table 15-5 lists some Boolean operators.

Table 15-5		Boolean Operators	
Operator	*Name*	*In Action*	*Description*
==	Equal operator	a == b	Returns true if these variables contain the same values
!=	Not-equal operator	a != b	Returns true if these variables do *not* contain the same values
>	Greater-than operator	a > b	Returns true if the expression to the left is greater than the expression on the right
<	Less-than operator	a < b	Returns true if the expression to the left is less than the expression on the right
>=	Greater-than or equal operator	a >= b	Returns true if the expression to the left is greater than or equal to the expression on the right
<=	Less-than or equal operator	a <= b	Returns true if the expression to the left is less than or equal to the expression on the right
!	Not operator	!a	Returns false if the expression is true
&&	Logical *and* operator	a && b	Returns true if both expressions are true
||	Logical *or* operator	a || b	Returns true if either expression is true

TECHNICAL STUFF

Shift workers and real operators

The shift operators (in the bottom two rows of Table 15-4) deserve a tad more explanation. You use these operators to take the binary value of the variable in question and move all the bits along by the number of positions indicated.

If a variable *i* holds the value 16, its binary representation is

    010000

If you apply the following expression

    i >> 1

all the bits move one place to the right and the value is effectively divided by 2, yielding the following result:

001000 (8 when converted back into decimal)

The reverse is true of the left-shift operator. Applying this operator shifts the bits to the left and subsequently increases values with each shift by a power of 2.

So the following variable (where the variable *i* again contains a value of 16)

    i << 2

provides the following binary pattern:

1000000 (64 in the human-speak decimal system).

Not all are created equal — assignment operators

Use an assignment operator (=) when you want to give a variable a value. Table 15-6 lists C++ assignment operators.

Table 15-6		C++ Assignment Operators
Operator	*In Action*	*Description*
+=	a += b	Adds the value of *b* to *a* and places result in *a*
-=	a -= b	Subtracts the value of *b* from *a* and places result in *a*
*=	a *= b	Multiplies the value of *a* by *b* and places result in *a*
/=	a /= b	Divides *a* by *b* and leaves the result in *a*
%=	a %= b	Sets *a* to the value of the modulo of *a* and *b*
<<=	a <<= b	Left-shifts *a* by *b* number of bits
>>=	a >>= b	Right-shifts *a* by *b* number of bits

Operator	In Action	Description
&=	a &= b	Performs a bitwise *and* on *a* and *b* and places the result in *a*
|=	a |= b	Performs a bitwise *or* on *a* and *b* and places the result in *a*
^=	a ^= b	Performs a bitwise *exclusive or* on *a* and *b* and places the result in *a*

When an operator performs a *bitwise,* it looks at each variable at a storage bit level. With the &= operator, if the bit on the left and the bit on the right are 1, the result is also assigned as 1. The result is set to 0 if either the left or right bit is 0. With the |= operator, when the bit on the left or the bit on the right is 1, the result is assigned as 1. It's set to 0 only if both left and right are 0. With the ^= operator, when one but not both of the bits on the left or the right is 1, the result is assigned as 1.

Flowing with the Go: Channeling Your Program Path

After seeing the operators that you can use for comparing expressions, you're going to want to be able to change the course of the programming ship according to the result of your comparisons. In this section, I introduce several code constructs for channeling the execution path of your program so you can play "program traffic cop."

Making decisions with if statements

The if statement is a powerful little critter that you use to make decisions within the code of your programs.

The following snippet of code shows this "tiny titan" — the if statement — in action. (You see this message only if the variable i contains a 0 value):

```
if (i == 0)
    ShowMessage("i has zero value") ;   // is return real
```

When you need to use more than one line of code to do a job, use { and } braces to bind your statements together, as in the following example (my preference for placing the braces is to have each one on a line of its own):

```
if (i == 0)
   {
   ShowMessage("i has zero value") ;
   return(0);
   }
```

Now you can place as much code as you need to into the code section of the if statement. (The assignment operator = is also valid inside an if statement.)

The following two code snippets are valid to the compiler, but entering the first one when you mean to enter the second one may trip you up!

```
if (j = 1)
              j++ ;

if (j == 1)
   j++ ;
```

Danger lies in the first two lines. You actually end up with j always containing the value of 1 with the first statement. The second if statement, on the other hand, performs just a comparison and does not interfere with the value of the variable j.

If not if, *then an* else *statement*

You can extend the if statement by using its companion else. The else statement is used when you want a particular action (or set of actions) to be performed when the condition that you provide for the if statement is not true. Here's an example of how you do this:

```
if (i == 0)
   ShowMessage("i has zero value") ;
else
   ShowMessage("There's something of value in your i!");
```

In this case, if the variable i contains 0, you are going to see the first message. When the variable i contains any value other than 0, the program executes the code segment inside the else statement and you see the message "There's something of value in your i!" instead.

You can extend the use of if and else by stringing together a number of these code constructs to build more specific control into your program. Consider the following chunk of code. If the variable i contained a value of 2, neither of the messages would be shown.

```
if (i == 0)
    ShowMessage("i has zero value") ;
else if (i == 1)
    ShowMessage("There's value 1 in your i!");
```

Try the following example steps. When you implement the if ... else statement, every time you click on the button the color of the panel changes.

1. **Choose File⇨New Application from the main menu to create a new form.**

2. **Drop a Panel and a Button component onto the form (see Chapters 3 and 4 for the steps to do this).**

3. **Select the Button and click on the Events tab on the C++Builder Object Inspector.**

   If the Object Inspector isn't already showing on the left side of your screen, press F11.

4. **Double-click on the empty** onClick **event handler name to get into the Code Editor, where you enter the following code:**

```
if (Button1->Caption == "Red")
   {
                Panel1->Color = clRed ;
   Button1->Caption = "Green" ;
   }
else if (   Button1->Caption == "Green" )
   {
                Panel1->Color = clGreen ;
   Button1->Caption = "Blue" ;
   }
else
   {
                Panel1->Color = clBlue ;
   Button1->Caption = "Red" ;
             }
```

5. **Press F9 to run the program.**

6. **Click on the button.**

   The color of the panel rotates through the colors that you've entered in the Code Editor, thanks to the decision-making that you assigned to the OnClick event.

Saving work with the switch *statement*

When you have multiple options to choose from and you don't have the energy to bash in all those if . . . else combination statements, rest assured that you don't have to. C++Builder has a much easier and neater way of building in such decision-making — the *switch* statement.

The switch statement can be broken down into three main parts.

✔ The *test* to see which variable you're examining for your decision

✔ The *case statements* to provide comparison values and corresponding code sections

✔ The *default code section* to sweep up any loose ends (anything you don't handle in the case statement)

For example, examine this code:

```
switch (expression)
   {
   case value1 :
      statement1 ;
   case value2 :
      statement2 ;
   case value3 :
      statement4 ;
   ...
   default :
      defaultstatement ;
   }
```

In this example code, the expression is first tested and compared against value1. If this doesn't work, the program then checks against the next value in line and so on, until it either finds one that does work, or it reaches the *default* statement, which would then be executed.

One thing to remember about switch statements: Once a match has been found, all the statements that follow it are executed. If you don't want this to happen, you must enter a break statement at the end of each case (as shown in the following lines of code).

You could replace Step 3 in the previous list of steps in this section with a switch statement. For example, examine the following chunk of code.

```
switch (Panel1->Color)
   {
case clBlue :
Panel1->Color = clRed ;
Button1->Caption = "Green" ;
break ;
case clRed :
Panel1->Color = clGreen ;
Button1->Caption = "Blue" ;
break ;
case clGreen :
default :
Panel1->Color = clBlue ;
Button1->Caption = "Red" ;
   }
```

Feeling a Bit Loopy — Building Loops

Have you ever had the feeling that you are repeating yourself unnecessarily? Have you ever had the feeling that you are repeating yourself . . . sorry, got carried away!

Computers are very good and very fast at repeating the same task over and over again, and unlike humans they don't get bored. You have two choices when it comes to repeating tasks in your programs:

- ✔ Cut and paste the operation as many times as you think that it will need to be performed — not the best option.
- ✔ Start building loops into your code to execute the same line of code as many times as required — a much more sensible way to go.

There are several different looping code constructs provided in C++Builder and this section covers each of them.

The for *loop*

To specify how many times you want a loop to go around executing the same line of code, use the for loop.

Here's a generic sample of a for loop:

```
for (expression1; expression2; expression3)
   statement1 ;
```

In this example, the loop begins by evaluating `expression1` — this is where you initialize the variables that are used in the loop. Next, `expression2` is evaluated and if it's true then `statement1` is executed. Once `statement1` has been executed, `expression3` is evaluated (this is usually used to increment counter variables). This process continues until `Expression2` is false; execution then continues to the statement following the `for` loop.

An example of this loop is shown in the following sample code segment below:

```
for (int i=0; i < 100; i++)
  strTemp[i] = ' ' ;
```

This `for` loop places 100 spaces in a character array. You must then provide the condition that is going to signal that you're dizzy with all this spinning around and are ready to end the loop. The last section controls the statement that indicates how large the step is going to be every time the loop is performed, so you can make the jump in steps of two or more, if you need to.

The while *loop*

Use this style of loop when you're not certain how many times the loop has to be performed to do the job, but you know what's going to finish it off. The `while` loop looks simpler than the previous section's `for` loop and uses the following construction:

```
while (expression1)
    statement1 ;
```

In this example, `expression1` is first evaluated; if it's true, then `statement1` is executed. This testing and executing process continues until `expression1` is false. The program execution then moves on to the first statement following the `while` loop.

Here's a common application for the `while` loop:

```
Table1->First() ;
while (!Table1->Eof )
    {
    // Do what you need to here!
               .

  .
               .
    Table1->Next() ;
    }
```

Taking control over your loops

Sometimes you need to provide an escape route inside a loop's code. A means of escape can serve either to prevent a chunk of code from being executed unnecessarily or to prevent the code from continuously running around a loop it can't finish. Two C++ keywords — continue and break — offer you this slip road to get more control over loops.

Use the continue keyword inside a loop to jump straight back to the loop test from anywhere inside the loop code. Here's an example of how you might use this keyword:

```
Table1->First() ;
while (!Table1->Eof )
  {
    if (!Table1->FieldByName("Friend")->AsBoolean )
      {
      Table1->Next() ;
      continue ;
      }
    // Invite to birthday party code here...
         .
         .
         .
         Table1->Next() ;
  }
```

In this case, the rest of the code is skipped if you are not looking at a record that contains details on a Friend of yours.

If you need to actually get out of a loop in a hurry, call on the keyword break for a quick "ejector seat." Here's how you could use a break inside a loop:

```
if ( x >= 50 )
    break ;
```

In this case, should the variable x ever return a value of 50 or more, out of the loop you'd leap.

In the preceding code sample, you move to the first row of the table, and then check to see that you are "not at the end row of the table." If that expression is true, the body of the loop is executed. In this case, it would perform some task on each row of the table. At the end of the body of code for the while loop, the Table1->Next() ; line moves you on to the next row of the table, and the process is repeated until the end of the table is reached.

The do . . . while *loop*

A variation on the while loop is the do . . . while loop. With this type of loop, you still don't know how many times you need to perform a loop to complete the task, but you do know that you need to perform the code inside the loop at least once. Here's what the do . . . while loop looks like in action:

```
do
   {
// repeating lines go in here
   x++ ;
   }while( x < y ) ;
```

In this case, the variable x is incremented at least once before the test is made to see whether x reached the same value as variable y. If not, the code is repeated.

Chapter 16

Power Building with More Advanced Data Types

· ·

In This Chapter

▶ Using arrays to hold data

▶ Grouping your data with structs and classes

▶ Encountering void and return functions

▶ Passing values to an argument with functions

▶ Handling strings with escape sequences

· ·

*B*y now, you're probably developing a taste for ordering all this code around with C++Builder in your holster. Declaring variables, wielding mathematical operators, controlling the behavior of your programs — it's all pretty heady stuff.

If you've read through the previous chapter, up until now you've been working with basic data types to run some fairly simple programs. Now you're going to find out how you can corral your data using arrays, structures, classes, and functions to get more processing power out of your coding and even build your own custom data types. (Chapter 15 introduces you to the basics of data types. You may want to familiarize yourself with the material in that chapter first before you dive into the following sections.)

Hip-Hip Array: Creating Arrays

Think of an *array* as a "street" lined with data items, and each data item is a house on the street with a number on the front door. You can create arrays of any basic data type (such as int, float, or char) and refer to each data item by their numeric *index*. An index is somewhat like a street address — if you know the house number, you can go to that house, knock on the door, and find out who lives there; with an index number you can get into the array and find out what the data value is at that location. This makes arrays ideal for holding lists of contiguous items such as names, numbers, or other kinds of more complicated data types such as structs.

Because you can refer directly to each of the data items in an array by its index, arrays are also handy for processing data using loops. For example, if you held a list of parts prices in any array and wanted to know the price of part Number 1, you would look at the data value at index1 in the parts prices array. If the price array in this example contained a list of *integers* (whole numbers), it would look something like the following:

Index	*Price*
0	25
1	32
2	99
3	18
4	59

Because computers consider 0 to be a valid number, array indexes always start at location zero. So when you create an array with x number of items, the last item will always have an index of $x-1$.

To declare this array of integers in C++ you can use the following code, which gives you an array of five integers.

```
int nPrices[5] ;
```

To access an element in the array, you use the array name followed by the index number of the element that you want. Here's an example of how to declare an integer array, how to assign values to array items, and how to retrieve a value from an array:

```
int nPrices[5] ;

nPrices[0]= 25 ;
nPrices[1]= 32 ;
nPrices[2]= 99 ;
nPrices[3]= 18 ;
nPrices[4]= 59 ;

Label1->Caption = nPrices[3];
```

A five-piece integer array is declared in the first line of this example. The next five code lines load the elements of the array with prices. The bottom line shows how you can access the fourth item in the array (remember that the index starts at 0) and load its contents into a Label component's caption property.

Another method of initializing arrays looks something like this:

```
int nPrices[5] = {25, 32, 99, 18, 59} ;
```

The following example uses another data type in an array called *character pointers* (see Chapter 15 for more on pointers) to hold the name for each day of the week.

```
char *DayNames[7] =
   {"Sunday", "Monday", "Tuesday",
   "Wednesday", "Thursday", "Friday", "Saturday"} ;
```

Given this pointer, you can say that the line

```
Label1->Caption = DayNames[5] ;
```

loads the string "Friday" into the Label's Caption.

When you have more than one row to organize into a two-dimensional matrix, you can build up what's called a *two-dimensional array*. You create a two-dimensional array just as you would a regular array, except that you add a second index number. In the example line of code that follows, the first bracketed number represents the number of items across one row; the second bracketed number indicates the number of rows. The following two-dimensional array can hold 100 numbers in 10 rows of 10:

```
int Prices[10][10] ;
```

If you have to represent up to ten product ranges of which each has up to ten different prices, you can show the third price for Product 2, for example, using this code:

```
Label1->Caption = nPrices[1][2] ;
```

What a handy price-lookup table this array has provided!

Grouping with Structure and a Touch of Class

The ability to group different data types and refer to them under one common type can be very useful. For example, if you maintain information on automobile parts kept in stock, you're going to want to hold the price of that part, plus the part number, supplier details, part description, the number in stock, and other details. Chapter 15 tells you how to hold these items individually; the following shows you how to bind them together.

Structuring your data

An important command used in C++ programs to declare data structures is `struct`. You define `struct` to bind together various data types that collectively refer to the same object, which makes processing information easier. Structures offer a way of organizing data items so that the whole entity provides greater benefits than the sum of its parts. For example, assume that you need to hold information on your friends to make sure that you don't miss their birthdays. You can create a structure that holds the following information:

Age

Name

Birth date

Street

Home phone number

E-mail address

To create this structure, you can enter the following code:

```
typedef struct MyFriend
    {
    int Age ;
    char Name[30] ;
    char BirthDate[6] ;
    char Street[30] ;
    char HomePhoneNo[20] ;
    char EmailAddress[30] ;
    } TBestFriend;
```

The first line of the code on the previous page indicates that you are defining a new type of structure — struct MyFriend. You then enter each item as you would if you were declaring them individually (see Chapter 15 for details on simple data types). Notice that the items that compose the structure are contained by braces — { at the beginning and } at the end. When all of the items are declared, the last line states what the name of the new composite type is going to be; followed by a semicolon. You can use whatever component items you'd like to make a struct, even other structs.

When you want to use your new structure inside your code, you are going to need to define it, just as you would with the simpler data types such as *int* or *char*. To do this, you can write a line such as the following:

```
TBestFriend bestfriend ;
```

You enter the new type name TBestFriend first, then enter the new variable name bestfriend, and then enter the semicolon. This is the definition of the new variable bestfriend. Just remember that it's the same method you use to define simple data type variables and you can't go wrong!

Once you create your own new data type and have a variable ready to roll, it's pretty likely that you are going to want to do something with it. The syntax for referring to items within a structure is the variable name for the struct first, followed by a period, and then the name of the data item within the struct that you want to access. Here are examples of how you can load information into the Name and Street items for your bestfriend struct.

```
bestfriend.Name = "Jake" ;
bestfriend.Street = "CoolCat Crescent" ;
```

You can also gain access to the contents of the structure after it's loaded. To access the internal data, use the same way of referencing (that is, assigning values to) the internal data items that's shown in this next line of code.

```
Label1->Caption = bestfriend.Name ;
```

This line of code places the contents of the Name data item into a Label on a form.

By using the same method to create pointer variables to simple data types (see Chapter 15 for more on this), you can also create pointer variables to structs. One difference is that you should place the characters -> between the structure variable name (bestfriend) and the data item name (Name in this example) instead of placing a period between them as was done in the previous example. Here's how it will look when accessing the Name item for a TBestFriend type:

```
TBestFriend *bestfriend=new TBestFriend;
bestfriend->Name = "Jake" ;
```

Getting classy: C++ classes

Structures have a serious shortcoming: They leave their contents open to use and abuse from anywhere in the program due to the lack of a mechanism to restrict access. You can alter any data item to any value any time you want, which is not necessarily a good thing. Because of this, developers now tend to organize and group data items by using *classes* instead of structures.

Because they contain functions as well as data items, classes enable C++ to increase its object-oriented programming power. This, in turn, enables you to build up autonomous data constructs that are more complete because they can contain their own processing rules. It doesn't matter how the data is stored internally to any code that uses a class, as long as you provide a set of "border patrol" functions. Code external to the class calls these functions that retrieve the data. External code is not allowed to access the internal data items.

The data items declared in the structure in the previous section will become data members of the class. (The official name for variables that are part of a class are *data members*.) Any actions that need to be performed on the data members can be written as member functions of the class.

A C++ class declaration looks like the following sample code (with pseudo-code explanations):

```
class ClassName
   {
   private :
      private data members and member functions go here
   public :
      public data members and member functions go here
   protected:
      protected data members and member functions go here
__published:
      specific to only C++Builder    } ;
```

ClassName refers to the type of name that you want to use to identify this kind of class. Following the line that uses the keyword private, you can enter your data items plus any internal class-processing functions. Following the line that uses the keyword public you place the "border patrol" functions that you want your outside code to be able to call. Basically, *public* data members and member functions are accessible from outside the class. Anything declared in the *private* section can't be called from any code outside of the class.

Besides public and private, another keyword — protected — can be used to control class access. Any members that are placed in this class are accessible to all member functions of the class and to those classes that *inherit* from this class. (Any data member placed in the published section is available through the Object Inspector.)

To stay hip in developer circles, you may want to revise the BestFriend structure in the example given earlier in this chapter to the following "classier" version:

```
class TBestFriend
{
private :
   int Age ;
   AnsiString Name ;
   AnsiString BirthDate ;
   AnsiString Street ;
   AnsiString HomePhoneNo ;
   AnsiString EMailAddress ;
public :
   int GetAge(void){return Age;}
   void SetAge(int NewAge){Age = NewAge;}

   AnsiString GetName(void){return Name;}
   void SetAge(AnsiString NewName){Name = NewName;}

   AnsiString GetBirthDate(void){return BirthDate;}
   void SetBirthDate(AnsiString NewBirthDate){BirthDate =
         NewBirthDate;}

   AnsiString GetStreet(void){return Street;}
   void SetStreet(AnsiString NewStreet){Street = NewStreet;}

   AnsiString GetHomePhoneNo(void){return HomePhoneNo;}
   void SetHomePhoneNo(AnsiString
         NewHomePhoneNo){HomePhoneNo = NewHomePhoneNo;}

AnsiString GetEMailAddress(void){return EMailAddress;}
  void SetEMailAddress(AnsiString NewEMailAddress)
         {EMailAddress = NewEMailAddress;}
};
```

You're probably saying to yourself, now hold on a minute! This is loads more code! How can this approach possibly be an improvement over the earlier BestFriend construct? Even though setting up a class initially involves more work than setting up a structure, the benefits of making this leap into object-oriented development abound.

Notice that the class declaration in this structure has two sections: private and public.

You can't easily access information on the age of your friends from any code external to the class; external code now has to call a function to retrieve the data contained in the age data members. That's what the GetAge and SetAge functions are used for — to provide a "border patrol" for the class. You don't have to know anything about how the class actually stores the data as you would using structures. You just know that if you call the correct member function (in this case, GetAge), the function returns the contents of the age data member as an integer value.

In the TBestFriend class created earlier in the chapter, all member functions are defined inside the class declaration. Functions declared in this way are called *inline* functions. For short class member functions inline functions are efficient, but as your member functions grow to be more complicated and larger, defining them inline isn't the best method.

Member functions for C++Builder forms are declared outside the class definition because they are expected to grow large and complicated; they are even placed in a separate file from their class declaration. A function is defined by the return type first, the class type name is prefixed to the function name with : : (two colons) separating them, and the parameter list is in the parentheses. Here's how you can declare the TBestFriend class GetAge function outside of the class declaration.

```
int TBestFriend::GetAge(void)
{
return Age;
}
```

Function Junction: Adding Functions to Code

If files hold the C++ language code that you write, how is all the code within those files organized? Like other programming languages, C++ splits code within these files into separate clumps, called *functions*. Each function performs a specific task. (You come across functions whilst constructing the examples in previous chapters in this book.)

In previous chapters of this book, C++Builder components are described and all of the event handlers for components are member functions of the forms that you create.

Even though C++Builder creates all of the function skeletons that you need to handle component events, you can also add your own functions straight into the Code Editor. C++Builder does not prevent you from diving into the code and creating whatever functions you need.

To increase the likelihood that you use the functions that you write more than once, write your functions to

✔ Perform a distinct task. If a function does just one job, you can add it to your "jobs-I've-got-code-for" list and call this function every time you need that particular task performed.

✔ Ideally not exceed one screen page in length. This helps to keep your functions small, which makes them more manageable.

The void function

What if you know that you just want a certain task performed, and you want to place the code for that task in a function of its own. If that's all there is to it, you can use what's called a *void function*. This construction is called *void* because it has no result to return to the code that called this function; it just performs a task. The following lines show how a void function can be constructed:

```
void FunctionName(void)
{
// Loads of lovely code go here!
}
```

In this example, the function declaration begins with the word void, followed by the name for the function (which should give an indication of the task that the function performs). The function name is followed by arguments within parentheses. In this example, the word void is placed within the parentheses because no arguments are being passed to the function. (See the later section "Don't you just love a good argument?" for more on the subject.) After the arguments') (closing parenthesis), the *body* of the function starts. This is where the actual coding grunt work of the function is done. The function's body starts with an { (open brace) and ends with a } (closing brace).

Return to sender: functions that return values

Some functions *return* values to the calling function as an indication of what they've discovered whilst doing their jobs. This return value can include data of any type. You can define a function that returns a value in the following way:

```
ReturnType FunctionName(arguments)
{
// Loads of lovely code go here!

return(value of ReturnType) ;
}
```

If you want to define a function that returns an integer you enter int and then a space prior to the function name.

At some point in the function, you need to say which value you want the function to return. This is done using the following line:

```
return(value of ReturnType) ;
```

In the case of a function returning an integer, the previous line looks like this:

```
return(1) ;
```

Here's an example of how an integer value is passed back from one function to another:

```
void CallerFunction(void)            // The caller
{
int x ;
x = myFunction() ;                   // The call
}


int myFunction(void)                 // Well, I Define!
{
// Do lots of things first here!
.

.
return(1) ;                          // The pass back
}
```

Here's how this example works: The function `CallerFunction` makes the call to `myFunction` using the line

```
x = myFunction() ;                          // The call
```

This line executes `myFunction`, which then does whatever it needs to do (not a lot in this case). When it reaches the return statement, it passes back a value of 1 (you can have as many return statements as you want in a function). This returns the program execution to the calling function and the variable x is set to the returned value (1 in this case).

Don't you just love a good argument?

You can't get enough of arguments . . . within the context of C++Builder that is! *Arguments* (or parameters, as they are sometimes called) enable you to pass values into functions so that you can make your functions operate on a level that's more commonly used.

You can use arguments to move values around in your programs. In fact, arguments are what the empty brackets that follow the first line of a function declaration yearn for! The following is one example of how you can use arguments in C++:

```
ReturnType FunctionName(argType1 argName1, argType2
            argName2, .....)
{
// Loads of lovely code go here!

return(value of ReturnType) ;
}
```

You can see by looking at the above sample code snippet that you state the argument type within parentheses (`int`, `char*`, and so on), followed by the argument name that you want to use to reference this argument. The argument name appears inside the body of the function, which appears between braces. You want to list arguments in this way within parentheses, separated by commas.

On the following page is an example that illustrates how to pass an integer and a string into a function:

```
void CallerFunction(void)
{
  int x=99 ;
  AnsiString strThis = "Space. The final frontier..." ;

  myFunction(x, strThis) ;

  // What do you think the variables hold now?

}
```

The call to myFunction in this example passes the values held in the variables x and strThis. This allows myFunction to act on these values once it receives them, as shown in the following lines of code:

```
void myFunction(int x, AnsiString strThis)
{
   // Use the arguments in here
  strThis = "Highly logical, Captain." ;
  x = 0 ;
}
```

In this case, the original variables in CallerFunction in the previous example are not affected by any processing that is done within myFunction because myFunction acts on only copies of these variables. So in the previous example, the variables still hold the same values (x and "Space. The final frontier...") they did when they entered myFunction.

Imagine that you are passing a string of characters into a function as an argument and inside the function you change the first character of every word to an uppercase letter. It would be a bit frustrating if you could not make those changes stick and reap the benefit back in the calling function. You'd be tempted to say, what's the point of making the call in the first place? If you want to keep the changes that are made to your roving variables during their spell inside the called function, you can pass the variables as pointers (Chapter 15 has more on pointers). To do this, you need to add an & (ampersand) character to the start of each variable when the function is called, which would look something like this:

```
myFunction(&x, &strThis) ;
```

This line of code passes the *address* of each variable in addition to its contents. In this example, you then need to change the first line of your function declaration to look something like this:

```
void myFunction(int *px, AnsiString *pstrThis)
```

Each argument has an * (an asterisk character that's sometimes referred to as a *star*) added between the argument type and argument name. The * turns these arguments into pointer types. Whenever you reference the arguments inside the function, you need to prefix the argument name with a *. This says that you want to gain access to the contents of the variable and not just the address (as passed by the calling function). Take a look at a complete example. Can you spot the difference in this version of the functions?

```
void CallerFunction(void)
{
int x=99 ;
AnsiString strThis = "Space. The final frontier..." ;

myFunction(&x, &strThis) ;

   // What do you think the variables hold this time?
}

void myFunction(int *px, AnsiString *pstrThis)
{
   // Use the arguments in here
 *pstrThis = "Highly logical, Captain." ;
 *px = 0 ;
}
```

In this example, pointers to the variables are passed into the function. So when the program returns to the calling function, the contents of the string and the integer are not what they were. Now when you refer to the variables inside the called function, you need to place a * character in front of the variable. This is how you eke out the actual variable data that is contained in the argument.

The Great Escape Characters

C++ *strings* (computer-speak for a bunch of contiguous characters) can accept more than just the visible letters of the words and sentences that the user sees. You can embed controlling characters (special characters that format your output), such as the New Line character (\n), as well as odd characters, such as quotation marks, into your strings. These special character combinations are called *escape characters*.

An escape character sequence can be placed directly into any of your C++ character strings and consists of two characters, the first always being a / (backslash). Upon seeing this character, C++Builder knows that it has to do something special with the character that follows.

C++ recognizes a variety of escape characters, as Table 16-1 demonstrates.

Table 16-1	Escape-Sequence Characters and What They Do
Character Sequence	**Description**
\f	New form or page
\n	New line
\t	Tab character
\b	Backspace
\0	Null character (zero)
\'	' character inside a string
\"	" character inside a string
\\	\ character

To see escape characters in action, imagine that you need to display a message on two lines with quotation marks shown in your program. You can use the following line of code:

```
ShowMessage("\"Feeling Lucky Punk?\"\n\"Make My Day\"") ;
```

Because double quotation marks indicate the beginning and ending of C++ strings, you need to use the \" escape character sequence every time you want to show the quotation mark itself; otherwise C++ thinks that you are marking the end of the string. To provide a split between two lines in this example, you enter \n, the new line escape sequence. This makes the second part of the message drop down to another line.

Programming is not a spectator sport; you can never attain C++Builder guru status from watching others or just reading about it. You have to roll up your sleeves and get on with it. Don't be afraid to make mistakes. You may find that when you make mistakes you often learn the best. To put your program right, you need to be able to get under the hood whilst the engine is running.

Chapter 17

Debugging C++Builder Programs

● ●

In This Chapter

▶ Dealing with compiler errors

▶ Getting inside your program while it's running

▶ Setting breakpoints

▶ Adding watches to keep an eye on variables

▶ Changing variables to avoid errors

▶ Call stacking to keep track of called functions

● ●

*T*ime to play "Spot the Bug." Choose the type of bugs that this chapter is about:

1. Hidden microphones in your boss's office

2. Your colleagues' annoying habits

3. Defects or unintentional program "features"

If you chose number 3, you win. (You didn't look ahead, did you?)

Computer programmers coined the word *bugs* to mean faults or errors within their programs that can cause nasty problems. So hold off on repel-lent; you don't need roaches nesting inside your PC to have bug-ridden code (even though you may find yourself repeating "But it worked perfectly last night!" when things mysteriously start to creak and pop).

At some time you are certain to experience two types of problems (or solution starting points, to put it euphemistically) with your code:

✔ Those that stop your application from compiling (syntax errors)

✔ Those that show up during program operation (run time or logical errors)

Obviously, you need to remove all of the first kind of bugs from your code before you can move on to finding the run-time kind (real bugs). Puns aside, this chapter's all about getting your program up and running smoothly after you've been stalled by bugs.

Special Delivery: Error Messages and Warnings

It isn't uncommon for your program to fail to run at all when you press the F9 key, especially the first time you press it after a long spell of writing software (what we programmers like to call "code cutting"). The program *compiler* often provides a list of messages or warnings (known as *syntax errors*) that tell you when your code is wrong or you simply typed something incorrectly. Compilers use the Message window that appears at the bottom of the Code Editor to convey these errors.

The compiler provides you with more than just the name of the file and the line number on which the problem was detected. C++Builder takes you straight to the problem, as well as providing a description of the error that it found (see Figure 17-1). (Usually compiler error messages are not bugs in the program, they're just syntax errors or typos.)

Figure 17-1:
The compiler takes you to the line of code on which it detected a problem.

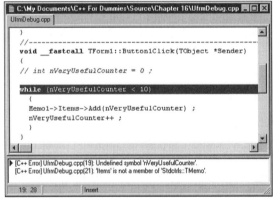

In the case of the code snippet in Figure 17-1, the declaration for the integer has been left as a comment line by mistake, and the property Items inside Memo1 appear to exist only in the programmer's imagination.

You need to do something about blatantly incorrect code before you can run it past the compiler again. If you don't edit the code using the Code Editor to try to fix it, the compiler just keeps repeating the cyber equivalent to "Surely you're joking!" and showing you the door. You need to make changes to the code to remove the syntax problems and then try to rebuild your program (pressing F9 is a quick way of compiling and running a program).

Sometimes the compiler finds that certain lines of your code are *syntactically correct* (meaning that they meet the rules of the programming language), but the compiler still cautions you with a warning. The example warning shown in Figure 17-2 is actually setting the value of the variable and not just checking the value that it contains, so you are asked whether this is really what you intended. You don't have to necessarily change any code when you see a warning message, but be sure to verify that the code that the compiler is highlighting is what you intend it to be.

Figure 17-2:
Warnings are messages in which the compiler draws your attention to code that could produce unexpected results.

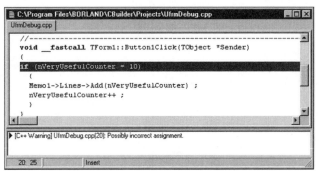

License to Kill (Bugs, That Is)

After you get all the compiler errors out of your code, you're in a position to run your program and test that it works as you intended. Code operates somewhat like a car; you may be able to back it out of the driveway, but that doesn't necessarily mean that it's running smoothly or that it's not going to conk out halfway up a hill. (Okay, so I've had some dodgy cars in my time!)

When you do come across run-time problems with your programs, neither the cause nor the solution may be immediately apparent. So how do you go about unraveling the knots that you can tie yourself up in? *Debugging* is part of the cycle of getting your fare to market, and a *debugger* is a tool that enables you to step through your code, line by line, as your program runs so that you can find those nasty run-time problems.

C++Builder has a fully integrated debugger, so you don't have to go jumping about running other programs to check out your code; it's all part and parcel of C++Builder.

Preparing for the hunt: the debug options

Before you can look under the hood of your code, you need to know some things — such as where the catch lever is! You have to make sure that you turn on the debug options for the project. (An application has to be compiled with debug options set to "on" before it is "debuggable.")

Make sure that you have the debug options set by following these steps:

1. **Choose Options⇨Project.**

   The Project Options dialog box appears.

2. **Select the C++ tab, as shown in Figure 17-3.**

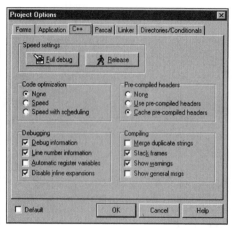

Figure 17-3:
Setting debugger options is one click away once you're in the Project Options box.

3. **Click on the Full debug button in the Speed Settings group.**

   C++Builder then saves your activated debug settings in the project make file.

4. **Click on OK.**

5. **Rebuild your program's executable file by choosing Project⇨ Build All.**

   By rebuilding the application, you allow the compiler to place extra information into the executable file, which allows C++Builder to perform its debugging operations.

Setting the debug options increases the size of your application's .exe (executable) file, so when you have tested your application and are sure that it's bug free and ready to roll out to your users, open the Project Options dialog box again and click the Release button to turn off the debugger settings. (Don't forget that you need to rebuild your application.)

Give your application a break: setting a breakpoint

Once you have your application on the operating table ready to dissect, where do you make the first incision?

You can set any executable line within your application to a *breakpoint*. A breakpoint is a code line that you can highlight in the Code Editor to literally stop your program in its tracks and hand control over to the debugger. Stopping the program gives you the opportunity to start poking around your variables to find out what's going on and what's not happening as you expect. When you think that you've found the section of code that's causing a particular problem, you can place a breakpoint on any line in the code that you suspect is a culprit.

You can set a breakpoint in a line in any one of several ways:

✔ Click on the first column of the code line in the Code Editor — this toggles the breakpoint on and off (see Chapter 1 for information on the Code Editor).

✔ Place the cursor in the code line in question and then press F5 — this also toggles the breakpoint on and off.

✔ Choose Run⇨Add Breakpoint to bring up the Edit Breakpoint dialog box. The line loaded into the Edit breakpoint dialog box becomes the Code Editor's current line.

✔ Place the cursor in the code line and right-click to bring up the speed menu and then select Toggle Breakpoint.

When you set a breakpoint in a line of code, that line becomes highlighted, as shown in Figure 17-4.

Figure 17-4: The program halts at a line with a breakpoint (shown highlighted) and hands control over to you and the debugger.

After setting a breakpoint, you can use the Edit breakpoint dialog box shown in Figure 17-5 by doing the following:

1. **Choose <u>V</u>iew⇨<u>B</u>reakpoints from the main menu to invoke the Edit breakpoint dialog box.**

2. **Select the breakpoint that you want to inspect by clicking on it in the dialog box.**

3. **Right-click on the breakpoint in the dialog box to bring up the speed menu.**

4. **Select the <u>P</u>roperties option from the speed menu.**

   You can see the Edit breakpoint dialog box with the details of the selected breakpoint line loaded into it.

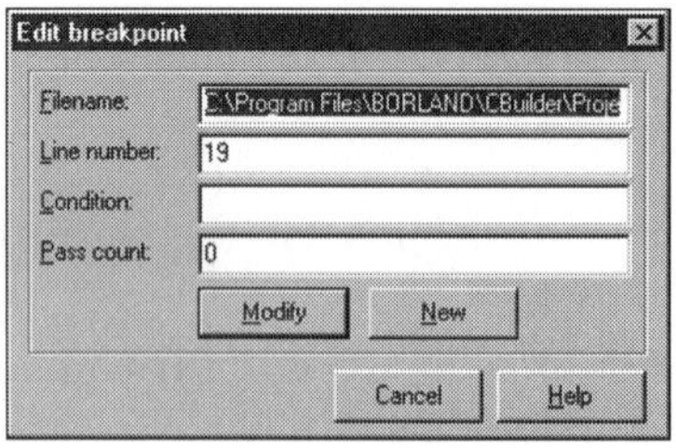

Figure 17-5:
The Edit breakpoint dialog box contains the details on a selected breakpoint line.

The Edit breakpoint dialog box provides more options than just a stop-at-this-line command. Suppose that you want to stop at a line only when a particular variable contains a certain value. You may want to enter a condition like the one shown in Figure 17-6. In this example, the condition specifies that the variable nVeryUsefulCounter must contain a value of 5 for the program to stop before executing the line to allow you to inspect the values currently contained in the variables.

Figure 17-6:
Adding some conditions makes this smarter than the average breakpoint.

Another sophisticated feature of the Edit breakpoint dialog box is the *Pass count setting.* This option is ideal for running through code that requires a great deal of looping, especially when you know you need to execute something a number of times before anything interesting happens. Simply enter into the Pass count text box the number of times the program should execute the line before it stops on the line. C++Builder does the rest for you. For example, if you were to set a Pass count value of 2, the program's execution stops at this line after executing it two times.

To view and navigate amongst all breakpoints, choose View⇨Breakpoints to access the Breakpoint list dialog box. As you can see in Figure 17-7, this dialog box also gives you a neat summary of what's set for each breakpoint.

Figure 17-7:
Surf the
breakpoints
with this
dialog box.

Breakpoint list			
Filename	Line	Condition	Pass
UfrmDebug.cpp	19	nVeryUsefulCounter == 5	0
UfrmDebug.cpp	22		2

When you have used a breakpoint, you may decide that you don't want to throw it away completely because you may need it again at a later stage. In this case, choose View⇨Breakpoints from the main menu again to show the Breakpoint list dialog box, select the breakpoint from the list, and then right-click to bring up the speed menu. Now click on Enabled to deselect the breakpoint. The breakpoint icon in the first column of the code line in the Code Editor turns gray and the breakpoint is put on ice for the time being.

To give all these debugging tools a go, follow the steps in this example:

1. **Create a new application by choosing File⇨New Application.**

2. **Select Options⇨Project from the main menu.**

3. **Select the C++ tab on the Project Options dialog box.**

4. **Click on the Full debug button.**

5. **Click on OK.**

6. **Drop a Button and a Memo control (from the Standard page of the Component Palette) onto the form. (See Chapters 4 and 5 for the steps on how to do this.)**

    Two controls are now on the form — Button1 and Memo1.

7. **Click on Button1, then click on the Events tab in the Object Inspector, and then double-click in the empty field next to** OnClick.

You're then in the Code Editor, where you enter the following code in the Button1 event handler:

```
int nVeryUsefulCounter = 0 ;

while (nVeryUsefulCounter < 10)
  {
  Memo1->Lines->Add(nVeryUsefulCounter) ;
  nVeryUsefulCounter++ ;
  }
```

8. **Now set a breakpoint by clicking on the following line and then pressing F5:**

```
while (nVeryUsefulCounter < 10) do
```

9. **Choose View⇨Breakpoints.**

   The Breakpoint list dialog box appears.

10. **Right-click on your new breakpoint in the Breakpoint list dialog box and select the Properties option from the speed menu that appears.**

    The Edit breakpoint dialog box appears.

11. **Enter the following code in the Condition edit box of the Edit breakpoint dialog box:**

```
nVeryUsefulCounter == 0
```

12. **Click on the Modify button.**

    You see your condition reflected in the Breakpoint list dialog box.

13. **Move back to the Code Editor by clicking on it.**

14. **Add another breakpoint by clicking on the following line and then pressing F5:**

```
Memo1->Items->Add(nVeryUsefulCounter) ;
```

15. **Select View⇨Breakpoint from the main menu.**

16. **Right-click on the breakpoint you created in Step 11 in the Breakpoint list dialog box.**

17. **Select Properties from the speed menu that appears to bring up the Edit breakpoint dialog box.**

18. **Enter a Pass count value of 2 and then click on the Modify button.**

    Well done. You have just set up your first C++Builder debug session.

19. **Press F9, wait until C++Builder rebuilds and runs your application, and then click on the Button1 button on the application.**

Notice that the program first settles (that is, stops running temporarily) on the second breakpoint because you set the Pass Count variable to 2. This line is now called the *execution point* — which is like a "twilight zone" for programs because the program is still loaded but has been "frozen" at the line where you placed the breakpoint.

If you just want to stop the debugging at this point, choose Run⇨Program Reset from the main menu or press Ctrl+F2. This comes in handy if the user gets confused and needs to exit out of debugging without rebooting the computer.

Restarting the program

After you create a breakpoint to stop a program, how do you get it going again? You have four choices, as shown in Table 17-1. (See Chapter 1 for the button equivalents for pressing the F keys.)

Table 17-1	Running Code That Contains Breakpoints
Key	*Description*
F4	Runs the program up to the line where the cursor is located
F7	Steps into the function at the execution point
F8	Executes one line of code at a time; steps over a function at the execution point, placing you on the next executable code line (also called "stepping through" the program)
F9	Runs the program so that it stops only when it hits a breakpoint or the program ends

Your program stops several times in the course of its execution. At this stage, you can't really see what's going on. What you really need is more information, which follows.

Spying on Variables with the Watch Property

When the application has paused at a breakpoint, you've got an ideal opportunity to start poking around under its hood. You can do more than just find out the value of variables at run time; you can actually *watch* them as they change.

To place a variable under surveillance, place the cursor on the variable in question and then press Ctrl+F5 or click anywhere on the variable in the Code Editor. Then right-click and choose Add Watch at Cursor from the speed menu that appears. Both actions display the dialog box shown in Figure 17-8.

Figure 17-8:
I spy with my little eye . . . the Watch Properties dialog box.

To view the list of watch values, choose View⇨Watches. Then rerun the application built in Steps 1–19 in the section "Give your application a break: setting a breakpoint," earlier in this chapter. As your program stops on the breakpoints that you have set up, you can discover the current contents of the watch items at each stage in your program's execution.

You can try out this procedure on the nVeryUsefulCounter variable in the program in which you just set breakpoints (if you followed the example in the previous section). Use these steps:

1. **Click on the Code Editor window.**

2. **Click on the** nVeryUsefulCounter **variable and then press Ctrl+F5.**

    The Watch Properties dialog box appears (refer to Figure 17-8).

3. **Click on OK.**

    Your variable is added to the watch list.

4. **Choose View⇨Watches to take a look at your watch list.**

5. **Press F9 to run your application again and then click on its Button component.**

    Now when the program stops for the first time, the Watch List dialog box shows the value that is contained in the nVeryUsefulCounter variable, as shown in Figure 17-9.

6. **Press F8 to step through the program.**

    You can see that the value of nVeryUsefulCounter increases as the loop progresses.

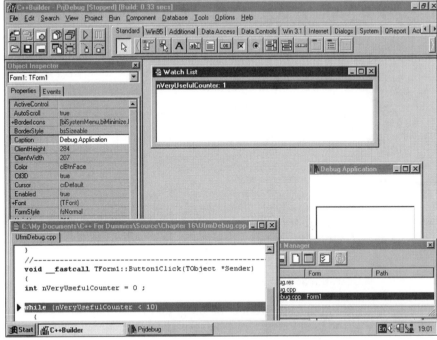

Changing Variable Values While a Program Is Running

C++Builder provides another extremely useful debugging capability — it allows you to not only look at variable values while you are debugging a program, but to also *change* those values. This means that you can prevent potential disasters by being able to load variables with a new value when the program has stopped at a breakpoint.

Before you finish running the sample application built in Steps 1–19 in the section "Give your application a break: setting a breakpoint," earlier in this chapter, try out this powerful part of C++Builder debugging.

1. **When the application is paused on a breakpoint, set the cursor on any reference of** nVeryUsefulCounter.

2. **Press Ctrl+F7 or right-click on the variable and choose Evaluate/ Modify from the speed menu that appears.**

   You see the Evaluate/Modify dialog box shown in Figure 17-10.

Figure 17-10:
You can
change a
variable
while the
program is
running by
using the
Evaluate/
Modify
dialog box.

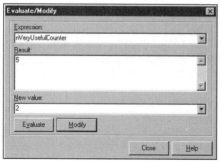

3. **Change the value of the variable by entering any value in the New value text box.**

4. **Click on the Modify button.**

   Watch as a change takes effect with the value shown in the Result box.

   Continue to step through the program by pressing the F8 key. You can see that the loop terminates when you get out of the loop and go back to the application because the nVeryUsefulCounter variable has exceeded 10. The original variable value of 10 was changed, so instead of terminating at 10, the while loop in this example terminates at the new value.

You can place whole C++ expressions inside the Expression edit box of the Evaluate/Modify dialog box if you need to find the likely outcome of an operation. For example, you could enter a new expression (such as, nVeryUsefulCounter*99 or nVeryUsefulCounter+45-40*99) in the Expression edit box, and see the answer in the Result box when you click the Evaluate button.

Using Call Stacking to Keep Track of Called Functions

As your programs become more complex, there may be many calls to a particular function. As such, you may not be certain which route through your code the program took to arrive at a particular breakpoint at a particular time.

You can keep track of which functions have been called within others by using the Call stack option under View in the C++Builder main menu. Call stacking provides a list of the functions that were called in order for the program to end up at the current line.

When you reach a breakpoint in a function, choose View➪Call Stack from the main menu. In the Call stack box shown in Figure 17-11, the current function is shown at the top of the list. The parameters that are passed to each function are shown as address values. You need to get a bit technical to interrogate these, so I won't be covering it in this chapter.

In Figure 17-11, values for arguments that are passed into functions are also shown — in this case, you can see address locations. An *address* is a reference to a location within the computer's memory where an application is executing.

Figure 17-11:
The Call
stack
feature
helps you
keep track
of the
functions
that have
been called
for a
program.

If you need to skip back to a function that is higher up in the call stack than your current location, follow these steps:

1. **Double-click on the line in the Call stack dialog box that contains the function you want to reach.**

2. **Move the cursor to the following line.**

3. **Press F4 to make the program run to that line.**

Chapter 18

Error-Proofing C++Builder Programs

. . . .

In This Chapter

▶ Anticipating where your program can go wrong

▶ Catching errors with `try...catch` statements

▶ Throwing your own exceptions

▶ Identifying candidates for exceptions

▶ Integrating exception handling into your applications

. . . .

You can always rely on one thing in application development, especially under Windows: You can never rely on anything. You may have spent many hours writing and debugging your program and may be absolutely sure that you've got it 100 percent correct, but the potential for problems always exists.

If you assume that every machine that your program runs on is set up in the same way as your own, you're bound to be in for a bumpy ride. Try to think of where your program is most vulnerable and then look to protect it against the worst.

A program's Achilles' heel can be found in any one of a few places:

- **User entry range and type errors:** What if the user enters numbers that you did not anticipate, such as negative or very large values?

- **Lack of disk space:** How will your program react if your hard disk becomes half-full while you're in the process of building something?

- **Database access errors:** What happens if a user removes one of your crucial tables or if the database server goes off-line for some reason?

Taking Some Preventive Measures

If you were looking to add both belt and braces to protect your program against the unexpected (such as dropping down around your ankles), there is a longhand way that you can go about this. You first need to think of all the ways in which the operations performed in your code can fail and then check every line in every function to see that the task in hand has been performed correctly before moving on to the next line of code. For example, assume you have three simple function calls such as the following:

```
myFunction1() ;
myFunction2() ;
myFunction3() ;
```

To provide any degree of real error protection, you have to change the three previous lines of code to end up looking something like this next code section.

```
ret = myFunction1() ;
if (ret == false)
 return(false) ;
ret = myFunction2() ;
if (ret == false)
 return(false) ;
ret = myFunction3() ;
if (ret == false)
 return(false) ;
```

That makes for a lot of return values and a lot of extra code, especially if you think that each line within these functions requires the same level of protection. This code is messy to write as well as to follow when it comes time to enhance further versions. Add to this that you may actually find yourself spending more time writing the error-handling code than writing the actual application, and you're entitled to wrinkle your nose at this method. This leads to the main subject of this chapter, and that's C++Builder's built-in method for effective and efficient error handling.

The following sections give you an introduction to the C++Builder error-protection techniques and then show you how C++Builder provides an error-protection approach at an application level.

Using Exception Handling

An *exception* is another term for an error (or any other unexpected result) and when an exception occurs (such as when you run out of disk space), you need to deal with the error in some way — that's when exception handling enters the picture. The implementation of exception handling comes in two parts:

- First, you have to state which areas of code you want to protect, so that when an error is detected, details of the exception can be passed to the section of code that can handle that particular problem.

- Depending on the type of exception, the program may be able to continue; at other times (such as the program not being able to locate its main data file) continuing with the program's execution may not be possible. Then there may be no choice but to bring down the curtain and close the program.

Try to protect your functions

You can determine which sections of code you want to place under the custody of exception handling. To do so, use a `try { }` block, as follows:

```
try
{
  myFunction1() ;
  myFunction2() ;
  myFunction3() ;
}
```

The program tries to execute the code contained in the braces, and if an error occurs the program's normal flow of execution is interrupted and moved to the end of the `try` section, indicated by the closing brace. An interruption such as this of the normal program flow is called *throwing an exception.*

Catch out any errors

Once normal program execution flow has been interrupted by an error, you need a mechanism to see what kind of error has occurred and what to do next. That's when the `catch` statement is introduced. It has a section of code associated with it that is delimited by opening and closing braces — {and }. The statement looks like the following:

```
catch(...)
   {
 // perform error handling code
 }
```

The (. . .) (three dots in the parentheses after the catch) means that no matter what type of error occurs, the code in the catch is expected to handle it. You can get much more specific by placing object types inside the parentheses of the catch statement. Here are some examples of what you can place within the parentheses:

```
catch(char *Message)
catch(const EDataBaseError &E)
```

In these cases, the program goes into the section of code that follows the catch only if the exception throws an object of the data type declared in the brackets (see Chapters 15 and 16 for more on data types).

You can use multiple catch sections for a single try section to handle several types of exceptions that can be thrown within a single code segment. The program then checks the error that occurs against each catch statement to see which one applies.

The following code structure shows how you can implement multiple catch sections:

```
try
   {
   // exception handling on
 .
 .
 .
 }
catch( exception_type_1)
 {
 // exception handling code here
 }
catch( exception_type_2)
 {
 // exception handling code here
 }
```

 When you use multiple catch statements, start by catching the most specific exceptions first and then gradually becoming more and more general. If you don't, the program is always lured into the general exception handler first and never gets to see the catch statements that follow.

Try . . . Catch *together*

You can put try and catch expressions together by using the following example of some real code. Assume that you are opening a data table inside a function. You can protect against the table open failing by using something similar to the following:

```
try
    {
  Table1->Open() ;
    }
catch(Exception &E)
    {
    ShowMessage("Bad News! " + E.Message ) ;
    }
```

C++Builder provides you with a whole family of exception objects to ease the job of using exception handling. The Exception referred to in the catch line is a class type in its own right; it's actually at the head of the whole family of exception types (you can even build your own exception-handling classes based on this exception class). Notice that you can use the Message property of the exception class to get the exception that was thrown to give you a description of itself.

Throwing an Exception

This exception stuff looks as though it can be pretty handy. What if you can take a situation inside a function, didn't like the look of what was going on, and create an exception of your very own to kick out of there? Well, you can.

Suppose that the user types something truly dumb (imagine that!). You can throw your own exceptions. Here's an example of how you can handle that situation by using an exception:

```
if (Edit1->Text == "")
  throw "Nothing Entered In Edit1" ;
```

You use the throw keyword to throw an exception of your own. In this case, you're actually throwing a message string out with the exception. The bigger code picture looks like this:

```
try
```

```
{
if (Edit1->Text == "")
throw "Nothing Entered In Edit1" ;

    .

    .

    .
}
catch (char *Message)
{
ShowMessage(Message) ;
}
```

Notice that the catch picks up a `char*` data type. That means the specific `throw` error message is displayed. You can use this technique to check user entries on controls in a form as part of the validation.

Don't think that you can throw only simple data types; you can also fit classes or objects into your exception-handler catapult. You can then pass over much more information and even provide the event handler built-in functionality.

Building an Exception-Handling Class

A couple definitions are in order here. *Exception handling* is how the program reacts when an error is encountered or unexpected results from an application occur at runtime. An *exception-handling class* is the program's reaction or the information provided to warn the user that some error has occurred or that the function's result does not match the program criteria.

Time to flex those fingers and put some of this theory into action by building your own exception-handling class. Just follow the steps in this example:

1. **Choose File⇨New Application from the main menu and place two Edit components and a Button component (from the Standard page of the Component Palette) in the form.**

   Three controls — Button1, Button2, and Edit1 — are now on the form.

2. **Click on the Code Editor (press F12 to get the Code Editor), and then press Ctrl+F6 to go to the new form's header file.**

3. **Enter the following lines in the header file following the list of `#include` lines:**

```
class UserError {
public:
  int Code ;
  AnsiString Message ;
void LogError(void)
  { ShowMessage(Message) ; }
} ;
```

That's the error-handling class.

4. **Press F12 to go back to the form itself.**

5. **Double-click on the Button1 component that you placed on the form in Step 1.**

You then end up in the Code Editor.

6. **Using the Object Inspector, enter the following lines in the Button1 component** OnClick **event handler:**

```
try
  {
  if (Edit1->Text == "")
  throw "Nothing Entered In Edit1" ;
  if (Edit2->Text == "")
   {
  UserError UErr ;
  UErr.Code = -1 ;
  UErr.Message = "Please Complete Edit2" ;
  throw UErr;
  }
  }
catch(char *Message)
  {
  ShowMessage(Message) ;
  }
catch(UserError Err)
  {
  Err.LogError() ;
  }
```

7. **Turn off Break on Exceptions by choosing Menu⇨Options⇨ Environment and then deselect Break on Exceptions.**

8. **Press F9 to run the program.**

If you clear out either of the Edit controls before pressing F9, you get a message informing you that the Edit control on the form has caused an exception. Notice that the exception type finds its own exception-handling statement according to the data type that was thrown with the exception.

One of the benefits of using exception handling is that any locally declared variables (the variables that you have declared within the function that the exception occurred in) are freed when an exception is raised.

Identifying Exceptions Candidates

So what about some real examples of how exceptions can change your coding life? Exception handling makes a real difference in three cases:

- ✔ Data conversion
- ✔ Code savers
- ✔ Database handling

I'm going to cover what I consider to be the most important of the three situations — data conversion. Converting data from one format to another, especially where the data has been provided by the user or any other nonvalidated source, can be fraught with danger. You can protect code lines that perform these operations as follows:

```
  try
{
int i = StrToInt(Edit1->Text) ;
}
catch (const EConvertError &convertE)
  {
ShowMessage(" Bong!") ;
  }
```

Don't assume that the user will enter what you expect. Using the example steps in the previous section, if a user enters letters in the Edit1 box instead of entering numbers, the conversion is going to go bust on you. But you don't need to worry, because you have protected the code from bad entries "blowing up" your program by placing the code within the braces of the `try` and handling rogue entries in the `catch` section.

C++Builder Exception Class Types

C++Builder provides you some ready-made classes that have been derived from the Exception class. It's worth getting familiar with these classes as they provide information pertinent to their type of exceptions. Use the following reference syntax to catch these exception types:

```
catch (const exception_class_type &exception_variable_name)
```

In the previous line of code, you specify the class type of the exception that you want to catch and provide a variable name that you want to use to refer to the exception within the catch section of code. A real-world example looks like the following code:

```
catch(const EDBEngineError &dbErr)
```

This statement catches all exceptions that were caused by a Borland Database Engine error using the EDBEngineError class (for more on the Borland Database Engine, refer to Chapter 10). References to this exception are be made through the variable dbErr, although you can use any name that you like.

Table 18-1 gives you an introduction to the ready-made exception classes that C++Builder provides for you.

Table 18-1	Exception Classes and What They Mean
EAbort	Throw this exception when you want to stop a sequence of events that has been triggered, but you don't necessarily want a whole "song-and-dance" routine performed to announce the fact.
EAccessViolation	Use this exception class if you need to check for invalid memory access errors.
EBitsError	Throw an exception object of this type if you use an invalid index on a Boolean array.
EClassNotFound	If you manually remove component references from your form's header file, you may see this exception.
EComponentError	If C++Builder cannot register or rename a component, this is the exception type that it raises.
EConvertError	If you try to convert a string to an integer, and the attempt fails, this is the exception class. Code such as int i = StrToInt(iABCi); is a prime contender for this exception.
EDatabaseError	This exception class covers a multitude of sins where database access is concerned. Always check out the message property contents for a clue when you get this exception!
EDBEditError	If you set a Mask property (Chapter 6 explains Mask properties) that does not fit the type of data that a data-aware edit box is placing below it, this is the exception class you get.

(continued)

Table 18-1 *(continued)*	
`EExternalException`	This is the class of exception generated for any exceptions that cannot be identified.
`EDBEngineError`	This exception class is derived from `EDatabaseError` and provides some extra properties.

Integrating Exception Handling into Your Applications

So much for using exceptions within the C++ language itself. It's a powerful enough technique using solely what you've seen already. In true C++Builder style, though, you're provided with more features that allow you to *fully* integrate exception handling into your applications. You have the Application object to thank for these features.

For an Application object, you can create your own handler and hook it in, as with any other event handler that you create. You first need to define an exception-handler function with the same signature as the Application object's. The function should take two arguments: one of `TObject` type and the other of `Exception` type. Here's an example of the first line of the function that you can use to start defining your own exception handler:

```
void __fastcall TForm1::myHandleException(TObject *Sender,
          Exception *E)
```

TECHNICAL STUFF

Count on loop control with the `ErrorCount` exception

There's an array of Error objects that you can interrogate using the `ErrorCount` exception class as a loop control.

The following code example shows how a `catch` statement can be written to provide you with information from a database error array.

```
catch (const EDBEngineError &dbErr)
  {
   for (int i=0; i < dbErr.ErrorCount; i++)
    ShowMessage(dbErr.Errors[i]->Message +" "+
  IntToStr(dbErr.ErrorCount) ) ;
  }
```

Any member functions that you add to a form also need to be declared in the form's header file.

Enough talk — the best way to understand this is to just work with it, so you're going see how to add an application-level exception log table to a program. You need to first create the table that's going to hold the log of program exceptions that are not handled directly by `catch` statements throughout your program. Here goes:

1. **Choose Tools⇨Database Desktop from the C++Builder main menu.**

   This starts the database maintenance utility called Database Desktop.

2. **Choose File⇨New⇨Table from the main menu of Database Desktop.**

   You are presented with the Create Table dialog box.

3. **Click OK to create a Paradox 7-type table.**

4. **Add the following fields to the table by entering** TimeStamp, **and then pressing the Tab key; entering @, and then pressing the Tab key twice; entering** Description, **and then pressing the Tab key; entering A, and then pressing the Tab key; and, finally, entering 255.**

5. **Click on Save As.**

6. **Select** BCDEMOS **from the Alias drop-down menu.**

7. **Enter** LogFile.DB **into the File name edit box that appears after Step 5.**

8. **Click on Save.**

9. **Close the Database Desktop utility by selecting File⇨Exit from the utility's main menu.**

   Now the Database Desktop has performed its duty. A table has been saved in the BCDEMOS database, which gets installed when you install C++Builder.

10. **Go back to C++Builder by clicking on the main form of the program.**

11. **Drop a Table component and DataSource component from the Data Access page of the Component Palette into the program's main form.**

12. **Set the** Alias **property of the Table component to** BCDEMOS **using the property's drop-down menu in the Object Inspector.**

13. **Select** LogFile.DB **from the Table component's** TableName **property drop-down menu.**

14. **Set the** Active **property on Table1 to** true.

15. **Set the** DataSet **property of the DataSource component to** Table1.

16. **Press F12 to get into the Code Editor.**

17. **Press Ctrl+End.**

   This command moves you to the bottom of the source file of the form.

18. **Enter the following function in its entirety into the Code Editor:**

```
void __fastcall TForm1::myHandleException(TObject
        *Sender, Exception *E)
{
 ShowMessage(" AppXHandler: " + E->Message) ;

 Table1->Append() ;
  Table1->FieldByName("TimeStamp")->AsDateTime = Now() ;
  Table1->FieldByName("Description")->AsString = E-
        >Message ;
 Table1->Post() ;
}
```

19. **Click on the main form for this example and then select the Events tab on the Object Inspector.**

20. **While still in the Object Inspector, double-click on the empty field next to the** OnCreate **event handler name for the form and enter the following line:**

```
Application->OnException = myHandleException ;
```

This step substitutes the myHandleException function for the default application exception handler.

21. **Go to the header file by pressing Ctrl+F6 to declare the** myHandleException **in the form class.**

22. **Add the following line in the public section of the form's class:**

```
void __fastcall myHandleException(TObject *Sender,
        Exception *E) ;
```

23. **Drop another Button component into the form and enter the following line in the component's** OnClick **event handler in the Object Inspector:**

```
 throw EExternalException("Generate Exceptions As U
        Like!") ;
```

You now have unhandled exceptions on tap for the example.

24. **Turn off Break on Exceptions by choosing Menu⇨Option⇨ Environment and then deselect Break on Exceptions.**

25. **Press F9 to run the program so that you can see the fruits of your labor.**

Now, every time you click on your new button, you are creating an unhandled exception, which causes the `myHandleException` function to be called. The code that you placed in the `myHandleException` function displays a message and then adds a record to the table noting that an exception has occurred.

When you get bored watching the message, turn your attention to the Database Explorer (choose Database⇨Explorer) and look at the log table entries. Not only has the exception message been added, but also you can see exactly when the exception occurred, thanks to the date and time entries.

Part V
The Part of Tens

The 5th Wave   By Rich Tennant

"RUMOR HAS IT THAT TOM'S COMPANY IS BEING BOUGHT OUT BY A MULTI-NATIONAL."

In this part . . .

By now, you're probably feeling like a C++Builder master architect, constructing nifty applications in record time. But even the pros can benefit from a few tricks of the trade.

In this part you can find lists of do's and don'ts (ten in each chapter, give or take a couple) that you want to commit to memory. The material here is brief and easy to digest, so I wouldn't be surprised if you read this part first!

Chapter 19

Ten Ways to Get the Most Out of C++Builder

*U*nderneath Borland C++Builder's modest exterior beats the heart of an industrial-strength C++ compiler. As you get more serious about building applications — and the applications that you build become more complicated — you'll probably want to let C++Builder expose more of its application development muscle. In this chapter, I mix direct coding tips with hints on coding practice, the intention being to prevent you from stubbing your toe on some of the hazards around your construction site.

Performing String Conversions

C++Builder provides more than one method of storing *strings*, the fancy name for a set of contiguous characters. Consider the difference between the two types of strings on the following page.

✔ **AnsiString class** — The Edit control, for example, has a Text property for holding users' entries that employs the AnsiString type. This AnsiString C++ class is used to implement strings throughout C++Builder components. A native C++ string doesn't play ball like AnsiString because it's nowhere near as sophisticated. A native C++ string is simply an *array* of characters (a data type that essentially acts like a bunch of cells to store information). It holds no information that refers to the string's size or any other string property.

✔ **Native C++ character array strings** — In native C++ character array strings, the first data element begins at 0 (zero). The character data for the string then continues until a special character acts as a "stop sign." This stop character has a value of 0 — the so-called *null character* or *terminating null.*

At some point, you may have to introduce these two types of strings to each other in one of your applications, especially if you want to hook in some existing C++ code. Because they go about holding their data differently you may have to do some converting between the AnsiString and Null Terminated string before you can copy a string from one type into the other.

To convert from a C++ character array to an AnsiString type is easy. Because AnsiStrings are smarter than C++ character array string types, you don't have to do a great deal to them; just assign the value of the character array straight to the AnsiString variable. The following lines of code give you an example:

```
char WhistleWhileYouWork[] = "Hi Ho, Hi Ho, it's off to
            work we go..." ;
Button1->Caption = WhistleWhileYouWork ;
```

The process for converting from an AnsiString type to a C++ character array string type is a little less obvious. Fortunately, the AnsiString type has a built-in member function called `c_str()`. Use the `c_str()` function as it returns the contents of the AnsiString in a null-terminated string format. When you need to, copy the result from this function to a waiting character array. The following snippet of code gets the user input from an edit box and places it in a null-terminated string:

```
strcpy( cTemp, Edit1->Text.c_str() ) ;
```

Using Third-Party Components

In addition to the components that come already installed on C++Builder's component palette, a whole industry has sprung up to provide extra components that you can buy and install. You can then use these additional components freely as you would any others. C++Builder components can be based on either C++ or Object Pascal (the language of Delphi — another Borland development tool), so you can also use any of the thousands of tried-and-tested Delphi components.

Most companies that offer third-party components offer the source code as well, often for an extra fee, so that you can see how the component is constructed (*source code* refers to the actual .cpp or .pas files that you write, edit, and compile). If possible, you should always buy this source code, too. Here's why:

- ✔ A company that makes its source code available obviously has nothing to hide about the way the product is built, so chances are good that the component is well-written.

- ✔ You can unearth massive amounts of useful information from looking through the source code written by experienced developers.

- ✔ If the company that supplies the component runs into trouble, you can always support your application if you have the source code.

How can you find out what sort of components are out there? Try trade shows, conferences, magazines, and other developers. For many people, one-stop shopping on the Internet provides the needed component. Thousands of components are available in cyberspace as freeware, shareware, and pay-and-download programs.

Obtaining components over the Internet has potential dangers. Don't assume that just because you download a component from an advertiser on the Web that it's well-written, thoroughly tested, and does what the developer claims. I'm not doubting the integrity of the many excellent developers who vend their wares over the Net, but don't forget that your end user must rely on whatever it is *you* choose to provide. Try out the downloaded component demo first and e-mail any questions you have about how you intend to use the component to the developer.

After considering the preceding words of warning, don't be disheartened. Using other people's components is a great way to leap-frog hours or maybe days of work.

Inserting Comments into Your Code

Suppose that you're asked to add some features and fix some problems in an application that you and a colleague wrote months ago. You have all but forgotten the project, but you vaguely remember the bits that you did write. The problem is that your partner has left the company, and you never got to see the code that she wrote.

Sound familiar? These kinds of situations do arise from time to time, and access to some answers (or even just a clue!) in the code can certainly make your job easier.

Intelligent and consistent use of commenting saves you and your colleagues a great deal of wasted time trying to remember what you were thinking about on that Friday afternoon a year ago when you wrote the program!

If you aren't sure how to actually place comments in C++ code, the following table shows the syntax for C++ comment lines and blocks.

Syntax	*Description*
//	Comments out the rest of the line
/*	Starts a comment block
*/	Ends a comment block

Here's an example of how a comment block can look in your code:

```
nAdjust = nValue - nFactor ; // This part of the line's a
            comment
```

```
/*
Here you can
 write a whole paragraph
      if you need to...
*/
```

One of the primary places you should religiously place comments is at the top of each C++ source file. The following is an example of a code file header comment block. At the very least, you know who to call to find out what's going into the code (unless, of course, you're the person who wrote it!).

```
//- - - - - - - - - - - - - - - - - - - - - - - - - - - - - -
// Unit Name:     Unit1.cpp
// Author: Your Name
// Date Created:  Christmas Day
//
// Purpose
// =======
// Explain here the job this unit does...
//
```

```
// Modifications:
//
// Date    Done By      Details
// ====    ======= =======
// 01-Jan-97     Your Name     Added a new widget
//
// Copyright (c) A.Company 1997
//————————————————————————————————————
```

Function header comments not only help separate functions within the source code file, but also provide an opportunity to state what you're setting out to do in a function and how you're actually going to do it. Think about how these comments could save you time if you haven't seen a particular function before and need to determine what the code is supposed to do. Here's a suggested starting point for a function header:

```
//————————————————————————————————————
// Function: myFunction
// Purpose: Brief explanation of what function does and
//   how it does it.
//
//
void myFunction
    .
    .
    .
```

Naming Objects and Variables

In the line of application development duty, you create objects and variables of all types (as you know by now, *objects* contain data and the routines that process the data; *variables* are names used to represent a piece of information). C++Builder provides default names (Edit1, Edit2, and so on) for the objects that you create using the Form Designer (the C++Builder tool that allows you to place and manipulate components, among other things), but these names are far from ideal for all but the simplest applications. Imagine having a form with ten edit boxes. You would soon be in trouble, wondering whether Edit7 holds the phone number or fax number.

A good habit to develop is to rename controls as you place them in forms. Indicate the type of variable by using an abbreviation as a prefix. All form names can begin with **frm,** all buttons with **btn,** and so on as you can see from the table that follows. Follow the prefix with a meaningful name that refers to the control's task, such as btnClose and edName.

Components renamed in this way also show up in an orderly fashion in the Object Inspector (you use the Object Inspector to modify a component's properties and events). The following table shows some common prefixes that can be used for basic C++Builder component types.

Prefix	Type
btn	TButton
cb	TComboBox
ds	TDataSource
ed	TEdit
frm	TForm
n	Integer
lbl	TLabel
pnl	TPanel
qry	TQuery
str	String
tbl	TTable
tim	TTimer
w	Word

Supplying User Interface Tips

If you're new to developing Windows applications, the choices you have available for what to include in the user interface may seem overwhelming. Keep in mind that your interface should be reasonably intuitive and user friendly. With that in mind, I offer the following suggestions:

- ✔ If you've built list boxes or combo boxes that allow the user to make selections within selections, think about providing a TreeView component for the user to navigate (see Figure 19-1). This type of component offers the user a way to not only view but also manage multiple-level data. (Chapter 8 has more information on TreeViews.)

Figure 19-1:
TreeView
components,
such as the
one in this
figure, help
the user
organize file
hierarchies.

✔ Most computer users are accustomed to Windows applications looking and behaving in a certain way. If you stick to these conventions, you make life easier for your users. If you ignore these conventions, you increase the frequency of users swearing at their computer screens while trying to work with something you built. The File⇨Exit command, for example, should always be assigned the shortcut keys Alt+F, Alt+X respectively, and F1 should always be the key to press for help.

✔ Provide your users instant access to menu options with *speed buttons* (that's the name for the buttons that are lined up under the main menu in a window within an area called a *speed bar*). The great thing is that you don't have to duplicate the code from menu command code; just hook the speed button's OnClick event to the appropriate menu event handler.

Don't be tempted to use oversize buttons and spread your application around numerous forms. This is a trap that snares many developers who are new to Windows. You can offer the same functionality using more-varied control types.

Using Delphi Code

C++Builder is capable of something clever that adds greatly to its flexibility. You can incorporate Delphi code and forms straight into your C++Builder applications. (Delphi is Borland's Pascal-based rapid application development tool.) There may be Delphi code that's just right for part of your current application. Ideally, you won't need to go through the rigmarole of rewriting the code in C++ or even having to make any changes in it.

If you want to include a complete form by using Delphi, choose Project➪Add to Project (or press Shift+F11) to display the Add to Project dialog box. Select Pascal Unit (*.pas) from the Files of Type drop-down list. Then select your Delphi code unit and click on the Open button. The form is now part of your project.

You can find out if the Delphi form has been added to your project by choosing View➪Project Manager.

Now that the form is part of the project, how do you go about using it? Just include it in the calling unit by choosing File➪Include Unit Header. C++Builder automatically creates a C++ header file for you. Then show the form by using code such as the following:

```
frmDelphiForm->ShowModal() ;
```

Avoiding Code Déjà Vu

What can be more frustrating than knowing you've already coded a task in another project and can't find the code that you wrote? Even worse, you find the code that you wrote, but you end up rewriting it anyway because extracting the pieces that you need would take just as much time. Obviously, the more code that you can reuse, the less code you have to write, and the faster you get the job done. Also, if you are using proven functions, classes, and components, your programs take less time to test and debug.

Building components is an obvious way of writing code that you can plug into your programs, but even when you don't package code this way, you can still benefit from a code-reuse strategy.

✔ Always try to solve a problem in the most general terms. When you come across a similar situation in the future, you may well have some code that goes at least part way toward providing a solution. Try to build functionality into classes that perform specific tasks (see Chapter 16 for more information on classes).

✔ While you're cutting your code, always express your ideas in small, simple code functions and source code files. You're more likely to reuse a small file that performs a single straightforward task than to reuse a large, application-specific source code file that performs several operations.

✔ Make sure each source code file does only one job. If you need to write a function that performs a task on two strings, for example, pass in the two strings as parameters rather than use globally accessible variables. In this way, you make the function more self-contained and easier to add to your list of the top 1,001 useful functions.

✔ To help yourself along the path of maximum code reuse, start thinking about accumulating useful code right now. Make sure that you add at least one entry to your useful-code library from every decent-size program that you write.

✔ Don't try to do anything too fancy. Your library addition can consist of just a folder in which you collect your own set of useful code units. Don't forget that you can include the location of your library folder in the Include path of your project's options.

Understanding Business Objects

Spot the workplace object in the following list:

✔ Fax machine

✔ Photocopier

✔ *Star Trek* desk clock

✔ Bill-processing rules class

I suppose that all these items are business objects in one way or another. But only the fourth item fits the bill as far as C++Builder is concerned.

You can create a business object as a class or (ideally) as a nonvisual component. Then you can just drop the object into a form, and reference the object's properties and methods to apply calculations and verification for the form.

Suppose that you are writing an order-processing system. You can write a class to verify that all of the conditions have been met to allow the order to proceed, as well as to provide functionality such as automatic discounting according to specific rules. The following code segment shows how you can organize these rules in a self-contained class. Other parts of the application gain access to these rules via the class member functions and do not perform these tasks directly.

```
class TOrderValidation
{
private: // User declarations
    int nOrderNo ;
public:    // User declarations
    TOrderValidation(void);
  int GetOrderNo(void) ;
    bool InStock(int PartNo) ;
  void ApplyDiscount(void) ;
};
```

No code outside the class has anything to do with *how* the validation process operates. Implementing a change means making a single visit to just the OrderValidation class. You still need to recompile the applications that rely on this object to implement the changes across the board, but you don't have to make any code changes in them.

Chapter 20

Ten Common Mistakes You Won't Make Again after Reading This

. . . .

In This Chapter

▶ Leaving off ending comments

▶ Skipping the `Next` statement in a loop

▶ Using = instead of == in an `if` statement

▶ Forgetting to place breaks in `switch` statements

▶ Forgetting that indexes start with zero

▶ Overlapping components

▶ Making errors in `FieldByName` references

▶ Putting TabStops in the wrong order

▶ Omitting the { and } braces when grouping code

▶ Overwriting memory with oversize variables

. . . .

I rounded up a bunch of common pitfalls that nearly all C++Builder programmers stumble into sooner or later. So don't be disheartened if you commit one of the goofs listed in this chapter when building an application. And, if you haven't encountered problems like these before, you can't say you weren't warned.

In each section I list the symptom first, and then the diagnosis.

Don't Leave Off Ending Comments

The symptom: Your program won't compile and the Message Window says `Unexpected end of file in comment started on line XX` (XX being the number of the line in question).

This compiler error message is telling you that you started a comment section using /* and forgot to end the comment with */. After you press F9 to compile, link, and run your program, C++Builder runs through your code, hits the end of the file without finding an end comment, and you get the error message.

To fix this problem, return to the line of code cited in the error message and look carefully to see where you need to add */ to end the comment section.

Don't Skip the Next *Statement in a Loop*

The symptom: The program "hangs up" your machine.

When you need to perform a section of code more than once, but you're not sure of the exact number of times you need to repeat it, use a while loop to test your code prior to executing it. When the while statement becomes false, the program execution moves on to the line of code following the closing brace (}) of the while statement (see Chapter 15 for more on while statements).

The catch is that you may inadvertently write some code in which the while loop tests a condition that will never change to false. The program winds up in a never-ending loop, which makes the program appear to have stopped.

An example of how a program can get hung up due to a never-ending while loop occurs when the program is stepping through the rows of a data table in your code. The following code shows you an example of how the while loop *should* be constructed.

```
            Table1->First() ;
while (!Table1->Eof)
   {
   // perform data processing tasks here

   Table1->Next() ;
   }
```

In this code sample, the program sets the table to the first record and then the while statement checks to see if this is the last record in the table. If it isn't, the code inside the { and } (the starting and closing braces) is executed to move the table onto its next record.

It's easy to inadvertently miss the `Table1->Next()` ; line of code. This oversight effectively stalls the program on the first record of the table forever, or at least until you stop the action by forcing the program to end. The best way to avoid this problem is to place the `Table1->Next()` ; line into the `while` loop *before* you type the rest of the body of the loop. Then, you can rest assured that the loop will eventually end!

Don't Use = (Instead of ==) in an `if` *Statement*

The symptom: The code section associated with an `if` statement is either always executed or never executed.

The `if` statement is used to test the condition of variables inside your program to allow program decisions to be made. Basically, you're telling the computer to execute a particular statement *if* a certain condition holds true.

Even though `if` statements can compare values higher or lower than one another, `if` statements are also often used to check two values for equality. The syntax for that comparison looks something like the following:

```
if (a == b)
```

Notice that in the previous line of code two = (equal) signs are entered next to each other. If by mistake you happen to use a single = character, like this

```
if (a = b)
```

you are going to get a different, and often unexpected, result. The previous line of code says the value of variable `a` is equal to `b` but does not test the two variables for equality.

Because the second `if` statement is syntactically correct, when you compile and run your program by pressing F9, C++Builder won't stop with a compile error. Instead, the warning message `Possibly incorrect assignment` appears with a reference to the line number that contains the `if` statement in question. That's your cue to take a good hard look at that line's syntax.

Don't Forget to Place Breaks in Switch Statements

The symptom: A switch statement calls more lines of code than anticipated.

You can use the switch statement to help organize complex decision-making inside your code. If you're new to C++ development, one potential stumbling block that may trip you up with the switch statement happens when you place a break statement inside each case branch. The problem lies in not having a break for each case, which causes the program execution to march onto the next case and execute it without jumping out of the switch. The following code shows a typical switch statement construct:

```
switch(j)
    {
  case 0:
      Function0() ;
      break ;
  case 1:
      Function1() ;
      break ;
  case 2:
      Function2() ;
      break ;
  default :
      DefaultFunc() ;
  }
```

When the program is running, the code in this example checks the value of the variable j and then compares the value of j to each of the values next to the case statements in turn. When the program finds a match, the function following the case statement is called. Each function call is followed by a break statement.

The break statements are placed after each function call to make the program immediately move to the next line following the closing } (brace) after each function is called. In other words, only one case section is executed every time the program passes through the switch statement.

If the break statements had not been included in the previous section of code, once the program finds a matching value for variable j in a case statement, all the functions for the case statements that follow would also be called. This can produce unexpected program behavior (to say the least).

So, if you have trouble with your `switch` statements, one of the first items on your troubleshooting checklist should be to make sure that `break` statements are where you need them.

Don't Forget that Array Indexes Start at Zero

The symptom: Array contents appear to be corrupted.

Computers consider zero to be as significant as the number one, so the first element in a C++ array has an index of 0 and the last item in an array has an index equivalent to the number of items in an array minus 1. (An *index* is the number assigned to each element in an array.)

If you create an array that holds ten integers, it may look like this:

```
int Numbers[10] ;
```

If you want to load these integers with numbers, you may decide to use a `for` loop. If you mistakenly code the `for` loop like this

```
for (i=1; i<11; i++ )
   Numbers[i] = i*2 ;
```

the `for` loop loads numbers into the array beginning from the second item in the array. It would skip the first array item altogether (the first array item being the integer with an array index of 0). This can cause some unpredictable results in your program because the first array item may hold absolutely any value left over from the last time that part of the system's memory was used. The correct code for this loop would be

```
for (i=0; i<10; i++ )
   Numbers[i] = i*2 ;
```

This loads array items 0 through 9 with the results of the calculation `i* 2 ;`.

Don't Overlap Components

The symptom: Components on a form don't show up where and when you want them to.

Assume you're placing a number of Panel components onto a form in your application with the intention of showing and hiding them in turn (to save on some window "real estate"). You may end up placing one Panel on top of another Panel by accidently clicking on the first Panel when placing the second one. The first Panel ends up being the "parent" of the second Panel. Then when the first Panel is hidden, so is the second Panel.

As you can see in Figure 20-1, Panel2 is contained within Panel1. If you are constructing a form that needs to show and hide overlaying Panels, you can avoid this situation by always leaving an area of the form background visible (the form background is the area marked with a grid pattern). Click on the form background area when you introduce new Panels onto a form. Once the Panel is on the form, then click and drag the Panel to where you need it.

Figure 20-1:
Be careful when placing Panels; otherwise, you may end up with something very strange (like this con-figuration) in your application.

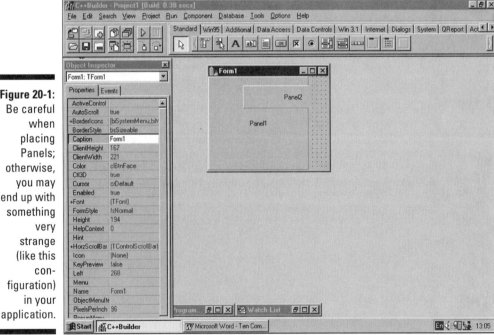

Don't Goof Up Your FieldByName References

The symptom: You get an error while accessing a data field only when your program is running.

The Table component has a member called FieldByName that you can use to reference individual fields within a data table. The FieldByName method takes one argument of a string type. That argument should hold the name of the field that you want to reference. Here's how it may look as code:

```
Table1->FieldByName("Name").AsString = Edit1->Text ;
```

This code line loads the field called "Name" with the contents of the Text property of the Component called Edit1. C++Builder can compile and link this line whether or not the actual data table has a "Name" field. If you place an incorrect string as the argument here, you get an error message that says Field 'Name' not found only when the program is running.

You need to first make sure that the arguments that you pass in these calls are correct because C++Builder cannot check these references for you as it compiles your program.

Don't Get Your TabStops Out of Order

The symptom: Pressing the Tab key when the program is running causes the cursor to jump out of sequence from control to control all over the form.

In Windows programs, users can move around the controls that you place on a form by using the Tab key. The order in which the application visits each control is called the *tab order*. Each control has a *TabOrder property* that enables you to determine the sequence that the Tab key follows when navigating the controls on a form.

C++Builder goes a long way in helping you with tab orders by providing each new component with sequential TabOrder property values. C++Builder's automatic ordering works fine as long as you add components in the order and location on the form where they will finally reside in the finished program.

Imagine that you've placed five EditBox components, one above the other, to form a column. C++Builder sees to it that the *TabStop property* for each EditBox holds a value one higher than that held by the TabStop property of the previous EditBox (you can access the TabStop property through the Object Inspector). When you compile and run the program, the user is able to use the Tab key to move down through the EditBox components in an orderly fashion.

If you need to move these EditBoxes around or change their order for any reason, you must first adjust the TabStop properties for each EditBox to reflect their new positions. Otherwise, when the user presses the Tab key, the program jumps from EditBox to EditBox up and down the form in no particular order.

The unordered navigation of the form can be easily cured by first right-clicking on the form to bring up the speed menu. Then select the Tab Order option from the menu to access the Edit Tab Order dialog box. You can then raise or lower the TabStop value of each control on the form by either using the buttons on the Edit Tab order dialog box or by clicking and dragging each control listed into the desired tab order.

Don't forget to check your program prior to releasing your software by trying out the tab ordering of the controls on your form. Just press F9 to run the program and then use the Tab key to navigate around your form before you pass the program on to others.

Don't Omit the { and } When Grouping Lines of Code

The symptom: The program does not compile and gives you a `Declaration syntax error` message.

Many code constructs within C++ require braces (`{ }`) to indicate the beginning and end of sections of code. Examples of code constructs that rely on these braces are functions, `if` statements, `while` statements, `for` loops, and others.

So what happens if you forget to provide a pair of start and end braces for a code section? The compiler picks up the fact that something is wrong in your program, but not at the place that you may suspect. The message you'll most likely get is `Declaration syntax error` and the line where the opening brace for the next function resides is highlighted. Even though this isn't the most informative error message in computerdom, you can at least deduce that something is missing from the function that immediately precedes the error message. You can then go in and add your braces.

Don't Overwrite Memory with Oversize Variables

The symptom: Strange values appear in program variables or unpredictable results occur when operating your program.

C++Builder does not prevent you from overwriting memory that you have not specifically allocated to a variable. For example, the following line of code shows a character array that has been declared with the capacity to hold ten characters.

```
char strTemp [10] ;
```

C++Builder won't give you a warning if you place a string longer than ten characters into the strTemp variable in this line. In fact, C++Builder would actually allow you to include the following line of code in your program.

```
sprintf(strTemp, "12345678912345678912345670") ;
```

If you do include this line of code in your program, you are effectively overwriting areas of memory that do not belong to this variable and could overwrite the values of other program variables as well. This results in data loss and there's no predicting how the program will react to these values overwriting the contents of other variables.

Make sure that you stick to the size capacities of the variables that you declare. The symptoms of memory overwriting problems can be very inconsistent and difficult to diagnose — so be especially careful with the size of your variables.

Appendix

About the Disk

●●

*W*elcome to the companion disk that provides you with source code for the program examples in *Borland C++Builder For Dummies.* There are two ways for you to access and use the helpful stuff on the disk that comes with this book. You can work with the files directly from the disk and then save them to your hard drive as you make changes to them, or you can copy all the files to your hard drive in one fell swoop with the self-extracting archive created just for that purpose.

If you don't want to copy the files to your hard drive, skip ahead to the section called "Loading Individual Project Programs." That section tells you how to find the files, whether they are on the disk or on your hard drive.

Two text files, License.txt and Contents.txt, are also included on the disk. Be sure to read these files for important information about both the IDG Books End User License Agreement and the files included on this disk.

Extracting the Files to Your Hard Drive

If you have Windows 95, and you want to copy all the files to your hard drive at once, first make sure the *Borland C++Builder For Dummies* disk is in your $3^1/2$" floppy disk drive, click on the Start button on the Windows 95 taskbar, and then select Run from the popup menu that appears.

Enter **A:\Cbuilder** in the Run dialog box that opens up (remember, if your $3^1/2$" floppy disk drive is not called A:\, be sure to use the correct letter for your drive). The files will be extracted automatically to your hard drive to a folder called C:\My Documents\Cbuilder.

Loading Individual Project Programs

If you decide not to copy the project files to your hard drive, you need to make sure the *Borland C++Builder For Dummies* disk is in your computer's floppy drive before you begin working with the files.

If the disk is in the drive, then just follow these steps:

1. **Open your Borland C++Builder program.**

2. **Select File⇨Open Project.**

   The files are on the disk in folders named "Chapter04," "Chapter06," and so on.

3. **Open the folder for the chapter you are interested in, and then select the project that you want from that chapter.**

If you make changes to the files that you want to save, just use the File⇨Save As option to save the files to your hard drive.

If you extracted the files to your hard drive, you don't have to worry about keeping track of your disk. Just put it away for safekeeping and follow these steps:

1. **Open your Borland C++Builder program.**

2. **Select File⇨Open Project.**

   If you have Windows 95, the files are on your hard drive in C:\My Documents\Cbuilder within folders named "Chapter04," "Chapter06," and so on.

3. **Open the folder for the chapter you are interested in, and then select the project that you want from that chapter.**

If you make changes to the files that you want to save, you can create new versions of the files using the File⇨Save As command, or you can replace the original files with your new versions. After all, if you ever need the originals, they are still on the disk and you can always recopy them to your hard drive.

Installation Questions?

If you have any trouble with installing the items on the *Borland C++Builder For Dummies* disk, please call the IDG Books Worldwide, Inc. Worldwide Customer Service phone number at 800-762-2974 (outside the U.S.: 317-596-5261).

Disk Directory Structure

When you examine the disk contents, you find that the directory structure looks like this:

A: — "Chapter 04," "Chapter 06," "Chapter 07," "Chapter 08," "Chapter 09," "Chapter 10," "Chapter 11," "Chapter 12," "Chapter 13," "Chapter 15," "Chapter 16," "Chapter 17," "Cbuilder.exe," "Contents.txt," "License.txt"

Directory Contents

The Directory contents include the following files:

Cbuilder.exe — This file is a self-extracting archive that copies the contents of the _Borland C++Builder For Dummies_ floppy disk to your hard drive. The files will be copied to C:\My Documents\Cbuilder and they require approximately 450K of hard-disk space.

Contents.txt — This file tells you what you can find on the disk.

License.txt — Be sure to read this file — it's the End-User License Agreement for this disk.

The Directory also includes the following chapter folders that contain files for the example projects developed in this book:

Chapter 4

prjColorSlider.mak — Creating a color selector using the ScrollBar component

Chapter 6

prjTrafficLights.mak — Creating a working "traffic light" with the Shape component

DatesMask.mak — Using the MaskEdit component for a data-entry program

TicTac.mak — Creating a working tic-tac-toe game with the DrawGrid component

StrGrid.mak — Using the StringGrid components for graphics as well as strings

Chapter 7

MainMenu.mak — Building a Main menu example program

PopMenu.mak — Building a Speed menu example program

MenuMerge.mak — Building a Menu merging example program

Chapter 8

prjTreeView.mak — Organizing entries with the TreeView component

prjProgress.mak — Tracking program status with the ProgressBar component

prjStatusBar.mak — Conveying information to users with the StatusBar component

prjRichEd.mak — Creating your own word processor using the RichEdit component

prjListView.mak — Viewing entries with the ListView component

prjPageControl.mak — Creating a multipage form with the PageControl component

Chapter 9
prjOpenSave.mak — Developing Open and Save dialog boxes

prjColor.mak — Selecting colors using the ColorDialog component

prjFont.mak — Selecting fonts using the FontDialog component

prjPrint.mak — Selecting print options using the PrintDialog and PrinterSetupDialog components

Chapter 10
prjSingleExpert.mak — Editing a single table

prjQParams.mak — Using a Query component with parameters

prjTableMthds.mak — Maneuvering around a table using member methods

Chapter 11
prjReports.mak — Checking out the QuickReport component

prjMultiExpert.mak — Creating a master-detail table form

Chapter 12
prjFTeam.mak — Building a program using the file/folder components

Chapter 13
prjTimer.mak — Building a digital clock using the Timer component

prjOLE.mak — Creating an OLE Container

prjSightSound.mak — Adding sounds to a program

prjVideo.mak — Showing video in a program

Chapter 15

prjIF.mak — Working with a short project to illustrate an if statement

Chapter 16

Developing with an example structure and class (includes example files but no specific project)

Chapter 17

prjDebug.mak — Checking out the C++Builder debugger tools

Index

Symbols

& (ampersand)
    in Caption property text
        for button, 86
    to pass address of variable, 288
    for shortcut hot key to
        menu items, 68, 128,
        232
&& (and) operator, 267
* (asterisk)
    for pointer, 264, 289
    as wildcard
        in file filters, 228
        in Query component, 199
< (less-than) operator, 267
= (assignment) operator,
        268
== (equal) operator, 267
!= (not-equal) operator, 267
{ } (braces)
    to enclose if statements,
        269
    for structures, 281
    troubleshooting, when
        missing, 338–339
> (greater-than) operator,
        267
... (ellipsis), in menu item,
        131
! (not) operator, 267
? button, on title bar, 41
– (minus-sign character), in
        Caption property of
        MenuItem object, 129
? (question mark), as
        wildcard, 228
\\ (or) operator, 267

• A •

Active property, of Table
        component, 188
ActiveX tab, in Component
        Palette, 60
Add to Project dialog box,
        18, 328
Add to Repository dialog
        box, 27–28
Additional tab, in Compo-
        nent Palette, 59, 101
address
    in computer memory, 303
    pointer-type variable to
        hold, 264
    of variable, & (amper-
        sand) to pass, 288
alias, BDE, 182
Align palette, 66, 67
Align property
    of Memo component, 73
    of OLEContainer compo-
        nent, 232
    of Panel component, 72
    versus Alignment prop-
        erty, 72
alignment
    of components, 66–67
    of text, code for, 148
Alignment dialog box, 66–67
Alignment Palette dialog
        box, 87
Alignment property
    of CheckBox component,
        96
    of Label component, 67
    of RadioButton compo-
        nent, 97
    versus Align property, 72

AllowAllUp property, of
        SpeedButton compo-
        nent, 93, 94
AllowChange argument, in
        OnChanging event, 159
AllowGrayed property, of
        CheckBox component,
        96
ampersand (&)
    in Caption property text
        for button, 86
    to pass address of vari-
        able, 288
    for shortcut hot key to
        menu items, 68, 128,
        232
and operator (&&), 267
AnsiString string class, 264,
        322
application entry point, 254
Application object, and
        exception handling,
        314
applications. *See also*
        projects
    adding progress bar to,
        143–144
    changing variable value
        during debugging,
        301–302
    integrating exception
        handling into, 314–317
    loading individual from
        companion disk,
        341–342
    potential error checks,
        305
    restarting when debug-
        ging, 299
arguments, for functions,
        287–289

(continued)

IDG Books Worldwide, Inc., End-User License Agreement

READ THIS. You should carefully read these terms and conditions before opening the software packet(s) included with this book ("Book"). This is a license agreement ("Agreement") between you and IDG Books Worldwide, Inc. ("IDGB"). By opening the accompanying software packet(s), you acknowledge that you have read and accept the following terms and conditions. If you do not agree and do not want to be bound by such terms and conditions, promptly return the Book and the unopened software packet(s) to the place you obtained them for a full refund.

1. **License Grant.** IDGB grants to you (either an individual or entity) a nonexclusive license to use one copy of the enclosed software program(s) (collectively, the "Software") solely for your own personal or business purposes on a single computer (whether a standard computer or a workstation component of a multiuser network). The Software is in use on a computer when it is loaded into temporary memory (RAM) or installed into permanent memory (hard disk, CD-ROM, or other storage device). IDGB reserves all rights not expressly granted herein.

2. **Ownership.** IDGB is the owner of all right, title, and interest, including copyright, in and to the compilation of the Software recorded on the disk(s) or CD-ROM ("Software Media"). Copyright to the individual programs recorded on the Software Media is owned by the author or other authorized copyright owner of each program. Ownership of the Software and all proprietary rights relating thereto remain with IDGB and its licensers.

3. **Restrictions on Use and Transfer.**

    (a) You may only (i) make one copy of the Software for backup or archival purposes, or (ii) transfer the Software to a single hard disk, provided that you keep the original for backup or archival purposes. You may not (i) rent or lease the Software, (ii) copy or reproduce the Software through a LAN or other network system or through any computer subscriber system or bulletin-board system, or (iii) modify, adapt, or create derivative works based on the Software.

    (b) You may not reverse engineer, decompile, or disassemble the Software. You may transfer the Software and user documentation on a permanent basis, provided that the transferee agrees to accept the terms and conditions of this Agreement and you retain no copies. If the Software is an update or has been updated, any transfer must include the most recent update and all prior versions.

4. **Restrictions on Use of Individual Programs.** You must follow the individual requirements and restrictions detailed for each individual program in the "About the Disk" section of this Book. These limitations are also contained in the individual license agreements recorded on the Software Media. These limitations may include a requirement that after using the program for a specified period of time, the user must pay a registration fee or discontinue use. By opening the Software packet(s), you will be agreeing to abide by the licenses and restrictions for these individual programs that are detailed in the "About the Disk" section and on the Software Media. None of the material on this Software Media or listed in this Book may ever be redistributed, in original or modified form, for commercial purposes.

5. Limited Warranty.

(a) IDGB warrants that the Software and Software Media are free from defects in materials and workmanship under normal use for a period of sixty (60) days from the date of purchase of this Book. If IDGB receives notification within the warranty period of defects in materials or workmanship, IDGB will replace the defective Software Media.

(b) IDGB AND THE AUTHOR OF THIS BOOK DISCLAIM ALL OTHER WARRANTIES, EXPRESS OR IMPLIED, INCLUDING WITHOUT LIMITATION IMPLIED WARRANTIES OF MER-CHANTABILITY AND FITNESS FOR A PARTICULAR PURPOSE, WITH RESPECT TO THE SOFTWARE, THE PROGRAMS, THE SOURCE CODE CONTAINED THEREIN, AND/OR THE TECHNIQUES DESCRIBED IN THIS BOOK. IDGB DOES NOT WARRANT THAT THE FUNCTIONS CONTAINED IN THE SOFTWARE WILL MEET YOUR REQUIREMENTS OR THAT THE OPERATION OF THE SOFTWARE WILL BE ERROR FREE.

(c) This limited warranty gives you specific legal rights, and you may have other rights that vary from jurisdiction to jurisdiction.

6. Remedies.

(a) IDGB's entire liability and your exclusive remedy for defects in materials and workmanship shall be limited to replacement of the Software Media, which may be returned to IDGB with a copy of your receipt at the following address: Software Media Fulfillment Department, Attn.: *Borland C++Builder For Dummies,* IDG Books Worldwide, Inc., 7260 Shadeland Station, Ste. 100, Indianapolis, IN 46256, or call 800-762-2974. Please allow three to four weeks for delivery. This Limited Warranty is void if failure of the Software Media has resulted from accident, abuse, or misapplication. Any replacement Software Media will be warranted for the remainder of the original warranty period or thirty (30) days, whichever is longer.

(b) In no event shall IDGB or the author be liable for any damages whatsoever (including without limitation damages for loss of business profits, business interruption, loss of business information, or any other pecuniary loss) arising from the use of or inability to use the Book or the Software, even if IDGB has been advised of the possibility of such damages.

(c) Because some jurisdictions do not allow the exclusion or limitation of liability for conse-quential or incidental damages, the above limitation or exclusion may not apply to you.

7. U.S. Government Restricted Rights. Use, duplication, or disclosure of the Software by the U.S. Government is subject to restrictions stated in paragraph (c)(1)(ii) of the Rights in Technical Data and Computer Software clause of DFARS 252.227-7013, and in subparagraphs (a) through (d) of the Commercial Computer–Restricted Rights clause at FAR 52.227-19, and in similar clauses in the NASA FAR supplement, when applicable.

8. General. This Agreement constitutes the entire understanding of the parties and revokes and supersedes all prior agreements, oral or written, between them and may not be modified or amended except in a writing signed by both parties hereto that specifically refers to this Agreement. This Agreement shall take precedence over any other documents that may be in conflict herewith. If any one or more provisions contained in this Agreement are held by any court or tribunal to be invalid, illegal, or otherwise unenforceable, each and every other provision shall remain in full force and effect.

Disk Installation Instructions

You can access and use the material on the disk that comes with this book in either one of two ways. You can work with the files directly from the disk and then save them to your hard drive as you make changes to them, or you can copy all the files to your hard drive at once with the self-extracting archive created just for that purpose.

Two text files, License.txt and Contents.txt, are also included on the disk. Be sure to read these files for important information about both the IDG Books End User License Agreement and the files included on this disk.

Extracting the Files to Your Hard Drive

If you have Windows 95, and you want to copy all the files to your hard drive at once, first make sure the *Borland C++Builder For Dummies* disk is in your 3¹/₂" floppy disk drive, click on the Start button on the Windows 95 taskbar, and then select Run from the popup menu that appears.

Enter **A:\Cbuilder** in the Run dialog box that opens up (remember, if your 3¹/₂" floppy disk drive is not called A:\, be sure to use the correct letter for your drive). The files will be extracted automatically to your hard drive to a folder called C:\My Documents\Cbuilder.

Loading Individual Project Programs

If you decide not to copy the project files to your hard drive, you need to make sure the *Borland C++Builder For Dummies* disk is in your computer's floppy drive before you begin working with the files. If the disk is in the drive, follow these steps:

1. **Open your Borland C++Builder program.**

2. **Select File⇨Open Project.**

   The files are in folders named "Chapter04," "Chapter06," and so on.

3. Open the folder for the chapter you are interested in, and then select the project that you want from that chapter.

If you make changes to the files that you want to save, just use the File⇨Save As option to save the files to your hard drive.

If you extract the files to your hard drive, you don't have to worry about keeping track of your disk. Just put it away for safekeeping and follow these steps:

1. Open your Borland C++Builder program.

2. Select File⇨Open Project.

If you have Windows 95, the files are in C:\My Documents\Cbuilder within folders named "Chapter04," "Chapter06," and so on.

3. Open the folder for the chapter you are interested in, and then select the project that you want from that chapter.

If you make changes to the files that you want to save, you can create new versions of the files using the File⇨Save As command, or you can replace the original files with your new versions.

IDG BOOKS WORLDWIDE REGISTRATION CARD

Visit our Web site at http://www.idgbooks.com

ISBN Number: 0-7645-0196-8

Title of this book: Borland® C++Builder™ For Dummies®

My overall rating of this book: ❑ Very good [1] ❑ Good [2] ❑ Satisfactory [3] ❑ Fair [4] ❑ Poor [5]

How I first heard about this book:

❑ Found in bookstore; name: [6] _____ ❑ Book review: [7]

❑ Advertisement: [8] ❑ Catalog: [9]

❑ Word of mouth; heard about book from friend, co-worker, etc.: [10] ❑ Other: [11]

What I liked most about this book:

_____

_____

What I would change, add, delete, etc., in future editions of this book:

_____

_____

Other comments:

_____

Number of computer books I purchase in a year: ❑ 1 [12] ❑ 2-5 [13] ❑ 6-10 [14] ❑ More than 10 [15]

I would characterize my computer skills as: ❑ Beginner [16] ❑ Intermediate [17] ❑ Advanced [18] ❑ Professional [19]

I use ❑ DOS [20] ❑ Windows [21] ❑ OS/2 [22] ❑ Unix [23] ❑ Macintosh [24] ❑ Other: [25] _____

(please specify)

I would be interested in new books on the following subjects:

(please check all that apply, and use the spaces provided to identify specific software)

❑ Word processing: [26] ❑ Spreadsheets: [27]

❑ Data bases: [28] ❑ Desktop publishing: [29]

❑ File Utilities: [30] ❑ Money management: [31]

❑ Networking: [32] ❑ Programming languages: [33]

❑ Other: [34]

I use a PC at (please check all that apply): ❑ home [35] ❑ work [36] ❑ school [37] ❑ other: [38] _____

The disks I prefer to use are ❑ 5.25 [39] ❑ 3.5 [40] ❑ other: [41] _____

I have a CD ROM: ❑ yes [42] ❑ no [43]

I plan to buy or upgrade computer hardware this year: ❑ yes [44] ❑ no [45]

I plan to buy or upgrade computer software this year: ❑ yes [46] ❑ no [47]

Name: _____ Business title: [48] _____ Type of Business: [49] _____

Address (❑ home [50] ❑ work [51]/Company name: _____)

Street/Suite# _____

City [52]/State [53]/Zip code [54]: _____ Country [55] _____

❑ **I liked this book!** You may quote me by name in future IDG Books Worldwide promotional materials.

My daytime phone number is _____

IDG
BOOKS
WORLDWIDE

THE WORLD OF
COMPUTER
KNOWLEDGE®

☐ YES!

Please keep me informed about IDG Books Worldwide's World of Computer Knowledge. Send me your latest catalog.

INFO WORLD
TECHNICAL BOOKS

...FOR DUMMIES™

BESTSELLING BOOK SERIES FROM IDG

3-D Visual

Macworld® Books

...SECRETS®